Final Whistle

THE PADDY RUSSELL STORY

Paddy Russell with **Jackie Cahill**

MAINSTREAM
PUBLISHING

EDINBURGH AND LONDON

First published in Great Britain in 2008 by
MAINSTREAM PUBLISHING COMPANY
(EDINBURGH) LTD
7 Albany Street
Edinburgh EH1 3UG

ISBN 9781845963910

A catalogue record for this book is available
from the British Library

Typeset in Champion and Palatino

Printed in Great Britain by
CPI Mackays of Chatham Ltd, Chatham, ME5 8TD

ACKNOWLEDGEMENTS

The problem with acknowledgements for the person writing them is always the big fear that you will leave someone out. This case is no different. In some ways, it is worse, because during the 32 years that I have been refereeing, so many people have helped me out. Some of them are mentioned in the book, but I know in my heart of hearts that there are others whom I called upon at very short notice to come umpiring with me to all parts of the country. If I have omitted their names, I apologise.

To Jackie Cahill, who convinced me that I had a story worth putting down on paper, I owe a huge debt of gratitude. The amount of research that Jackie conducted and his attention to detail were just phenomenal. It has been a pleasure working with him, and I have gained a friend into the bargain.

To the people who have kept me going throughout all these years: I am deeply indebted to my mother and father, Betty and Larry, whose role in my career I have touched upon in this book but whose importance in my life can never be adequately expressed. To my siblings, Margaret, Michael, Tommy, Mary, Larry, Jimmy and John, and their families, a big thank you. I must, of course, mention my wife Margaret's family: her late father Mikey, her mother Mary, her sisters Lena (who was always at the end of a phone line after a match), Marie and Teresa, and her brothers Michael and Noel, and their families.

My deepest debt of gratitude is owed to Margaret, who was at my side through good times and bad, and who never complained when my obsession with the GAA got in the way of family life.

Last but not least, our two boys Shane and Mark. How much these two mean to me would only embarrass them if I put it down on paper. I hope this book will give them an insight into why their father was so honoured to be involved in what is the greatest sporting organisation in the world bar none.

Paddy Russell

To begin, a sincere thanks to all who agreed to go on the record for *Final Whistle*, including Stevie O'Donnell, who first 'hopped the ball' off Paddy. To John Gough, Tony Jordan and Dermot Deasy, a sincere thanks for your permission to reproduce those touching letters. And to Ray McManus at Sportsfile, thanks for the photographs. I owe a debt of gratitude to GAA president Nickey Brennan, who penned the foreword to this book, and to Tipperary county board chairman John Costigan for his words of tribute to Paddy. Thanks also to Jerry Ring, Séamus King and Ed Donnelly for their help with some of the research. Thanks to the staff of Lion Print in Cashel. To my loving family – Mam, Dad, Rose, Brian and Andrew – for being there from the very start. To my wonderful fiancée, Chris, your patience, love and tolerance over the last few months have been truly amazing. Thanks for putting up with me. To the other members of the Stapleton clan, thanks for your kindness and friendship. In the world of journalism, Damian Lawlor and Vincent Hogan are two real confidants. Once again, your advice and input proved invaluable. To my great friend Iver, congratulations on the new arrival – another Liverpool fan in the making! And to Jimmy, who has felt the pain of loss this year, your strength inspires me, and our friendship is a treasured one. The last words, fittingly, to the Russells – Paddy, Margaret, Shane and Mark. I have made friends for life. Paddy, I could never do your career justice simply through words, but attempting the impossible has truly been an honour.

Jackie Cahill

CONTENTS

···

FOREWORD

A dhaoine uaisle, táim fíor-bhuíoch go bhfuil deis agam réamhrá a scríobh don leabhar seo ina bhfuil scéal réiteora agus saol iomlán Phádraig Ó Rúiséil á léiriú ag Seán Ó Cathail. Chaith Pádraig cuid mhór dá shaol mar réiteoir. Uaireanta is uaigneach saol an réiteora ach mar sin féin is fíor a rá gur bhain Pádraig an-shásamh as an saol chéanna. Tá deis agaibh anois bheith páirteach san saol sin. Bainigí taithneamh as.

I am honoured to have been asked to write a foreword to this fine book, which chronicles the tremendous refereeing career of Paddy Russell. I congratulate Jackie Cahill on this excellent publication; but then, as a Tipperary man himself, he is immensely proud of the achievements of his fellow Tipperary native.

The level of scrutiny that referees undergo these days is unprecedented. Everyone seems to have an opinion on the subject of refereeing, especially those who write on Gaelic games every day. The papers nowadays feature not only their dedicated GAA correspondents but also many guest writers, including former players, all of whom give their opinions on every aspect of refereeing. This analysis is part of the increased coverage that Gaelic games get these days, but on occasions the referee can receive very unfair criticism. Referees do not have the benefit of TV replay when making a call, so split-second decisiveness is required in even the most intense of games.

The ability to stay cool when under pressure from players, team mentors and supporters is a critical characteristic of any referee, and Paddy Russell has it in abundance. Gaelic games have never been more competitive than they are today, with players honed to a level of fitness much higher than was usual in years gone by. This has put increased pressure on our referees to match our players for speed. I regularly attend meetings of referees, and I have also witnessed their fitness programmes. All referees take the fitness tests very seriously, and I can tell you that Paddy Russell has come through on every occasion with flying colours.

Every referee at intercounty level harbours ambitions to referee an All-Ireland final. The high standards reached by Paddy have seen him referee two All-Ireland senior finals, a minor and a junior final, plus provincial finals in all four provinces. Add in a couple of National League finals and a Railway Cup final, and it is clear that Paddy Russell has achieved everything in his long career. Paddy's intercounty refereeing has now come to an end, but I have no doubt that he will continue to perform to the very highest level on the local club scene in Tipperary.

This book covers many angles of Paddy's life and career, including away from the hustle and bustle of the intercounty refereeing scene. The common trend coming across at all stages is Paddy's great love for the GAA and Gaelic games. They have been a huge part of his and his family's lives for so many years.

The book does, of course, examine some incidents that made national headlines, and which, to be honest, we could have done without. However, when leadership, assertiveness and control were called for, Paddy Russell was not found wanting. Hard calls had to be made, and Paddy made them. I have met no referee yet who gets any pleasure from having to issue a sanction against a player, but sometimes, thankfully not that often, tough decisions have to be made. Refereeing is not a popularity contest, and without these officials, our games could not take place.

I am sure this book will inspire others to take up the whistle. The GAA is constantly looking for new referees, and there is no better role model today than Paddy Russell. I am sure Paddy would also be the first to acknowledge the assistance he receives from the great back-up team of umpires who travel with him Sunday after Sunday. Thanks, Paddy, for your dedication and commitment.

Nioclás Ó Braonáin
Uachtarán GAA

Prologue

···

THY KINGDOM COME

There are two futures, the future of desire and the future of
fate, and man's reason has never learned to separate them.

John Desmond Bernal

The phone call from the Vodafone representative took me by
surprise. A television advertisement was in the pipeline for
transmission during the 2008 All-Ireland football championship,
and a number of top players had come on board for filming.
With Monaghan official Pat McEnaney, I was one of two referees
earmarked for the shoot at Dublin's Parnell Park. It was nice to
be asked, and I agreed pretty much without hesitation.

On Thursday, 12 June, I took the day off work and boarded
a 6.20 a.m. train bound for Dublin. We had been told to be at
Parnell Park at eight o'clock, but it was closer to half past when
I finally arrived in a taxi from the capital's Heuston Station.

Kerry captain Paul Galvin flashed me a cheery smile when
he spotted me.

'Well, Paddy, how are you?'

'Good, Paul, and yourself?'

I togged out alongside Meath player Darren Fay and Dublin
players Alan Brogan, Tomás 'Mossy' Quinn and Paul Flynn.
Parnell Park is the same venue where Dublin and Meath had
clashed in a fiery National Football League encounter in April. I

had been the referee when all but one of the thirty players on the pitch had become involved in an infamous brawl. Five had been sent off and a further eleven booked on that fateful afternoon, and lengthy suspensions had been imposed on a number of players.

There was no mention of that game as we got ready to face the cameras. There wasn't much talk at all, in fact. I don't think the players knew what to expect any more than I did. Pat McEnaney was ready to go. His scene involved a Dublin player being caught in the middle of two Meath men, and Pat was to blow for a free. Six takes later, and the directors finally seemed satisfied.

Filming stopped for a while until the sun reappeared from behind the clouds. Now it was our turn. Paul Galvin and Mayo's Ronan McGarrity stood on either side of me for a re-creation of the pre-match coin toss. I was to shake hands with Paul and Ronan, toss the coin, place it on my hand and nod to the winner. I would have thought that it would be a straightforward scene, but it took much longer than expected.

During a break in filming, Paul asked me, 'Where did that row break out between Dublin and Meath? Was it up around here?'

'No, down in that corner there, where you go into the dressing-rooms.'

As time ticked by, my fingers went numb from the cold and the coin fell from my grasp a few times. There wasn't much sympathy on offer here, though, and numerous retakes were ordered and recorded before filming was finally complete, for me at least.

It had been a long day. I left Parnell Park before three o'clock, but Pat later informed me that he was kept there until twenty to six. Before I left the North Dublin venue, Paul Galvin waved goodbye.

'I'll see you, Paddy.'

I replied, 'I'll see you on Sunday.'

He asked, 'Are you doing the game? I was wondering who was doing our match. I'll see you then.'

* * *

Sunday, 15 June: Munster and All-Ireland champions Kerry v. Clare at Fitzgerald Stadium, Killarney, in the provincial senior football championship semi-final. I had been linesman for the recent Galway–Sligo tie in Connacht, but this would be my first time refereeing an intercounty fixture since Dublin v. Meath at Parnell Park on 20 April. I certainly hoped there would be no drama here. I wasn't expecting any, either. Kerry were expected to win comfortably. It was a game expected to pass off without major incident.

I was ready for my first championship game of the season, wired up to my two linesmen, Mike Meade and Pat McGovern, and to an umpire at each end of the field. Another coin toss. Paul Galvin was present. We smiled at each other. We must have shaken hands at Parnell Park 100 times the previous Thursday.

Before the game started, I looked down towards the Clare goalmouth and noticed that Clare's full-back and captain for the day, Conor Whelan, and Kerry full-forward Tommy Walsh were pushing and shoving each other. I decided to get this one under way at 3.29 p.m., a minute before the scheduled throw-in time. Better to start it a minute early than have guys waiting around and becoming increasingly agitated.

With the ball thrown in, my nerves vanished completely, but it was a tough game with a real undercurrent of needle. I knew that I needed to get on top of this one early. I couldn't afford to let too much go. The fact that there were eight frees in the first five minutes tells its own story. The late, great John Moloney, who was such a huge influence on my career, used to say, 'Blow for everything in the first five or ten minutes. Ease off after that and see how it goes.'

Clare corner-back Gordon Kelly was booked for a foul on Kerry star Colm 'Gooch' Cooper. Pat McGovern informed me that Kelly had been tugging at Cooper's jersey off the ball. Kelly marked Cooper tight after that, but fair. There was no more off-the-ball stuff. If you nip something in the bud early, it generally tends not to happen again.

15

I booked Paul Galvin after 14 minutes for a foul on his marker, John Hayes, who was moving forward with the ball. 'That's not a booking,' Galvin protested, but it was a clear case of 'pulling down an opponent', an offence punishable by a yellow card.

It was a poor, scrappy first half, and Kerry led by just three points at the break – 0–7 to 0–4. At half-time, I spoke to my fellow officials and asked them the usual questions: 'How's it going? Am I blowing too much?' The general response was that I was doing fine and should continue 'keeping it tight'.

Predictably, Kerry asserted their authority on proceedings after half-time and, aided by a goal from Cooper, were coasting to victory with 15 minutes of normal time remaining. I had just sent off Clare's Conor Whelan for a late tackle on Darren O'Sullivan, but that was nothing compared to what came next.

MICHAEL MEADE: *'After Kerry's number 10 [Paul Galvin] had played the ball, he got into a scuffle with the Clare number 7 [John Hayes]. It went on for a couple of seconds. By the time Kerry had scored a point, it had broken up, but the Kerry 10 continued to point his finger at his opponent in an intimidating manner. I had to wait for the break in play before I could come in and tell Paddy what was going on. They had been jostling standing up and had each other caught by the collars of their jerseys. Number 7 was the instigator but number 10 reacted, and you can't do that.'*

In his official report on my performance, which arrived ten days after the game, assessor Eddie Cunningham wrote: 'I felt the second yellow card to Kerry's number 10 was a bit harsh, as I thought both the Clare number 7 and Kerry number 10 were just pushing and shoving each other, but the linesman was much nearer than me.'

Mike told me that Galvin was held by Hayes, and the two players became entangled and were jostling off the ball. That meant a yellow card for both. I dealt with Hayes first and was just about to book Galvin when he began remonstrating. I don't recall exactly what he said, but he did shout, 'You can't be serious!' I had my notebook out, ready to open it up, when Galvin slapped it to the ground.

Having to bend down and pick up my notebook was a degrading experience. People asked me later why I didn't make Galvin pick it up, but that never entered my head. Notebook safely back in my possession, I issued Galvin with a second yellow and was reaching for the red when the player marched towards Mike Meade.

MICHAEL MEADE: *'Galvin was highly strung. He was aggressive and confrontational in his manner. I was taken aback and made to feel very low. He was in my face, abusing me. "I did nothing, you fucking bollocks," he said. It was the luck of God that I didn't say anything back. I don't know what would have happened if I had opened my mouth. I didn't acknowledge him high up or low down, but he degraded me, cut the two legs out from under me.*

'I knew he had lost it when he slapped Paddy's notebook away. And that prepared me when he came across to me. There was no point in me doing anything. I had to blank it out. When a man is in that state, you don't acknowledge him or confront him in any way.'

Following Galvin's exchange with Mike, Kerry player Tomás Ó Sé tried to pull his teammate away, but he swung back at Tomás before finally making his way off the field. I was shocked, but although my wife, Margaret, told me later that she was worried that Galvin might hit me, I knew that he would never do something like that.

Even now, I find it difficult to understand why Galvin reacted the way he did, particularly for a second yellow card. He could have played in another game that evening having been sent off for two yellows, but instead he missed five championship matches. It was crazy stuff. He's a lovely guy off the field, and filming that Vodafone ad, we got on very well, but something snapped that day, and the repercussions were enormous. If Kerry had been playing Cork in a tight Munster final with one or two points separating the teams, perhaps I could understand a reaction like that, but they were cruising to victory against Clare.

I never considered a red card for the book-slapping offence alone. That would have led to huge confusion, because a red had already been issued. I'm sure I would have been accused of throwing cards around like confetti, and issuing a yellow followed by two reds would have looked ridiculous and led to further questions.

MICHEÁL O'DWYER (MATCH UMPIRE): *'If it had been anyone else but Paddy, the referee would have lost it with Galvin. I can certainly think of a couple of guys on the local scene in Tipperary who would have retaliated!'*

Hayes was sent off for a second yellow card deep in stoppage time – another story in itself. When I was booking Hayes for the initial incident with Galvin, I mistakenly marked Hayes down in my notebook as number 10. I'm not sure why this happened. It may have been the case that I was looking at Galvin while booking Hayes. Close to the full-time whistle, the Clare man caught a Kerry opponent with a high challenge – a definite case of rough play, punishable by a yellow card.

'Name?'

'John Hayes.'

I noted Hayes' number, checked my book for any previous offences by the Clare number 7 and issued a yellow card. Pat McGovern's voice came through in my earpiece, with a sense of urgency. 'Paddy! Paddy! He's after getting a yellow card already! You have to give him a red!' My umpires, John O'Brien and Stevie O'Donnell, were through seconds later with similar advice.

STEVIE O'DONNELL: *'Paddy had booked number 7 for Clare, but he told me afterwards that he put him in as number 10, so that this would have appeared as Hayes' first offence. When Paddy yellow-carded Hayes, I told John [O'Brien] that this was his second yellow. John went on the speaker to Paddy's earpiece straight away.'*

Before Kerry took the free, I returned to Hayes and showed him a second yellow, followed by red. Clare's manager, Frank Doherty, made it clear to Pat McGovern that he was unhappy that Pat, a fellow Galway man, had drawn my attention to the fact that Hayes had been booked earlier. Pat reminded Frank that if my error had slipped through the net, there would have been far more serious consequences. Frank later apologised to Pat for his comments.

After the Galvin sending off, Kerry midfielder Darragh Ó Sé trotted past and remarked, 'You're having a stinker. You're evening it up.' That was the final straw as far as I was concerned. I rarely, if ever, engage in chat with players, and my quick reply surprised even me: 'You're having a stinker yourself.' Sometimes, there's only so much that one can put up with. I had reached the end of my tether. Gaelic football was no fun any more.

1

....

CHARACTER FORMING

There is always one moment in childhood when
the door opens and lets the future in.

Deepak Chopra

Step back in time. Back to 1958 when the United States launched its first satellite, Explorer 1, a revolution in Iraq overthrew the monarchy, Brazil won the soccer World Cup and a 14 year old, Bobby Fischer, won the US chess championships.

That was the year I was born, at home in Rodas, Emly, West Tipperary, on 8 May. I was a fine, healthy-sized baby, the fourth in what would be a family of eight children. Margaret is the eldest, followed by Michael, Tommy, myself, Mary, Larry, Jimmy and John.

My father, Laurence, better known as Larry, is a local man from Ballinacree, while my mother, Elizabeth Brennan, hails from Ballingarry in South Tipperary. Mum, a housewife, and Dad, a builder, certainly had their hands full with eight children. Although times were hard and we didn't have an awful lot, I believe we were happier than the youth of today, many of whom seem disaffected.

We didn't have running water in the house when I was a child (the scheme from the Galtee Mountains came in later years), but we managed to source water from a well a half-mile from home.

That was one of the main evening chores when we arrived home from the local National School, and it helped us to appreciate the value of material possessions later in life.

I have noticed incredible changes in the last 20 years, and the vast majority of people do not want for much now. Today, however, there is so much pressure on people to succeed and compete. When I think of my childhood, I remember the innocence of long summers that stretched out like a giant blanket. Life these days is incredibly fast-paced, but it was gloriously slow when I was growing up. Piking hay with a local farmer, Mikey O'Dwyer, and bringing it home on the horse and float was hugely enjoyable and a handy source of an extra few bob. There were trips to the creamery on the ass and cart with another farmer, Paddy Burke. People back then were much more appreciative of what they had and understood the value of money. Every Sunday, three pence given to me by my mother or father on the way to Mass were deposited in the till of Paddy Hayes, a local sweetshop owner, in exchange for penny bars.

My best friends were Pascal Dawson, Seán Lonergan (who would later join me as a referee), Séamie Cunningham, Tom Nugent, Michael Kiely and Dermot Mulhall. I'm glad to say that I'm still in touch with some of the old school buddies. Seán was a Fethard-based garda and is now living on the outskirts of Clonmel, in Moyle Rovers country. Seán is also involved in refereeing administration, while Dermot owns the well-known Golden Thatch hostelry in Emly.

The world-renowned Grand National horse race was a source of great annual excitement for this bunch of friends. Preparations would begin weeks in advance, and when the dust had settled on the race at Liverpool, it was time for the main event as Russell, Dawson, Lonergan, Cunningham and Mulhall burst from the stalls for the Emly Grand National and Dawson's field became Aintree. Becher's Brook and The Chair were constructed from local foliage, and to this day I believe that Pascal's father enjoyed our race more than the famous steeplechase with the big fences!

CHARACTER FORMING

I loved all sports. Soccer, rugby, GAA – it really didn't matter as long as I could put foot to ball. Before televisions became a common item in almost every household, we would travel to Mary Carroll's house; she was a local woman who owned a prized set. All-Ireland semi-finals and finals in August and September were huge highlights, and playing on the road later in the evening, we'd pretend we were the players who graced Mary's screen. I had a particular fascination with the emerging Offaly teams of the late 1960s and early '70s, and I also remember Cork's Jimmy Barry-Murphy, a gifted dual player, taking a starring role for the Rebels in 1973.

When the TV age dawned and most households owned a set, each spring, the Five Nations rugby internationals were beamed into our homes, and after those games it was time for our own version. For us, Dawson's field was Lansdowne Road, Twickenham, Cardiff Arms Park, the Parc des Princes and Murrayfield all rolled into one. Gulping in the fresh air after watching the games, I'd imagine I was the legendary Irish international Mike Gibson. In later years, I adored the current rugby pundit Tony Ward, and when he vied for the coveted number 10 shirt with Ollie Campbell in the late 1970s and early '80s, I was firmly entrenched in the Ward camp. His all-action style of play excited me.

I was an altar boy for seven or eight years in Emly, and the local curate, Father Robert Mullally, was a great servant of the community for seventeen years. There is a plaque erected in his honour near the local tennis court, and he played a huge role in the construction of that particular amenity, as did my father, who helped to construct the pavilion. Father Mullally was a huge inspiration, raising funds and engendering a real spirit of solidarity in his parishioners.

When the local people met in Emly, the GAA was always the main topic of discussion, and whenever a big match was pencilled in for the town, it seemed that everybody rallied together, picking stones off the field, removing weeds, cleaning out the dressing-rooms and painting them, as well as cleaning the banks that surrounded the playing area. Getting a big match was a bonus because an overdue spring clean for the Emly GAA pitch was guaranteed. We're lucky nowadays that we have FÁS workers who do a tremendous job, but in my young days we relied totally on the goodwill of neighbours and friends. The community spirit was very special.

A Roscommon man, Seán McManus, was the driving force behind Gaelic football at my primary school. He would join us for soccer in the yard at breaktime, and lunchtime was spent on the Emly GAA pitch. A new field had just been purchased at the time, opened in 1968, and my father did a lot of the work on it, along with Paddy Walsh, putting down seats and building walls.

SEÁN MCMANUS: *'Coaching the young pupils was part of the school's extracurricular activities. I'm what's known as a "blow-in" around these parts. I'm originally from a place called Arigna in North Roscommon, a former coal-mining area near the borders of Leitrim and Sligo. I came down to Emly in January 1965, having spent a number of years teaching in Dublin. I joined the local GAA club and things progressed from there. I recall that Paddy, as a student, was very diligent. He just got on with it, a quiet kind of fella, really. He certainly never caused me any problems in his time here. I would have had him here as a pupil from the age of four right through to twelve or thirteen. He was always mad keen for playing games, and kicking a football gave him great satisfaction. I have great time for Paddy, and in later years I would have soldiered alongside him as a player and a club member. We were in contact quite a lot. A sound man and a very sincere individual who always tried 100 per cent.'*

Pascal's older brother Patsy Dawson was the big star in local circles. He wore the blue and gold of Tipperary and played Railway Cup football with the province of Munster. At the Dawsons' house, as a young boy, I'd get to see the red Munster jersey, which was often hanging up there, and I was spellbound by it. I spent a huge amount of time in that house, and I looked up to Patsy as a hero. He ate oranges in his car, never drank alcohol or smoked and really looked after himself. A superb footballer and hurler, Patsy came from a large family who were all blessed with their own individual talents. Pascal was a good player in his own right, but music had a greater hold on him.

SEÁN MCMANUS: *'Patsy was the real star, all right, and he was on the Emly junior football team that defeated Lorrha in the county final in 1968. I was a selector alongside Mick Frawley [former Tipperary football board chairman]. Patsy's brothers Mickey and William were handy players, too, on that successful team.'*

Secondary school was a daunting prospect, but the blow was softened by the presence of some of my old Emly chums. Very few boys from National School went to the Abbey CBS in Tipperary town, opting instead for the vocational college in Hospital, three miles from Emly. We went there to learn a trade. The well-known comedian Jon Kenny, who was one half of the much-loved double act D'Unbelievables, was one of my school chums. Jon attended the nearby convent for a year before joining us, and it wasn't long before he formed the band Gimmick. That was the start of a fine career in the entertainment business for Jon, and visiting the RTÉ studios in Dublin for his special school-reunion TV show a few years ago was an unforgettable experience.

I wouldn't say I was very strong academically at school. I didn't have a whole lot of interest, and, because money was scarce, the main aim was to find any kind of job after school, rather than to learn for learning's sake. I disliked Irish classes and found that I could pick up French far more easily than our native tongue. It would have been nice to have the cupla focail, but I never got to grips with the Irish language.

I wasn't a bad footballer, but hurling was definitely not one of my gifts. Football was undoubtedly the most popular sport in the school, and that suited me just fine. I managed to get on the school team, and although centre-back or wing-back were my favourite positions, I played at centre field. The school team wasn't taken too seriously then, not like today, when there is such an emphasis on preparation.

I see Tipperary footballer Damien O'Brien doing some great work with the boys in the Abbey, where my sons Shane and Mark go to school. Paddy O'Kelly, Conor Reale and Jim Ryan are putting in the hours too, and they need to be on their toes because of the attractions of rugby and soccer. The glitz and glamour associated with those sports, particularly in the midst of a highly successful period for the Munster rugby team, are extremely attractive to the young kids.

When I was in secondary school, the alternatives to Gaelic football were volleyball or basketball, hardly sports to capture the hearts and minds of the youth, and there was no rugby or soccer at all. Now you have rugby coaches in the schools, and even at National School level, tag rugby is a popular pursuit.

I recall that FÁS had a scheme for a good number of years whereby coaches were paid to come to the National Schools. The legendary Kerry player Mick O'Connell was a regular visitor around West Tipperary. It's difficult to get people from local clubs involved in the schools now, unless they're retired.

I can't say that my family boasted a huge GAA background, although my uncle Jimmy, an army man, was renowned as a good hurler in Naas, County Kildare. My parents had only a passing interest in Gaelic games, but when we began playing at juvenile level, they attended most of our matches. And in the early 1970s, Emly started to make progress at underage level, which would lead to some decent success in the intermediate and senior ranks.

Inspired by our coach, a local man called Johnny Aylmer, we captured the county rural and urban-rural titles at Under-13 level in 1971. I'm not quite sure how Johnny got involved, because his family would not have been steeped in the GAA either, but we were certainly glad that he wove his magic with us. Patsy Dawson assisted in training, too, and that was quite a thrill because we looked up to and respected a man of his talent. A year later, we repeated those successes at Under-14 level, and our reward was a visit to Croke Park for the replayed 1972 All-Ireland final replay between Kerry and Offaly, two teams I loved. The whole day just blew me away. Before I entered the famous stadium for the very first time, we played a challenge match against a team from Meath in the Phoenix Park. Then we stood on the famous Hill 16 terrace for the big game. Although I had a real fondness for Kerry, Offaly were my favourites. They had some fantastic players – Tony McTague, Willie Bryan, Kevin Kilmurray, Martin Furlong and 'the Iron Man from Rhode', Paddy McCormack. I'd grown up hearing about the heroic deeds of these men. I stood on a 7-Up can during the big game for an extra few inches of height, as the view down towards the front of the Hill wasn't great.

Of course, following the Tipperary senior hurlers was another huge part of the summer. I listened to the 1971 Munster final on the radio, a famous day when Tipperary beat Limerick, with Michael 'Babs' Keating's famous 'dry ball' incident. That was probably a game that Tipperary should have lost, but Limerick would have their revenge two years later. The 1973 provincial final at Semple Stadium, Thurles, is the first big Tipperary game that I can recall being present at. I was stood on the bank, before the New Stand was built, and Limerick's manager for the last couple of seasons, Richie Bennis, scored a late winning point. At the time, it was difficult to attend many of the big games, but the unmistakable voice of the late Micheál O'Hehir brought the action to life in our living rooms. Listening to O'Hehir was the next best thing to being there.

Even then, the GAA consumed me, while my siblings had varied interests. Jimmy played football and hurling, and was good at both. John and Michael played a bit too, and while Larry's main passion was for cars, he now does a lot of work at underage level with Kilteely.

In 1975, I got my hands on a precious West minor football championship medal. However, it wasn't long before elation was replaced by despair. Clonmel Commercials were our opponents in the county minor football final, and glory beckoned as we led by eight points at half-time. I thought we had the game won, but the wheels came off in the second half and Commercials stormed back to beat us by five points, a thirteen-point turnaround. I remember lying on the field for what seemed like an eternity afterwards, and when I blow the final whistle to signal the end of massive games at intercounty and club levels, I can certainly identify with that nauseating feeling of defeat. I sampled intermediate success with the club in 1975, but losing the minor final was a particularly hard blow that I have never forgotten.

An Emly-Lattin combination won the West Tipp minor championship in 1977, but this team never had a chance to really build on that success. In the years that followed, many were forced to emigrate in search of work, and, as for many other GAA clubs at the time, it was often a struggle to field a team. However, that group of minor players formed the backbone of a senior team that saw success on the divisional and county stages in the 1980s.

The undoubted highlights of my playing career were first in 1983 when Emly won the West and county intermediate football titles, and then in 1987 when we won the West senior football crown. In that 1987 final, I even managed to kick a point – a rarity in itself! It was one of those days when absolutely nothing could go wrong.

TOM-JOE O'BRIEN (FORMER UMPIRE WITH PADDY): '*There were two really good crops in the club, the first being the team that won the Under-14 county final in 1972. A second wave came through after a two-year juvenile ban for the club, and we contested three minor and five Under-21 West finals. Mike Burke bridged the gap between the 1968 and 1983 county intermediate championship-winning teams, playing on both. Paddy Russell and Timmy Bourke, experienced players by that time, played in the wing-back positions on the 1983 team. Research shows that 63 matches were played between 1981 and '83, and both Paddy and Timmy played in them all. That's a phenomenal record.*'

SEÁN MCMANUS: '*I played alongside Paddy up until the 1980s. We played together for many years, and that would have been the case with a good number of lads: I would have taught them and played football with them later. Those boys from the mid-1970s really developed in the 1980s as adult footballers. It took us a long time to bring through some really good hurlers, though.'*

I always felt that our day would come, because men like Seán McManus had laid the foundations and put in tremendous work. Seán became much more heavily involved at club level in the 1970s, and he placed greater emphasis on hurling, which had been neglected for too long.

TOM-JOE O'BRIEN: *'Seán McManus was to leave for Australia in the 1970s, but he played in a tournament, was knocked unconscious and that seemed to change his mind. That was certainly the locality's gain, as Seán brought athletics into the National School. Some girls won All-Ireland medals. A camogie team was started up and the girls were taken to the Community Games finals. Hurling had been played before, but there was no real emphasis placed on it, and Seán changed that. I can remember our Under-11 team being taken to Golden, where the former Tipperary hurler Donie Nealon showed us a video of the skills of the game.'*

SEÁN MCMANUS: *'In the early 1970s, the Emly club was involved in a bit of controversy for playing overage players at juvenile level. The club was suspended from competing in all juvenile competitions for a year and a half, which was very harsh. Since then, the rule has changed so that only club officials and the players involved can now be suspended. I came on the scene from then on, not because of what happened, but because it was a natural progression, really. I was promoting hurling and football in the school, and that followed on to the club. From the time I came to Emly, I was a player with the club, but I had a choice to make around 1974: whether to stay involved in coaching the Tipperary senior footballers or to throw in my lot with the club. Football would have been my main interest in the beginning, but I took responsibility for all juvenile teams and started promoting hurling, too. There were some great hurlers produced in Emly once the game gained a foothold. Mike Cunningham and Mike Corcoran won Munster minor and Under-21 medals with Tipperary, and Corcoran also won a National League title. Brendan Corcoran was beaten in minor and Under-21 All-Irelands but he won Munster medals, and my eldest son Shane won an All-Ireland junior title with Tipperary in 1991.'*

It was football all the way with me. I played a small bit of hurling later in my career, but I would have considered myself a dangerous hurler! The 'highlight' of my days wielding the ash came in an outing against local rivals Lattin-Cullen, when I had the dubious honour of marking an emerging Nicholas English. Nicholas, an elusive and supremely gifted player, went on to become a real star for Tipperary, winning All-Ireland medals in 1989 and 1991 before becoming an All-Ireland winning manager in 2001. I went to block Nicky during the game, but his hurl slid down along mine and connected with my finger, breaking it. It's my claim to fame: I had my finger broken by Nicky English! It was totally innocuous, of course, and it is a genuine honour to say that I marked Nicky in a game at a time when he was just starting out on the path to greatness.

By then, I had embarked on a path of my own, a new and unexpected path that would change my life forever. As a club player, I had to be particularly careful not to find myself in trouble. For, now, I was a referee.

2

....

THE FIRST WHISTLE

Motivation is what gets you started.
Habit is what keeps you going.

Jim Rohn

It starts innocently enough for some. The referee fails to turn up, and an unwitting volunteer picks up the baton and decides to run with it. From there, he never looks back.

I never took a huge amount of interest in refereeing as a young player. As far as I was concerned, the referee was there to do a job but he was a peripheral figure, an irrelevance in many ways. But there was one man who made me see things differently, a man respected by players, supporters, officials and fellow referees alike. His name was John Moloney.

My refereeing career began when I was a 17 year old in 1976, when I took part in a Bórd na nÓg training course in Bansha under the guidance of John and the juvenile-board chairman at the time, Brother Michael O'Grady, who would later manage Dublin's senior hurlers.

SEÁN MCMANUS: 'Michael was recruiting referees and Paddy, Seán Lonergan, who is still involved with the Referees Association in South Tipperary, and John O'Meara took up the invitation. I thought that was great. They were very young lads, but they went off and became referees. John later left this locality, and for a while he worked as a *fisherman in Donegal. He's been back down in Cork for a good number of years. Seán and Paddy kept at it, though, and Paddy is still going strong, of course.'*

As a teenager, I was already hooked by the GAA on various levels. My playing career was progressing quite nicely, but I was also interested in the administration side of the Emly club. As a committee member, I was present for the various meetings, which were generally very well attended in those years. The highlight of the club year at boardroom level is the annual general meeting, and, as youngsters, my friends and I were always amazed by the huge crowds that would flock to the local hall for this event.

SEÁN MCMANUS: *'I have always admired Paddy's commitment to refereeing, and he was a committed player as well, an individual who would give you 100 per cent. He always worked to his limits; there was no holding back. He was and is a great club person and would have been hurling secretary at a very young age. He wouldn't have had much to do in that role, but he was on the committee for a long time and was always interested in club activities outside of refereeing. He was an all-round GAA person.'*

While I was attending a run-of-the-mill monthly club meeting in 1976, fate grabbed me firmly by the hand. The West Bórd na nÓg wanted referees to take charge of juvenile games, and the various clubs had been contacted and asked to put names forward. The letter was read out, and a few of us decided to go along, out of pure curiosity. It was a shot in the dark, but that's exactly how it started. Each graduate received his very first refereeing kit after the course in Bansha: a black jersey with a white pocket and white collars, black togs and black socks.

The refereeing course lasted for five weeks and my brother Michael was a great help, driving me everywhere as my fledgling career took off. Mike Hennessy, too, a clubmate and former teammate of mine, was often on hand in his Morris Minor to give me a lift. Bansha or Seán Treacy Park in Tipperary town were my most frequent venues in the early days, and the very first match

I can remember refereeing was played in Bansha, an Under-12 game between the local team and Cashel King Cormacs.

I remember John Moloney after the match: on that particular evening, John was very definitely wearing his Bansha hat, and he wasn't best pleased with the performance of this novice referee! That was John; when Bansha were playing, he just couldn't help letting his passion shine through. But what a help he was to me, always there for a chat and a piece of valuable advice. I couldn't but learn from the master.

Of course, a referee needs four umpires, and I owe a huge thanks to Seán O'Brien, a local farmer who always allowed his sons Tom-Joe, Seánie, Mikey and Liam to join me for evening games. The four brothers were all younger than me, and even though they might have been needed for milking or other farming chores, their late father Seán always allowed them to travel to the various matches.

TOM-JOE O'BRIEN: *'We liked going to the matches with Paddy. He would ring us up and tell us that he had an Under-12 game the following night and ask were we available. It wasn't so much that we enjoyed umpiring as such when we were young, but it was something to do in the evenings. It would be the craic of going somewhere, a group to be in, and there was a lot of scuttin' and blackguarding! I always blame Paddy for starting us smoking! We would have known every footballer and hurler in West Tipp as Paddy progressed through the ranks, and many more in the rest of the county. Paddy got a fair bit of abuse refereeing, but the craic afterwards was great. And Paddy always took our word as umpires for what had happened if we had witnessed an incident, waved a ball wide or disallowed a goal for a square ball. He always stood by us.'*

A car fast became a necessity to get around to matches, and pretty soon I was doing a fine impression of a taxi driver – minus the plate and the few bob at the end of the ride, mind you! There was a brilliant feeling of independence that came with owning a car, and driving around was no penance whatsoever.

TOM-JOE O'BRIEN: *'When the Under-16 players arrived for a match away from home, there was a rush of four or five fellas for Paddy's car.*

We travelled around looking at underage games with Paddy, and that group of young guys became his regular umpires. I remember Paddy had a black-and-white Escort, and Timmy Bourke, who was umpiring too, had a Morris Minor. There could have been six or seven in each car driving to tournaments around the county. Moyle Rovers used to run a very successful sevens competition in the late 1970s, and Seán McManus would share the driving with Paddy and Timmy.

'I remember going for coaching with the Tipperary minor team – I was sixteen at the time – and every Saturday for eight weeks before Christmas, we left Emly for Clonmel at ten past nine in the morning. The timetable was a session of coaching in the morning, lunch at one, back again for more theory and then a match at three o'clock. Paddy would wait all day to bring us home. He did that for the two years we were training there. He was the designated driver, wasn't drinking, and so he was an ideal person for parents to send young lads off with. We went to see so many tournament games. I remember watching Tipperary v. Cork on one occasion, and, after returning by train to Limerick Junction, we hopped in the car and went to see Solohead and Galbally playing in a tournament final in Galbally. Paddy was also the hackney to the discos in Ballylanders and was always good for a couple of loads!'

There were many others who helped me out as umpires: Paddy Clancy, Pa Sheehy, Johnny Martin, Paddy Brennan, Martin Condon, Eamonn O'Meara, Jack Hennessy, Seán McManus, Davy Crowe, Mick Concannon, John and Mike McGrath, Liam Burke, Joe, Denis and Donal Heelan, and Timmy Bourke, men who would make themselves available at the drop of a hat – and often at very short notice. Mickey Collins and D.D. Cremins, from outside the parish boundaries, were also brilliant. The late Sammy Ryan from Golden umpired for me, ran the line for me and even drove a minibus containing the refereeing team to some games. The list goes on: Connie Lorigan, Paddy Maher, Eamonn Buckley, Brendan Lohan, Connie Sullivan, Gerry Cummins, Nicholas Lonergan, Richard O'Connor and Lar O'Keeffe from Solohead, right through to my right-hand men of the present day – John O'Brien of Arravale Rovers, Liam and

Micheál O'Dwyer from Annacarty (an uncle-and-nephew team) and Stevie O'Donnell. Michael Forrester from Golden, Jim Ryan of Arravale Rovers and Seán Bradshaw from the Knockavilla Kickhams are three great guys, always on standby and ready to fill in if the need arises. There were so many people who helped out, and I owe them all my thanks. Some of them I'm sure I have forgotten to mention here, and if I have, I sincerely apologise.

Timmy Bourke and I went to school together. He worked hard, but, as my career progressed to the intercounty stage, I recall him joining me in far-flung Killarney, Castleisland and Páirc Uí Chaoimh for Munster Under-21 championship matches. Eventually, Timmy became self-employed, and even though the number of games increased, he still felt obliged to travel with me. I felt guilty about this, dragging Timmy from his work at three or four o'clock in the afternoon. In the end, I didn't ask Timmy to travel with me any more. He may have wondered why, but I can assure him that it had nothing to do with the standard of his umpiring. I felt he needed to be at his place of work rather than traipsing all over the province of Munster with me.

TOM-JOE O'BRIEN: *'The more Under-21 games Paddy got, the harder it became. The local matches were no problem. You could get the milking done beforehand or do it later, but leaving at three o'clock in the afternoon became increasingly difficult. I missed out on some of the intercounty matches.'*

Two cars were often needed for those fixtures because the referee was obliged to supply not only umpires but also linesmen. We would often have to leave Tipperary at 3 p.m. for a 7 p.m. start, and but for the selflessness of some of the guys who travelled with me, I would not have survived long as an intercounty referee.

In many ways, refereeing was more demanding at club level, where I might be taking charge of a game five or six nights a week. I couldn't expect the same four umpires to join me every night, so it was important to have a good few men to pick from.

Sometimes I could get away with two umpires, one at each goal, and draft in a couple of spectators to make up the quartet. That was never an ideal situation, but sometimes it was either that or no game.

I don't think I was ever nervous in the early part of my career; I was more likely to be excited when I was given a fixture. It was like playing, in many ways. I didn't know what to expect from one game to another. Because a large number of guys had completed the refereeing course, there was a plethora of new, young referees on the local scene, and that was exciting too.

There was the odd occasion when I was thrust into the fray at short notice. After I'd purchased a car, a few of us went over to Golden for a match, and when no referee turned up, I was asked to fill in. The local club officials spotted me coming through the gate and provided me with boots and socks.

There were no official assessments of referees at the time. The assessment was basic word of mouth. Somebody at the game might tell colleagues, 'He's not a bad referee,' and the word would spread from there. There were always people who would complain about my performances, although most games seemed to go pretty well for me. I would notice at juvenile games that you would get people who had never attended a GAA match in their lives until their little Johnny appeared on the scene and then suddenly they were experts on the rules of the games. The other side of the coin, of course, is that a lot of people start following the GAA because their kids are playing, and, at a time when it is so difficult to find new volunteers within the Association, that can only be a good thing.

I've witnessed so much on the juvenile scene, good and bad. I've seen mentors literally dragging young kids off the field and putting in substitutes. That's bound to leave a mental scar on a young player. Kids need encouragement at that age, not embarrassment. The vast majority of parents and team mentors are great, but there is a small minority who really do not know how to behave.

After an initial period of refereeing juvenile games, my first major assignment came when I took charge of the 1978 West junior football final, when Aherlow defeated Golden in Bansha. That was a massive afternoon, as the game was the curtain-raiser to a National Football League tie between Tipperary and Clare. Two years later, a wet Saturday evening in Dundrum was the backdrop to my first West minor football final, as Arravale Rovers defeated Cashel.

They were great times, although far removed from the glamour associated with the modern intercounty scene. There were occasions when I togged out in the car, because the facilities at some clubs left a lot to be desired. To this day, some clubs really don't know what to do about the referee. When new clubhouses are being constructed, the referee is an afterthought. I've often prepared for matches in the janitor's room.

By 1981, I had handled my first divisional senior football final, involving Arravale Rovers and Solohead – another memorable milestone, as the game took place in Emly. My first senior final in my own back yard. It could hardly have been scripted better: the game finished in a draw, and I had another day out, in Emly again. Bonus territory.

TOM-JOE O'BRIEN: *'The games I would remember more are the ones where there were incidents. At a junior hurling game in Aherlow in the early days, John Moloney was umpiring, with me at one end. We had given a goal that the Bansha goalkeeper felt should have been disallowed for a square ball, and we awarded another one that crept behind the line. The goalie reckoned we were out to do him. At one point, the ball came in around the square, and, instead of picking it up and clearing it, he picked it up and drove it at us! There were some hairy ones like that.*

'I remember the day myself and Eamonn O'Meara ran off after an intermediate final between Moyne-Templetuohy and Father Sheehy's. Before half-time, we gave a goal against Father Sheehy's when the goalie stepped behind the line. We went to put up the green flag, but play continued, and it took a few moments before people realised that we

had signalled for a goal. By now, people had gathered around us, and that was one of the few times when I did not feel safe. The half-time whistle blew, and, as we walked off, the Father Sheehy's crowd told us that we weren't going home if they were beaten. When Paddy blew the final whistle, Eamonn and I ran!'

Bearing in mind that I was still a player, I had to be aware of my conduct on the field of play. Indeed, many people felt that I should have packed in my playing career after becoming a referee. I vividly recall a senior championship game between Emly and Solohead at Seán Treacy Park in Tipperary town when my direct opponent hit me a slap. I was itching for revenge, but I knew that if I went there, I would be sent off and my refereeing career would be placed in immediate jeopardy. Also, if I were to receive a lengthy suspension from the GAA, I would be banned from all activities, refereeing included. I had to watch my step.

I would never have considered myself a dirty player, but I went in hard and saw no danger. That's the way I played the game, and, because I was so consumed by the GAA, I wanted to do both, burn the candles at both ends. I wanted to play the game *and* referee it. There were times when I had to decide between playing and refereeing, but the club almost always came first, most notably when I passed up the chance to referee a glamour All-Ireland Under-21 semi-final between Kerry and Galway in 1987. Emly were involved in the county senior football championship, and, I'll be honest, it was a no-brainer for me. I often wondered if that would be held against me at Croke Park, but it's often the case that referees are unable to do fixtures, for a variety of reasons. And on many occasions, I have stepped in at the eleventh hour for other referees who have had to cry off, injured, sick or because of a prior engagement.

Another time, when I was chairman of the Emly club, we were due to play Fethard in the county junior football final in Clonoulty; however, I was also asked to referee the Munster senior club football final replay between Nemo Rangers and St

Senan's Kilkee, after I had taken charge of the drawn fixture between the two sides. I gave up the provincial decider in favour of Emly's county final.

If a local league match involving Emly clashed with a National League fixture I was down to referee, I would choose the National League game. It was a painful choice at times, but Emly were struggling to make headway as a club and I was moving up the refereeing ladder.

TOM-JOE O'BRIEN: *'From the very first day that Paddy refereed, he reffed as he saw it, even if he had to take charge of an Emly game. And Paddy has stepped in at short notice so many times. If he gets a late call to do a game because the appointed referee fails to show up, he drops everything. Then, when he's refereeing the game, everybody's having a go. I think it will become the biggest problem for the GAA, getting people to referee. The numbers in West Tipperary are falling rapidly. My own daughter told me about a series of four Under-12 games this year where on three occasions no referee turned up.'*

After learning my trade for four years at local level, the opportunity I had been waiting for finally arrived in 1981. It was time to clamber out of the shallow end of the refereeing pool and dive in head first at the deep end. I was about to become an intercounty referee. Time to sink or swim.

3

....

DARBY DAY

> History is merely a list of surprises. It can only
> prepare us to be surprised yet again.
>
> Kurt Vonnegut

From humble beginnings to the biggest stage of all: that neatly sums up my first season as a senior intercounty football referee. The Division 4 National Football League tie between hosts Limerick and Longford at the Gaelic Grounds in October 1981 was a dream fixture for a cub referee like me.

In truth, it was a mundane match, far removed from the media spotlight, attracted a paltry attendance and passed off without incident. Nevertheless, my intercounty debut filled me with excitement and was the start of a lengthy career that spanned 28 seasons. And just 11 months after that Limerick city opener, I was appointed as linesman for the 1982 All-Ireland senior football final, when Offaly scored what I regard as the most famous goal in Gaelic football history to deny Kerry a fifth successive crown.

Not long after my debut, I took charge of another Limerick game in Kilbeheny. Paddy Ryan from Galbally, Limerick's delegate to the GAA's Central Council, was on the gate collecting the entrance fee from patrons. The takings for the match were £30.50, and as I was entitled to a meal allowance of £6 per head for myself and my four umpires, I ended up with the £30. Paddy threw in the 50p for good measure!

I believe that my early career benefited from my remaining patient. I knew that I had to start at the bottom and work my way up through the ranks, but some referees starting out now want an All-Ireland final in their very first year. And if they don't achieve immediate success, they walk away from the whistle.

Of course, everybody needs a break, and I was lucky in that top officials at Croke Park were aware of my capabilities as a referee. They were heavily reliant on word of mouth, and, through the years, Liam O'Dwyer of Boherlahan, John Doyle, Mick Maguire, Con Hogan and Noel Morris have flown the flag for Tipperary within the corridors of power. I'd compare the situation to a Tipperary selector pushing players for interprovincial representation with Munster. I was lucky that Mick was from the West division. He would have touted guys from the Mid, North and South if he felt they were good enough, but he obviously had a bit of time for me. Mick also helped the former intercounty hurling referee Willie Barrett on his way. Both of us started off on the national circuit at around the same time.

It was a great honour to run the line in the 1982 All-Ireland final, but I got more of a buzz out of doing matches towards the end of my intercounty career; I was very young back then, too young to appreciate it, perhaps. It was a cracking game of football, but if the matches were as intense then as they are now, it would have been a much more difficult job. Crucially for big-match referee P.J. McGrath and his team of officials, these were two teams intent on playing football the way it should be played. I loved Offaly's style but Kerry were the game's true aristocrats, as they are today. Privately, I was hoping that Offaly would win the game, because I had been fascinated by them as a child; but, on the flipside, Kerry came from the province of Munster, and I was aware of the game's historical significance. It's a shame that they didn't complete the five-in-a-row, because that Kerry team deserved it. It's probably the one time that I would not have minded seeing Offaly lose.

It was my second visit to Croke Park, but this time I was gracing the hallowed sod. Eleven years before, I had strained from my perch on Hill 16 for a look at these two teams battling it out, but now here they were, right in front of my very eyes, with Sam Maguire gleaming on the Hogan Stand presentation podium. This is what I had dreamed of: an incredible atmosphere and a game that would go down in the annals as one of the most dramatic ever played. So good, in fact, that a book was published about it in 2007.

I received notification from Croke Park that I had been appointed to run the line in the form of a letter from the GAA's Pat Quigley. I must admit that I didn't make a particularly big deal of it at the time. Being awarded a big game at Croke Park meant a whole lot more to me in later years.

On the morning of the game, I rose early and linked up with Mick Maguire at his place before travelling on to collect Donie English, father of Nicky. We went early to avoid the Kerry traffic on the way up, and, on arriving at Croke Park, I found that a gleaming set of gear was waiting for P.J. and his linesmen in the dressing-room.

There was a tremendous atmosphere and I was completely taken aback by the speed of the game. I hurtled up and down the touchline. At one point, John Egan lost his football boot and I handed it back to him. On the match video, Micheál O'Hehir referred to a blacksmith helping Egan out in his time of need.

P.J. MCGRATH: *'The Kerry v. Derry minor clash in 1975 was my very first All-Ireland final. The great Jack O'Shea was full-forward for the Kerry minors that day, and Paddy's old mentor, John Moloney, did the senior match that followed. I was delighted to get my first senior final in 1982, and a guy called Mick Maguire, who was on the GAC [the GAA's Games Administration Committee] at the time, proposed Paddy for a linesman's job. "We have a young fella from Tipperary, he's in great shape and he'll be a great help to you." That's what Mick said to me at the time. The first time I met Paddy was in the dressing-room before we went out to do the game. In previous years, all of the All-*

Ireland final linesmen came from Dublin. It was handy for the GAA, and they rotated it among a group of Dublin guys. But they decided to try a few fellas from other counties, and it was a great experience for a budding referee because it's a daunting task running the line. You have 10,000 people in the stand behind roaring at you. It would have been intimidating for Paddy officiating in a game of that magnitude for the first time.'

Mick Maguire went on to become county-board chairman in Tipperary. I didn't know him terribly well at the time, but he played with Lattin and would have been aware of my refereeing. Mick was Tipperary's representative on the GAA's powerful Central Council and a member of the GAC, which appointed referees and linesmen. Since we came to live in the parish of Lattin, we've been delighted to count Mick among our friends. His late wife Eileen, RIP, always had a great welcome for us, and he has a lovely family. Gerry, his son, who played hurling for Tipperary, is one man our two boys really look up to. One thing I really like about Mick is that if he feels that I made a bad call in a game, he will say it to my face, not behind my back or shouting from the sideline. We have great chats over a cuppa, and he is always a welcome caller to our home.

MICK MAGUIRE: '*Watching Paddy from a young age, he reminded me of a fellow who saw a foul before it happened. He had that kind of instinct in him, something special, a foresight. At club games in the county, I latched onto him. I did give him a lot of advice, and I would have told him straight out if he made mistakes. I was a member of the Activities Committee of the GAA, and I pushed him well. I knew that I could push him, because I felt I was on safe ground – I was sure that he wouldn't let me down. He looked so assured on the field, and he would always look back after a ball was cleared to spot any possible "afters". He was mature from a young age. The one thing I saw about Paddy, and I've always maintained this, is that, regardless of the way a match is going, he always referees the game on a straight line.*'

P.J. MCGRATH: '*Paddy did very well. He was very helpful. He was up with the play from the start, and when he gave a decision, he was within yards of the incident. He wasn't dawdling along. I had spoken to him before the game and filled him in on what to expect. I told him to keep up with the play and give the right signals. Paddy was a fit young fella, and he needed to be. I'm sure he remembers that day with great fondness. For anybody who ever takes up refereeing, the first day out at Croke Park is a great day. He's a solid guy is Paddy, courageous and courteous, and he commands respect from players and officials alike. As chairman of the National Referees Association now, I'd have Paddy refereeing every day of the week if I could. He was starting out when I was finishing up and was still involved over a quarter of a century later. He really has given it his all.'*

I was a club footballer when my refereeing career really took off at intercounty level, but nonetheless I was really struck by the speed of the game. There was such a difference between intercounty and club. Players weren't as fit as they are now, but Dublin and Kerry had brought fitness to unprecedented levels in the 1970s before Offaly emerged once again to challenge the big two.

Martin Furlong famously saved a second-half penalty from Kerry's Mikey Sheehy, and that was a huge moment in the match because if the Kingdom had netted, there would have been no way back for Offaly. The 1982 final was decided by that famous goal from Offaly's Séamus Darby, and Kerry were denied the five-in-a-row in dramatic fashion. However, many people believe to this day that Darby pushed Kerry's Tommy Doyle while climbing high to gather possession.

I had a reasonable view of the incident, but I couldn't see if there was a push or not. I was running the line on the Cusack Stand side of the field, and it looked a perfectly good goal from where I was situated. It's still very hard to judge, even if you look back at slow-motion video footage, but my view is that if it really was a push, the defender would have lurched forward in an obvious fashion. I took it for granted then that Darby had timed his jump to perfection. P.J. was happy enough that no offence had been committed, but none of us realised just how big a deal the 'push' would become. It was similar to my own situation in the 1995 All-Ireland final, when I was involved in two much talked-about incidents. You return to the dressing-room after the game confident that you have performed capably, and then the storm blows up.

P.J. MCGRATH: *'All of my officials were totally unanimous that it was a perfect goal. The game itself has stood the test of time. It was one of the great games, and it's one of the most requested for the reruns on TG4.'*

P.J. is now chairman of the GAA's National Referees Association, and to this day we maintain a good relationship. He still says to me, 'You were with me in 1982.' That was his finest hour, and it's nice to have been a part of it.

Offaly were, naturally, ecstatic at the final whistle, but we were there to do a job, and we quickly retreated to the dressing-room as spectators raced onto the pitch. We togged off on the Hogan Stand side of the field, had our shower and headed for home. Of course, the day was an obvious milestone in my career, but, at the time, it was just another match to me. The All-Ireland final is a much bigger occasion now, with huge media interest. Look at how many reporters attend matches now compared to when I started out refereeing in the 1970s. Even the secondary provincial competitions, the McGrath Cup in Munster, Leinster's O'Byrne Cup, the FBD League in Connacht and Ulster's McKenna Cup, are given huge space in the newspapers now. They barely registered in the past. I can recall newspapers giving maybe a page to an All-Ireland final, but now you have entire supplements previewing and reviewing the big day.

The 1982 final gave me a real taste for Croke Park. It's the place where everybody wants to be. It was a dream come true, but, as I was just 24 at the time, I was too young to fully appreciate the occasion. In his autobiography, the soccer referee Graham Poll spoke about having officiated in both the old and new Wembley stadiums, and it's the same for me. I was a referee and a linesman at the old and new Croke Park stadiums, and every time I walked out on that pitch, it was an honour. One of my umpires, Stevie O'Donnell, often thanked me for bringing him to the best venue in the country when we were preparing for games at GAA headquarters. I'll take good and bad memories from the place, but one thing's for sure: I'll certainly miss it.

4

....

A VIOLENT RIVALRY

Life is 10 per cent what happens to you
and 90 per cent how you react to it.

Charles R. Swindoll

In the career of any referee, there are surely defining moments.
For me, the first of these came in 1983 when I refereed the West
Tipperary senior football final between Galtee Rovers (Bansha)
and Solohead. It ranks as one of the most violent games in the
history of the GAA.

The Nationalist newspaper, a local publication in Tipperary, ran
the banner headline: 'The most disgraceful display ever seen on
a GAA pitch'. The edition date was Saturday, 30 July 1983, six
days after I sent off five players in what should have been one
of the best games in the local GAA calendar.

During my intercounty career, I have refereed two matches
that were marred by mass brawls involving both sets of players.
The 2006 National Football League clash between Dublin and
Tyrone is remembered as 'the Battle of Omagh', while Dublin
and Meath's meeting in April 2008 is referred to as 'the Dust-
Up in Donnycarney'. Both pale into insignificance when placed
alongside the sheer naked thuggery witnessed at Seán Treacy
Park in Tipperary town on that Sunday afternoon in 1983.

It's fair to say that trouble was anticipated before Bansha's

Galtee Rovers and Solohead locked horns in the final. The previous meetings between the teams had been explosive encounters, so bad that referees were being drafted in from outside the divisional and county boundaries in an attempt to bring some order to proceedings.

Normally, a West senior football final does not draw a massive crowd, but the clash between Bansha and Solohead packed them in. During the week leading up to the game, both sets of players were talking about what they would do to each other, but nobody could have predicted in their wildest dreams what would follow.

JERRY RING (WEST GAA SECRETARY): *'At the subsequent West board meeting of 25 August, where players and clubs were dealt with, Solohead chairman Michael Ryan Cooper said that because of pre-match reports [anticipating violent behaviour], he had called a club meeting, attended by 50 people, on the Thursday before the game to warn against any indiscipline on the day. This warning was repeated in the dressing-room before the game by team manager Billa Stapleton. Galtee Rovers delegate Larry Roche said that they knew they were in for a tough match and that they also warned their players before it. So what was rumoured in the pubs beforehand certainly had some truth in it. The gate for this game was the second-highest for a West senior football final behind the 1991 Lattin–Cashel decider. More than 500 people attended the game and the takings were in the region of £1,000. That's significant, and people came in the knowledge that something was going to happen. The incidents and the indiscipline were the worst I have ever seen. Jack Fogarty from Cashel was the local correspondent for the* Cork Examiner, *and he hit the front page with the story of the game.'*

The *Examiner's* report ran as follows:

APOLOGY FOR VIOLENT FINAL

Five players were sent off and another was carried off in what a senior GAA official described as the worst scenes he had ever witnessed on a sports field at yesterday's final of the West Tipperary senior football championship.

At one stage all 30 players were involved in fighting which led to the chairman of the West Tipperary board, Mr Brendan Ryan, apologising to spectators at the end.

Galtee Rovers beat Solohead 0–9 to 0–2 in the game which was held up for quite some time as referee Paddy Russell sought to restore order. Three players from Solohead and two from Galtee Rovers were sent off and another Galtee Rovers player was carried off with a nasty facial injury.

Mr Ryan, speaking at the presentation of the Brother Hennessy Cup, strongly condemned the players' behaviour and said the West Board would make an example of them.

The Nationalist printed this report by J.J. Kennedy:

Five players sent off within the first five minutes and a further seven booked during the hour was the very sad scenario to a West Tipp senior football final that will surely go down as one of the most disgraceful exhibitions ever witnessed on a GAA pitch. On the football side Galtee Rovers won their 13th West title by 0–9 to 0–2 but this game will be more remembered as a running battle from start to finish – and even before the start – with two teams ignoring the football and indulging in all that is sinister, vicious and entirely disgraceful.

The infamy of this game has now spread far and wide; it was one of the main topics of conversation at the Crosco Cup game in Cappawhite on Sunday evening and its coverage in Monday's *Irish Independent* has put the West in the headlines in a most regrettable way. It would be nice to be able to challenge the reports, rumours and much of the exaggeration but what happened at Seán Treacy Park was like a chapter from the faction fights of old and it would be difficult to overstate its severity. It is true that people were seen leaving in disgust with their children at the height of the fracas and listening to many older patrons with a lifelong association with the game there was unanimity that this was by far the worst exhibition of vicious thuggery that was ever witnessed.

The game was only about three minutes old when sanity departed and uncivilised barbarism took over. Most of the 30 players became locked in a battle of fists, boots, knees, elbows, anything that was available, and the miracle is that there wasn't a list of serious injuries. It was like a saloon scene from a Wild West film – all that was missing was the smashing of whiskey bottles. It was impossible to say that it was started in one position or another – almost simultaneously the punch-up began in numerous different areas and a bewildered referee could only watch on as the battle raged and two teams clattered each other to a standstill. When the dust settled, the most serious victim was the Rovers centre-forward Séamus McCarthy, who had to depart for immediate medical attention with closed eyes; the rest had burst lips, bleeding noses and swelled faces.

With peace restored the referee Paddy Russell, who must have had thoughts of calling a halt to proceedings entirely, decided instead to move courageously into action. He marched five to the sideline when he resumed play – Michael Ryan, Pat Ryan and Timmy Dwyer from Solohead and Séamie Grogan and Mickey Seán O'Connell from Galtee Rovers. It had been a horrific start to a game of football and coming so rapidly one cannot avoid the conclusion that it was premeditated. The signs of trouble were clearly visible from even before the throw-in. The normal cursory handshakes as players take their positions were in a number of cases replaced by a nudge of the elbow or boot. A pair of Solohead half-backs in particular made their intentions for the day known even before the ball was thrown in. The first action after the start, which was a prelude to the real explosion, saw a Solohead corner-back on the turf and his marker being booked. And the trouble in the early minutes was not an isolated incident for, despite the referee's strong action, the game could have continued in the same vein. The desire to have enough players to finish the game must have been the only reason why another five at least weren't sent to the line as the tackles continued late and dangerous, as did the intimidation and the occasional bout of fisticuffs.

Where does one apportion blame for what happened? In my opinion the main provocation came from Solohead and, when it did, the Rovers weren't slow to respond. Prior to the game one heard rumours of what was about to ensue – old scores having to be settled and this or that player having to be dealt with before any football was played. Galtee Rovers have a record which is well documented and has been publicised through heavy suspensions but Solohead have some shining examples of the kind of rowdies who should not be allowed on any team. What happened to Séamus McCarthy was barbaric and indeed if the behaviour in general which we witnessed was perpetrated outside the security of a sporting occasion, jail sentences would be no surprise. One can only shudder to think what would have happened if hurleys had been in use and another very minor consolation was the fact that no spectators got involved.

Out of the whole sad episode there is one thing, however, to praise – the referee. In impossible circumstances Paddy Russell showed his courage and nerve and, like in the semi-final of the same competition, when it came to sending off players he did not try to balance the books with even numbers from both teams, like so many other referees do. I doubt if he will ever experience more intimidating circumstances again and he for one can be proud of his performance.

TOM-JOE O'BRIEN (MATCH UMPIRE): *'This had been built up for weeks beforehand. It was quite clear from the team that Solohead put out [that they were expecting trouble]. Philip Ryan and Martin Ryan would have been young, talented players but they did not start. In my view, the team seemed to have been picked not to beat Bansha but to have a real cut at them. The person on the public-address system was pleading with the players to stop, but it made no difference. There were a few incidents in that game that were very, very unsavoury. Down through the years, we would have witnessed shemozzles and 'handbags' stuff, but this was different. This was vindictive. Sometimes when you hear talk before a game that something is going to happen, it passes off relatively quietly, but this time the pub threats came to pass. Nothing really sparked it. There was no incident where a guy was fouled and it went from there. They had just decided that they were going to sort each other out. I was afraid that the whole thing would spill over onto the sidelines. It was fortunate that it happened in the first couple of minutes, because I feared that the subs would have got involved had it broken out later.'*

MARGARET RUSSELL: *'I went to the game because I had just started going out with Paddy at the time. I knew nothing about the history between these two teams, and I could not believe my eyes. The Battle of Omagh received huge press coverage, and that almost spread to the stands, but I never in my life witnessed anything like that West final. Omagh was handbags in comparison. I was worried for Paddy. He didn't seem too perturbed, but he was still relatively new to refereeing. I was new to the whole scene, too, and it never crossed my mind before then that a referee might actually get a belt, too. I feared that Paddy would be struck. I thought that referees were above that; in my eyes, it would be like assaulting a member of the Garda Síochána, but, years later, I did see a local referee, Eamonn Browne, being assaulted during a game between Seán Treacy's and Cappawhite.'*

EAMONN BROWNE: *'It was the 1990 West semi-final between the Treacys and Cappa in Cashel. At the time, certain clubs had their hatchet men, and Cappa were one of the teams that the Treacys particularly liked having a cut off. Some of the games between the teams at the time were disgraceful. Maybe I had a reputation for being fairly strict, but I think that Cappa looked for me to protect them during that semi-final. Every foul and dirty swipe, I whistled for, and the first 20 minutes was riddled with frees. A very dirty pull was drawn, and as I was booking the offending player, he verbally abused one of my umpires, and I then decided to send him off. I was writing the name and number in the book when I was struck from behind, with what I am led to believe was a fist. I was caught totally off guard. I had my dentures broken and was in a fairly sorry state, but I would not give in. I got up again and finished the game. If some of my clubmates from Knockavilla Kickhams hadn't been there, it could have got very nasty. They prevented some of the Treacys people coming in off the line. They were really fired up. After the match, there was no trouble, and I went off to Fethard to referee a camogie match. Duty called. The matter ended up in Cashel district court later. The perpetrator was ordered to pay my medical expenses.'*

A couple of weeks before the game, Jerry Ring, the amiable, long-serving secretary of the West Board of Tipperary GAA, informed me that I would be refereeing the West final. I was aware of fierce animosity between the two clubs; in previous years, Solohead and Bansha clashes had been fiercely contested. I heard later that even before the ball was thrown in, and during the national anthem, players were niggling at each other. The game commenced at a frantic pace, and, after a couple of minutes, this 25-year-old referee noticed that one of my umpires, the late Ailbe Burke, had his hand raised to signal for my attention. I walked in to speak with Ailbe, who said quietly, 'Paddy . . . look out.' Mick Maguire was the other umpire at that end of the pitch. Players were going at it all over the field. Solohead's Pat Redigan, just 17 years of age, sat on the field while all hell broke loose around him. Bansha's Séamus McCarthy was pinned to the ground by his opponent, who was punching him repeatedly with both fists.

I've never seen anything on the field of play before or since to match the levels of violence I witnessed that afternoon. It was a surreal scene when I looked out across the pitch after talking to Ailbe. It was like something out of a movie. Almost every player on the field was fighting at the same time.

JERRY RING: *'I'd say that one of the things that helped Paddy was that Mick Maguire was at the upper goals, at the Hospital End. Mick was umpire, and he advised Paddy to finish the game with the remaining players if possible. Paddy could have sent off three or four others, but he handled it well. He came in to consult his umpires every now and then, and that cooled things down. Thank goodness that we don't have to blood all of our referees in a situation like that. Paddy was a good learner, and he got to the top on merit.'*

MICK MAGUIRE: *'Paddy did well that day. I'll always remember after an incident in the square, I caught a Solohead player by the two hands to stop him fighting again. I'd say the whole thing was planned beforehand. Afterwards, I knew that strong action had to be taken, and I said that to the West board chairman at the time, Brendan Ryan, who was seated on the sleepers near one of the teams and witnessed the violence. The appearance of Séamus McCarthy coming off the field was desperate. That was the end of Solohead; they never really came back from that. All of the old stalwarts that had kept the club going never went back. I met several of them afterwards who told me they never went to a Solohead match again. It was an awful day.'*

I sent off five players and tried to calm the situation as best I could. I kept a tight rein on proceedings after that, because there was always the fear that the game could explode again. By sending off five, I acted pretty decisively. I was a young referee, and, in the middle of something as big as that, people might think that I feared for my own personal safety, but that was not the case. The players were not interested in me. They had their own scores to settle. I'm sure that in sending off those players I took the violent sting out of the game, and that probably ensured that no more would follow. I could have sent off more, of course, but it was impossible to see everything.

JERRY RING: *'Séamus McCarthy was brought into our house and cleaned up. We live across the road from Seán Treacy Park. He was unrecognisable. Picture a man with slits for eyes and a puffed-up face. He was conscious and walked across from the field, but he could not see. His face, mouth, nose and eyes were filled with blood. We cleaned him up as best we could, but he needed more help. That was the first time I met his wife, Margaret (who, incidentally, had a brother playing for Solohead on that day). We have been great friends with them ever since.'*

Nobody realised at the time how badly injured Séamus was. Somebody remarked afterwards that he needed a panel beater that day, not a doctor. With the great advances in sports medicine that have happened since then, people are reluctant now to move an injured player on the field before he or she has been checked out, but it was commonplace then for injured players to be physically dragged off the pitch in order for the game to continue.

In J.J. Kennedy's match report for *The Nationalist*, he was fulsome in his praise of my handling of the game, and that piece kept me going as a young referee. I read it a few times when I was feeling low, and it gave me a genuine lift. We all need a boost now and then, and J.J.'s words were a tonic. It's like getting a good report from an assessor. He is somebody in the stand, completely neutral, and he's praising my work. That's always a satisfying feeling.

That game defined my early days as a referee. My intercounty career was definitely boosted as a result, and any doubts about my ability to reach the very top in this difficult game were dispelled. I had my doubts for a few years after starting out, when I was itching for a big break. I was continually handed juvenile games, while Seánie Lonergan was getting some senior O'Donoghue Cup matches in the West. Maybe that was an indication that he showed more potential than I as a young referee.

The West board launched an immediate investigation into the violent scenes that marred the final. Mike Ryan Cooper, the Solohead club chairman, appealed on behalf of his players, claiming that I was too young and inexperienced for a game of that magnitude. The implication was that premeditated violence broke out because I was inexperienced. Brendan Ryan, the West board chairman, gave that theory short shrift. Solohead were in action again the following Sunday, and, before that game, club members protested outside the main gate of the Knockavilla Kickhams GAA grounds against this perceived injustice.

JERRY RING: '*Repercussions from the whole sad affair went deeper than the game of football. There were so many social and personal facets. Relationships were affected in the parishes, and people fell out. Some of the players involved were also warned by their employers. However, time is a great healer, and that episode has now largely been forgotten. The only match I ever saw like it since was the 1999 Munster Under-21 hurling final between Clare and Tipperary in Ennis. There was real badness in the air.*

'*The investigation into that West final was wide-ranging. Eyewitnesses went to the investigation meetings at the Royal Hotel in Tipperary town* to give evidence. Some wanted their names attached to their statements; more didn't. Oral and written accounts were taken. The Solohead club was suspended for six months and fined a hundred pounds. Brendan Ryan described them as "a disgrace to the division and the Association". Galtee Rovers were told that their retaliation was unjustified, and they received a fifty-pound fine. I myself was later personally targeted on occasion by some who claimed we had all been against them. There were serious repercussions for the Solohead club. They never recovered. They have tried hard and have had some great workers, but it has never been the same from the mid-1980s on.

'Brendan Ryan had attended the game. He was seated around the middle of the field. At that time, there were no dugouts. The subs and mentors were on either side of Brendan but oblivious to his presence. Brendan saw a lot of what happened, and at the subsequent board meeting he was shocked when certain individuals claimed that they'd done nothing.

'I was young myself at the time, refereeing the year before, too, and also interested in taking the odd photo. When the investigation was set up, every action shot I'd taken was dumped, the negatives destroyed. I didn't want to be embroiled in it. Two photographs survive, I think: the Bansha team photo and Paddy with the team captains before the match.

'Two-year suspensions were handed down to Pat Ryan, Martin Ryan and Paul Lynch. A lot of the Solohead guys just didn't play any more. The West board was accused of being a lynching mob but the main conclusion of the investigation was that Solohead were the instigators. Some of their delegates walked out of the meeting saying that they would play soccer and rugby in their GAA field the following day. Of course nothing like this ever happened!'

That West final is a game that I have never forgotten. So much happened in the first few minutes to test the resolve of a young referee like myself, but I believe that I handled the situation well. Certainly, I have never since witnessed violence on a similar scale. There could surely have been no better learning experience.

5

....

CARRYING THE FLAME

Show class, have pride, and display character.
If you do, winning takes care of itself.

Paul Bryant

It is a proud boast for West Tipperary that a referee from the area
has taken charge of an All-Ireland final in every decade since
the 1940s: Bill O'Donnell refereed the 1941 hurling decider; Seán
Hayes was the man in the middle for the 1952 football showpiece;
George Ryan refereed hurling finals in 1979 and 1985; and in 2008
Eamonn Browne kept the flag flying when he took charge of the
All-Ireland senior camogie final. My inspiration was John Moloney,
whose career began in 1957. When John finally hung up the whistle
after almost half a century of service, he had refereed six All-Ireland
finals, five football and one hurling. He also officiated at nine
Munster football and two Munster hurling finals.

With that history in mind, it was lovely to uphold a proud
local tradition when I was chosen for the 1990 All-Ireland senior
football final, a potential powder-keg of an encounter between
Meath and Cork. The two counties had built up a huge rivalry in
the late 1980s, and some of their clashes were extremely volatile.
Croke Park was nothing new, but I was sailing into uncharted
waters with my selection as referee for an All-Ireland senior final.
This was the pinnacle of my career, what I had dreamed of since
first picking up a whistle.

I was told of my appointment less than a fortnight before the game. When I arrived home from work that afternoon, the post made for most pleasant reading.

4 September 1990

. . . Congratulations on your appointment to referee this year's All-Ireland senior football final at Croke Park on 16 September 1990. Go n-éirí go geal leat.

Seán O'Laoire
Secretary of the GAC

Acting as a linesman alongside P.J. McGrath at Croke Park in 1982 had been a fantastic experience, and two years after that I had refereed the All-Ireland junior final between Wexford and Cork in Dungarvan. Incidentally, Brian Tyrell, the promising Tipperary referee, took charge of the same two counties in the 2007 decider. It would appear that our careers are running along parallel lines. Whether Brian will look upon that statement as a good or a bad thing is debatable! On a more serious note, Brian is doing well for himself on the intercounty circuit, renowned as a decisive referee. Also in 1984, Tipperary's Johnny McDonnell refereed the All-Ireland junior hurling final – a nice double for the Premier County in the GAA's centenary year.

The 1989 minor decider was the first of three All-Ireland finals that I refereed at Croke Park. Derry won that game, with a certain Anthony Tohill in their team, a fine player and now TV pundit who won a senior title in 1993.

I was playing football and pretty fit, but when I received notification of the 'big one', I put in some extra yards around the GAA field in Emly, with plenty of cycling thrown in for good measure.

On the night before the game, Margaret and I stayed in Dublin's Clarence Hotel, along with my umpires Davy Crowe, Ailbe Burke, Mickey Collins and Lar O'Keeffe. The well-known former referee Tommy Sugrue popped in to wish us the best of luck for match day. Tommy knew all about Cork v. Meath clashes, having refereed the drawn and replayed finals between the teams in 1988. In the drawn match, Tommy awarded a controversial late free to Meath, which Brian Stafford converted to gain a draw. And in the replay, he sent off Meath midfielder Gerry McEntee with only minutes on the clock. Yet, as is so often the case, the 14 men found something extra, and at the end of another close, hard-fought game, Meath had edged home by 0–13 to 0–12.

Tommy told me to keep the game tight and not to let it go too far. The media had hyped this one into World War Three, and there had been speculation as to who would take charge of such an explosive match. Supporters of both counties and neutrals alike wondered who would be chosen for the final because previous clashes between the two teams had been vicious. The competition between Meath and Cork was bitter. Some of the team members have talked in recent years about how, at one point, they would not even speak to players from the other county. Their rivalry captured the imagination of the GAA public from 1987 until 1990, and this final was seen as the ultimate battle for bragging rights. Meath had captured All-Ireland titles in 1987 and 1988, both at Cork's expense, before Cork made a real breakthrough by defeating Mayo in the 1989 decider.

A referee who takes charge of an All-Ireland semi-final is not generally considered to be in the running for the final, but 1990 was an exception to the unwritten rule. Donegal v. Meath had gone well for me. Two years before, I had been named as Munster's referee of the year for football, but, nonetheless, an All-Ireland senior final would be a serious test of my credentials.

The cards and best wishes arrived thick and fast from near and far. A good luck card from Michael Burke in Sligo, a former Emly teammate, summed up my appointment nicely. Inside, the popular, zany TV aliens Zig and Zag urged me to 'Just go for it, buster!!'

Michael added:

> Hello, Paddy,
>
> I'm delighted to hear the good news. Heartiest congratulations and the best of luck on the big day. Some neutrals will cheer for Cork, others for Meath; this neutral will be cheering for the referee. As Z and Z say, just go for it, buster, and to hell with the begrudgers.

A postcard from Killarney read:

> Hi Paddy,
>
> I wish you the very best of luck on Sunday and hope you enjoy your first All-Ireland and everything goes well for you on the day. See you on Monday at the function, will be there with the Kerry minors.
>
> All the best from Dan O'Sullivan, Co. Kerry

From the hurling referee Willie Barrett, I received the following message:

> Paddy,
>
> Congratulations on achieving the ultimate honour in refereeing. I wish you and your team the very best on the 16th. I know that as usual you will do a great job.
>
> Joan and Willie Barrett and family

My parents sent a Mass card with a beautiful message:

> To Paddy,
>
> With every good wish and God's blessing on you. Good luck for Sunday.
>
> Dad and Mam

One of my childhood friends, Patsy Dawson, sent his good wishes:

> Dear Paddy,
>
> Congratulations on appointment for All-Ireland final on Sunday week. I'm sure you will do a good job and we are all with you. I could do with a ticket if you had one to spare – they are scarce as you well know.

And there was a kind word from a former Tipperary board secretary:

> Delighted you got the honour. I was very impressed by you in the semi-final. 'Play it cool.'
>
> Tommy Barrett

My boss also sent a card to wish me luck:

> Dear Paddy,
>
> When I wrote to you recently following the All-Ireland semi-final, I expressed the wish to see you appointed to referee an All-Ireland final in the future. Little did I know that wish would be fulfilled so soon.
>
> Congratulations, Paddy, and good luck for the match, and I look forward to seeing you from somewhere in Croker on the 16th.
>
> Best wishes,
> Bill Lilley

Weather-wise, the day of the final was not pleasant. Wet and miserable conditions ensured that the Croke Park pitch was greasy. But there was a phenomenal atmosphere, and the Cork crowd, with their various banners and flags, brought wonderful colour to Croke Park, as the Meath fans added to the tremendous backdrop with their green and gold.

I kept a tight rein on it and didn't let a terrible lot go. I blew the whistle quite a bit; there were 69 frees over the course of the 70 minutes. I just felt that if I had allowed any leeway to either side, the game could have boiled over very quickly. It takes just one bad tackle to spark a flare-up. The two sets of players didn't exactly like each other.

The tackles came in thick and fast and the game was on a knife-edge. Paddy Downey, the Gaelic games correspondent with the *Irish Times*, wrote that he could feel the tension from his perch in the Hogan Stand press-box. The atmosphere was electric, the crowd, the singing. There were a couple of incidents where players tumbled to the ground, but I was in pretty quickly to separate them before they became entangled and got stuck into each other.

I was pleased with my performance, but, unfortunately, I did have to send off Cork forward Colm O'Neill. The incident occurred on the Hogan Stand side of the pitch; O'Neill punched Meath player Mick Lyons. I was left with no choice, but I felt genuinely sorry for Colm. He wasn't that type of player; the *Examiner* newspaper reported that he had left his sick bed – he had been suffering with a virus – to aid the Cork cause.

After the game, Colm told reporters: 'I would have bet my life savings that what happened to me out there would not have occurred in a million years. But, in retrospect, I suppose something was bound to happen sooner or later, because, right from the start, I thought that I was taking part in a boxing match rather than playing in an All-Ireland football final. I really have no excuses to offer. What I did was totally stupid, and the referee had no other course of action open to him but to send me off.'

Sending off a player, particularly in a game of that magnitude, is a terrible feeling. I dismissed a player in both of the senior All-Ireland finals that I was in charge of, and it ruins the game for a referee to an extent. It's a nightmare moment for the player but not exactly a barrel of laughs for the ref either. All-Ireland finals don't come around too often for players – indeed, they are once-in-a-lifetime opportunities for many – and I'm sure for almost all of them, the prospect of being sent off is unthinkable. But, as the referee, I am there to know the rules and apply them accordingly. And if a player strikes an opponent, that is a sending-off offence.

Colm's actions were out of character, but I had no choice but to put him out of the game. It's typical of the man that he never held it against me. I met him in Killarney a couple of years later, at a Munster final, and when we bumped into each other in the car park, one of my umpires took a photograph of the two of us together.

After the 1990 final, there were some rumblings of discontent about my performance, and the GAA journalist Donal Keenan commented: 'The referee, Pat Russell, discarded the opportunity to use the advantage and halted play for every indiscretion. That did not help the game as a spectacle.'

I didn't really mind as long as the powers that be at Croke Park were happy, and the following letter arrived just days after the final:

A Chara,

I enclose a copy of the referee's assessment for the senior All-Ireland football final.

I would like on behalf of the referees committee to thank you for the part you played in making the All-Ireland football final the very fine spectacle that it was.

If you require any further information on the assessment or if you have any observations to make on it, don't hesitate to submit them to me.

Pat Daly

Official assessment . . .

Control/Authority: very good in what could have been a difficult game. In his efforts to control the game the referee was caught a few times when players in possession and fouled broke free. This was understandable.

Overall the referee had a very good game and must be commended. He is quick, firm, decisive and looked cool. Two things: 1. Always indicate free's direction first. 2. Don't turn your back completely in walking away after giving a free.

In controlling the game the referee can be well satisfied with his contribution to this All-Ireland.

The year finished on a personal high note as John Moore and I, the referees in the All-Ireland senior hurling and football finals, were invited to Jury's Hotel in Cork over the Christmas period for a special function to honour Cork's double success of that year. We were presented with a medal each for refereeing the finals, and that was a lovely touch from the Cork county board. That piece of bronze is a prized memento in the Russell household and a fitting tribute to the many men and women who helped me to reach the very top as a referee.

Five years passed by before the 'big one' came my way again. When it did, my experience of All-Ireland final day would be very different. Never before had the old saying that 'just a few inches separate a pat on the back from a kick in the backside' rung truer.

6

....

THE GOOD NEWS

The world of achievement has always belonged to the optimist.

Harold Wilkins

The 1995 All-Ireland senior football final was played at Croke Park, Dublin, on Sunday, 17 September. Paddy Russell was named as match referee for the clash between two of Gaelic football's biggest names: Dublin and Tyrone. This appointment should have set the seal on a remarkable season for Russell, who had already taken charge of that year's All-Ireland club final, National Football League decider and Munster football final.

* * *

Life was good, couldn't have been much better, in fact. My son Mark was born in 1995, and a memorably warm summer provided numerous opportunities for an evening run, the perfect tonic after a long day at work. My preparations had gone very much according to plan. After receiving the welcome news that I was to take charge of September's All-Ireland senior football final, I was also anxious to referee as many local games as possible. Jerry Ring duly obliged with the fixtures list.

I was informed of my appointment when I was at a match. Tipperary captured the All-Ireland B title in Birr, and, attending the final, I bumped into Seán O'Laoire, secretary of the GAA's Games Administration Committee. Seán almost knocked me off my feet when he informed me that I would be the man in the middle for the glamour senior decider just a couple of short weeks later.

'We are pleased to inform you', the letter from Croke Park began. Seán wasn't pulling my leg after all. This was very much for real, and not entirely unexpected when I look back on it now. It had been a good year, and the fact that no team from my province was involved in the final must have helped my cause, too. I had also been linesman for the semi-final between Cork and Dublin.

I knew of so many top-class referees who had retired with just the one final under their belts, and I appreciated that I was in exalted company, having been handed a second. It was indeed a huge honour, and, naturally, I was anxious to do well.

It wasn't long before well-wishers began to pick up the telephone to congratulate me on the good news. Those calls were punctuated by enquiries from representatives of the media looking to find out a bit more about Paddy Russell from Emly. I recall speaking to the *Irish Times*, expressing my heartfelt desire to remain as anonymous as possible on the day of the game.

A week before the final, I stepped back from the club scene and began to focus on the big game. The countdown had begun in earnest. Dublin and Tyrone were set to battle it out for the biggest prize in Gaelic football – the coveted Sam Maguire Cup. The stakes were sky high as Dublin, the media darlings who had been knocking on the door in previous years, prepared to take on Tyrone, who had never won an All-Ireland senior crown. Dublin were looking for their twenty-second title, and their first since the 1983 final, when they finished with twelve men in an ill-tempered match against Galway. The twelve players who finished the game are fondly remembered in Dublin GAA circles as the 'Twelve Apostles'.

Every team has hard men, but I never made a habit of studying the participants before any match. The rules were there, and it was up to me to apply them. Of course, there were guys with reputations for bad behaviour, but it didn't matter to me if a player had struck an opponent in a previous game. As long as he didn't do it when I was in charge, we would have no problems. Naturally, I was aware of the huge hype surrounding the Dublin football team, but at home in West Tipperary, I was cocooned from it.

Dublin's Green Isle Hotel was our base for the All-Ireland weekend, and, after driving from home, my wife Margaret and three of my four umpires – Lar O'Keeffe, Jerry Cummins and Nicholas Lonergan – checked in at around five o'clock on the Saturday evening.

My fourth man, Davy Crowe, was not due to arrive until the morning of the game, as he had cut short a holiday in England to get home for the match. Davy, a man quite proud of his appearance, had even decided to get his white umpire's coat tailor-made for the final, even though four had been specially supplied by Croke Park!

After tuning in to the traditional Saturday night TV preview programme, *Up for the Match*, we turned in for the night, blissfully unaware of what was to take place the following day.

The portents were not very good. I was nervous and anxious for sleep, but at one o'clock in the morning the hotel's fire alarm went off in ear-splitting fashion. I had just managed to drift off to sleep when all of the hotel's occupants had to be evacuated. After we had finally returned to our beds, the alarm went off again, at four o'clock. There was no evacuation on this occasion, but once again my night's sleep had been interrupted.

MARGARET RUSSELL: *'There's so much spoken about what the players do the night before a game. For example, they might go to the dogs or, in the past, one or two of them might have had a pint. But everything is done and everything is in place to ensure that their night is a peaceful one. Now, I'm sure that Paddy's decisions would not have changed even if he had slept all night, but it was hardly the ideal preparation. And I'm sure there would be hell to pay if players were roused in such a fashion twice the night before a massive game.'*

I don't think I would have slept well anyway. The enormity of the final build-up engulfed me like a giant shroud. It was suffocating, but whatever fatigue I felt was swallowed up by the sense of occasion. We rose early and went to Mass at eight o'clock in the city centre. It was quiet then, but just a couple of hours later the streets came alive.

MARGARET RUSSELL: *'At Croke Park – and this is a much bandied about statement – you could have cut the tension with a knife. There was a heaviness in the air. I will never forget it as long as I live. It was incredible.'*

I must have arrived at Croke Park around midday. Fresh gear for the final was waiting for me in my dressing-room, and I felt very much at home. The big fixture had dominated my thoughts from the moment I'd received the official notification from GAA HQ, but I knew that once the ball was thrown in and the game was under way, the nerves would disappear immediately.

CHARLIE REDMOND (DUBLIN FORWARD): *'The whole week was bad for me. I didn't think that I was going to play. I pulled a muscle in my thigh kicking a 21-yard free in training on the Friday evening. I was finishing off a light session, half an hour or forty minutes done, when I hit one from the right-hand side of the goal, five yards in from the touchline. After I clipped it, I knew that I had done some damage. On Saturday, I couldn't move, never mind kick a ball. I spent Sunday morning on a physio's table in Castleknock getting work done on the injury. I had a dash back to Ashbourne for my gear, and then back to meet the team before Croke Park.'*

I watched some of the minor final between Westmeath and Derry, but it wasn't long before I returned to the sanctuary of the dressing-room. Mentally, I zoned in on the 70 minutes that lay ahead and, in time-honoured fashion, prayed that things would go right and that no team would be blackguarded.

Minutes later, safe haven no more. Into the light and the pre-match protocols: a quick warm-up, the coin toss, the pre-match parade, meeting the president, Mary Robinson. Then, a final word with my match officials, and we're ready for the off. Nerves churning up my stomach. Inhale, exhale. A sharp blast of the whistle, ball in the air, and we're away.

7

....

THE MATCH

When anger rises, think of the consequences.

Confucius

THE INCIDENT

*Cult hero and terrace favourite Charlie Redmond, who had been
a pre-match doubt with a calf-muscle injury, scores a first-half goal
that helps Dublin to a 1–8 to 0–6 half-time lead.*

* * *

CHARLIE REDMOND: *'I couldn't miss from three yards! When Jason
Sherlock went in on Finbarr McConnell, the ball was going in, and
I was trying to hold Paul Devlin back as he went for it. But, at the
same moment, both of us realised that the ball wasn't going to go in.
Suddenly, I was dragging him forward, and he was pulling me back.
Thankfully, I was a little bit bigger, and I was able to drag him with
me and kick the ball in. There's a photograph of me kicking the ball into
the back of the net, and I have one stud missing from my boot. I don't
know how that happened; I certainly didn't go onto the field with one
stud missing. The boots got sold later for a few thousand pounds.'*

* * *

*Ten minutes after half-time, Dublin hold a 1–9 to 0–9 lead when a
dropping ball breaks off full-back Paddy Moran to Paul Bealin, who
transfers quickly to Paul Curran, now a* Sunday Game *analyst but
in his time one of the finest attacking half-backs in the game.*

73

Curran looks for options and plays a right-footed pass along the Cusack Stand touchline, and as Jason Sherlock runs to gather possession, he is fouled on the 45-yard line. Just a couple of yards away, Redmond is on the floor after being fouled by Paul Devlin. Fergal Logan arrives on the scene and lands on a grounded Redmond, who takes immediate offence. Linesman Willie O'Mahony moves across to restrain Redmond, but the Dublin player aims a head-butt at Logan. Paddy is left with no choice. He checks Redmond's number before motioning with his right arm towards the touchline. Dublin's number 13, Charlie Redmond, is sent off.

* * *

CHARLIE REDMOND: *'I remember coming out for the ball when Paul Devlin fouled me from behind and Paddy gave the free. I was lying on the ground, and, a few seconds after the whistle had gone, Fergal Logan came up and fell onto the back of my neck with his elbow. I took grave exception to that and charged at him.'*

I was following play when I saw Redmond throwing his head at Fergal Logan. I consulted with my linesman, Willie O'Mahony, who confirmed that Redmond had aimed a head-butt. It was a definite sending-off offence. 'You're off,' I told Redmond, pointing to the line. It was the normal way I would send off a player.

Redmond knew that he was off, but he continued to argue. Dublin manager Pat O'Neill was irate, but I was not listening to any of it. Once a referee's decision is made, there is absolutely no way that it will be overturned. Arguing the call is folly. O'Neill could have gone down on his knees and begged, but it would have made no difference.

I made the correct call by sending off Charlie Redmond for what he did, and Fergal Logan would have gone too, had he been identified. I returned to Willie and asked if he knew who the Tyrone player involved was. He told me that he didn't get the player's number. I had to let it go. In the heat of the moment, as players and officials alike converged on the incident, Logan escaped.

WILLIE O'MAHONY: *'There was a collision along the sideline. Fergal Logan dropped on Redmond, all right, but I didn't catch his [Logan's] number. I couldn't report the player to Paddy because I didn't have the number. He would have got the line, too. Redmond was incensed. When he got up, he made a drive for Logan and attempted to head-butt him. It was a red card. In the rule book, the offence is "striking or attempting to strike". I held Redmond until the incident died down. Paddy asked me, "Did he do what I thought he did?" Paddy had no hesitation. Redmond had gone mad. In a way, you couldn't blame him, because Logan had hurt him, but you can't go for a guy with your head.'*

When Willie confirmed that he had not caught the identity of the Tyrone player, I then had the option to consult my umpires or the linesman on the far touchline, Francis Finan. I am happy that I did not do that. It would have been a pointless exercise, running like a wild rabbit from touchline to touchline, from goalmouth to goalmouth. I recall speaking with the other officials after the game, and none of them had seen what happened. Willie and I were best placed.

CHARLIE REDMOND: *'I can't tell Paddy that what he did was right or wrong. He made a decision, and I'm sure he stands by that. Somebody tried to put me out of the game when I was lying on the ground, and Steve Collins, the boxer, told me later that I should have decked him with a dig. If Logan had hit me standing face to face, Steve would have had more respect for him. I can't see why Paddy didn't act. What Logan did at least deserved a booking. I was angry, upset and annoyed. I felt that I was being treated unfairly by Paddy. I don't think that I deserved to be sent off. The linesman also said to Paddy that no, I didn't deserve to go. So why did Paddy send me off? And why did Fergal Logan walk away scot free when, in my view, he caused it all?'*

MARGARET RUSSELL: *'The game itself meant nothing to me. I prayed all the way through, rosary after rosary, praying for it to be all over. Watching from the opposite side of the pitch, in the Hogan Stand, I thought to myself, "Jesus, what's going on now?" But I didn't feel any sense of foreboding. I just felt that it would lead to more time added* on. I was right in the centre of the stand, in a very good position, but I couldn't see what was happening over there. And never in my wildest dreams would I have thought that the incident would be blown up the way it was.'

THE RESTART

Paddy decides to restart play by throwing the ball in. Because of Redmond's retaliation, Dublin have lost the free they were initially awarded for the foul on Sherlock. However, Redmond is still on the field, just a couple of yards from where play recommences.

* * *

I throw the ball in, oblivious to the fact that Redmond is standing in close proximity hoping to latch onto any breaking ball. TV footage shows that he's literally right in front of me.

MARGARET RUSSELL: *'People couldn't understand how Paddy couldn't see Charlie Redmond in front of him from the throw-in. Paddy might not remember what he said to me about it afterwards, but it was like this. To everybody looking at the TV that day, the player was Charlie Redmond. To them, Charlie Redmond was clearly still on the field. I'm not trying to put words into Paddy's mouth, but what he said to me was, "I only looked to throw in the ball between two players." So, to Paddy, it wasn't Charlie Redmond per se standing there. It was a Dublin player. Paddy said to me later, "If he was sent off, then why would I be looking for him on the field?" And then when Paddy spotted him on the field soon after, he said to himself, "Number 13? Sure, I've sent him off."'*

CHARLIE REDMOND: *'The linesman said that I didn't head-butt Logan, and that's why I thought that I wasn't being sent off after Paddy had indicated that I was to go. I thought I was to stay on, hence the reason why I did. To this day, I'll never understand why nothing was said to Fergal Logan. He wasn't even booked for the incident. I was the one fouled twice, and yet I got sent off. I heard the linesman saying "no, no, no". I assumed that he was referring to me, saying that I hadn't head-butted. I just assumed that I wasn't being sent off, but obviously that wasn't the case. Paddy rectified the error, or my mistake, as soon* as he became aware of it. But it wasn't as if I was trying to pull the wool over his eyes. He threw the ball in the air, and I was actually there contesting the breaking ball. Paddy's like myself, he's only human, and we all make errors. I've done things that I look back on later and think, "Why did I do that? That was silly." Paddy wasn't looking out for me, so why would he have seen me?'

WILLIE O'MAHONY: 'Redmond claimed that I told him to stay on, but I had no conversation with him at all. I wasn't near him when he was going off. The only words I said to Paddy were "yes, he did" when he asked me if Redmond committed the offence. When I said "no", it was probably when Paddy asked me if I caught the Tyrone player's number. I might have replied, "No, I didn't get his number." But I think Redmond was bould, he was chancing his arm. I don't know how he could have heard any of our conversation, with the noise of the crowd. You can imagine what it's like on the day of an All-Ireland final. He must have had super-hearing.'

THE REALISATION

> Nineteen seconds after the game restarts, Charlie Redmond, who has been sent off less than a minute before, gains possession of the ball and delivers it towards the old Nally Stand at the Hill 16 end. In the corner, Tyrone defender Chris Lawn is fouled by Dublin attacker Dessie Farrell.

* * *

The penny drops. Dublin's number 13, the player I had sent off, is still on the field. I return to the Cusack Stand touchline to consult with Willie O'Mahony.

'Willie, did Charlie Redmond go off the field?'

Willie replied, 'He did.'

I was looking towards the sideline and Willie was looking in.

I asked, 'Was it number 13? Number 13 is still on the field.'

Willie looked out and said, 'Jesus, Paddy, he is.'

I didn't say any more.

WILLIE O'MAHONY: 'I can remember the incident [that resulted in Redmond's sending off] like it was yesterday, but everything else about *that day is a blank. I can't even remember leaving the pitch at the end of the game or anything like that. In the general melee, Redmond seemed to get away. I didn't even notice that he was gone. I was standing in the same position where the incident occurred, on the Cusack Stand side of the field. The ball was delivered into the corner over on the other side. Paddy gave a free-out, and, the next thing, I saw him running over. I'll never forget him running across, and he had to run a long way, because the ball had been kicked a distance of 50 or 60 yards from the middle of the field into the Nally Stand area. I didn't know where Paddy was running to at the time, but, Jesus, it was to me he was heading. "Did number 13 kick in that ball?" he asked.'*

I went back to Charlie Redmond and said, 'Charlie, you're off.'

CHARLIE REDMOND: *'There's a famous story going around, which isn't true but which I propagated to a degree, that when I was sent off for the second time, he said, "You shouldn't be here." I'm supposed to have said, "I know. I failed a fitness test earlier on!" It didn't happen, but I thought it was a good story so I stuck with it.'*

He said to me: 'Jesus, Paddy, please don't send me off. It's my last game.' I said, 'I can't do anything about that. You're off.'

CHARLIE REDMOND: *'I watched it on video and I did have a couple of words with him. What I said, I don't know. I might well have said something like that, clutching at straws. I can't verify 100 per cent, but that is possibly what was said.'*

I motioned towards the sideline. Redmond left the field of play, for good this time.

CHARLIE REDMOND: *'When I was coming off, Pat O'Neill said to me, "Well, you got two chances."*

'"No, I didn't. He sent me off for the first incident."

'Pat thought that something else had happened. He was taken aback by that.'

THE FIST

Deep into stoppage time, the remarkable Peter Canavan has just kicked his eleventh point of the game and urges his Tyrone teammates to keep going. 'One point,' he roars, as Tyrone trail by the bare minimum. From Dublin goalkeeper John O'Leary's kick-out, Tyrone's Fay Devlin pounces on the loose ball before Ronan McGarrity is fouled. The free is quickly taken and Ciarán Corr, the Tyrone captain, launches a speculative delivery into Dublin territory, which is fisted clear by O'Leary straight to the gifted Canavan, who slips on the 21-yard line as he attempts to gather possession. Dublin corner-back Ciarán Walsh moves in to put pressure on a prostrate Canavan, who knocks the ball with his fist to Tyrone's wing-back Seán McLaughlin. Paddy whistles up immediately, before McLaughlin receives the pass and pops the ball over the bar for what he thinks is the equalising score.

The Tyrone number 7, wearing a beaming smile, jogs back to his defensive position, blissfully unaware that the score has been disallowed. Seconds later, and with three minutes of injury-time played, Keith Barr launches the resultant free up the field and Paddy blows for full-time. Dublin are All-Ireland senior football champions.

* * *

Peter Canavan scooped the ball to a teammate, who kicked it over the bar. I was in a perfect position, close to Peter. The ball was on the ground. A free kick to Dublin. No doubt about it. Looking back, wouldn't it have been grand to let it go to avoid some of the controversy that followed? But the Charlie Redmond thing became more of an issue later. And nobody ran after me and queried the Peter Canavan call.

WILLIE O'MAHONY: *'The Peter Canavan incident? I still can't decide. I've seen it so many times, but Paddy was right beside it and I take his word for it. I think Canavan accepted it, and fair play to him for that. And he got his medals in later years.'*

CHARLIE REDMOND: *'The whole furore was not just about what happened to me; there was also the Peter Canavan incident at the end of the game. Some say getting one decision wrong is careless but getting two wrong is really careless. But did he get them wrong, or did he get them right? People have their opinions. I have mine. I'm sure Peter has an opinion there. Paddy was very close to the incident.*

There's no clear-cut view on the TV footage as to whether the ball was on the ground or not.'

When I first watched the incident on television, I doubted myself for a moment. But the angle from behind the Canal End goal makes it clear, in my opinion. I was convinced at the time, even more so now. I'm strict on that particular offence. I always blow when players touch the ball on the ground.

PETER CANAVAN: *'The fact that I won two All-Ireland medals [2003 and 2005] made it a bit easier for me personally not to look back on that one decision. As for the guys that played and never won one, that was their chance. They would look back and say that that decision may have cost them an All-Ireland. For a county that had never won one, to get so close to the Holy Grail and to be denied by a referee's mistake was definitely hard to take. There was no other way around it. It was devastating. I've seen it on TV, but at the time I was confident that it was marginally off the ground. Take the fact that when I punched the ball, I slightly elevated it. It would be very hard to do that if the ball was flat on the ground. There was no doubt in my mind that it was slightly off the ground. In fairness to the referee, the whistle went straight away. He didn't wait for the ball to be kicked over the bar. But that didn't take away from the fact that he got the call wrong.*

'I was bitterly disappointed that we didn't get the chance of a replay. It wasn't a great game of football, and there had been that contentious moment when the man that was sent off didn't go. Nine referees out of ten in a situation like that would be waiting on the chance to make a draw out of the game. At the time, 13 years ago, a replay would have guaranteed another £1 million for the GAA. They would have been patting him on the back. I don't think the supporters of either side would have been too unhappy. Dublin didn't play to their full potential, and we certainly didn't. It would have given the two teams another day to play up to standard and to put on a better show on All-Ireland final day. Hopefully, Paddy will confirm this, but a Tipperary source informed me a few weeks after that Paddy thought the game was a draw at the time, that the sides were level when he blew the final whistle. I never got to ask Paddy if that was the case or not.'

I can confirm, Peter, that nothing could be further from the truth. Speaking on TV on the night of the final, Pat Spillane, the former Kerry player and presenter of *The Sunday Game*, reckoned that I was 'balancing the books' with the call against Canavan. That was totally wrong, because I whistled up before the ball was kicked over the bar.

CHARLIE REDMOND: *'It's funny, at the end of the game, Pat O'Neill didn't realise for a few moments that we had actually won. He thought that it was a draw, that Paddy had given the point to Tyrone and that we were taking a free kick, and not a kick-out.'*

PETER CANAVAN: *'Some referees like to make themselves the centre of attention, and if Paddy fell into that category, I would definitely have held it against him. But from previous games, I knew that he was not that type. He was never out there to be seen. I would have accepted that it was a genuine mistake on his part and never held it against him as such. Most players would agree with me when I say that Paddy was impartial and generally considered a good referee. And he refereed important games that we were involved in later well.'*

8

....

THE ARTICLE

A wise man makes his own decisions; an ignorant man
follows public opinion.

Chinese proverb

Charlie Redmond's refusal to leave the pitch during the 1995 All-Ireland football final would make the list of 20 Moments That Shook Irish Sport, a two-hour countdown show aired on RTÉ in October 2007. Leaving the pitch on that fateful afternoon in September 1995, Paddy had no idea of what lay in store in the days to come.

* * *

MARGARET RUSSELL: *'I would always go into the dressing-room after a game. That day, I asked the question I have asked many a time: "How are you?" Things seemed fine.'*

I could never have envisaged what was about to explode. We attended a post-match function at Croke Park, where Margaret overheard a leading official passing a remark that I had cost the GAA a million pounds by not making a draw out of the game.

MARGARET RUSSELL: *'That really stuck in my head. That's all that man was thinking of: money. My husband had just made such a courageous, honest-to-goodness call, and he'd done as good a job as he could have done out there. That's what I loved about Paddy and his refereeing. And this man was thinking about money.'*

That official's comment was my first inkling that trouble was in store. Driving back to the Green Isle Hotel later, there was talk about the game on the radio but nothing untoward, as far as I could gather. We ate, chatted for a while and retired to our room to watch *The Sunday Game* on TV. There was heavy analysis of the Redmond incident and the Peter Canavan pass. Pundit Pat Spillane advised me to switch off my set if I was watching. It wasn't long before we were taking calls to our hotel room from home urging us to ignore the pundits, who were highly critical of my performance. Easier said than done. A living nightmare had begun. I recall a state of total bewilderment, a sense of impending doom. It felt like my entire life was collapsing like a giant house of cards.

MARGARET RUSSELL: *'I couldn't sleep that night with the sick feeling. I just wanted to go home and cover my head. I always try to smile, to convey the impression that I don't give a monkey's, but that night I was dying inside.'*

I remember that Margaret wasn't able to sleep. I felt that the criticism was attacking my very being. I had a fitful night's sleep, too, and the agony intensified the next morning. My umpires, who had surfaced before me, reluctantly informed us that I was the hot topic of conversation on the morning radio phone-ins.

WILLIE O'MAHONY: *'I arrived home on the Sunday night. The next morning, it was all over the radio. Pat Kenny was on with GAA journalist Martin Breheny. I went down to the local shop, and John Landers, a man now involved with the Munster council, told me that they were talking about us on the radio. "These were experienced officials. How could this happen?" That kind of stuff.'*

People were ringing in to radio presenters Gerry Ryan and Pat Kenny, asking, 'What would a Tipperary man know about refereeing a football match?' I had been playing the game for the best part of three decades and refereeing since 1976, but it didn't matter. I was cannon fodder.

The media were whipping up a frenzy. Margaret went for the newspapers. The *Irish Times* carried an extensive post-match interview with Charlie Redmond. His words fanned the flames of this raging inferno for days to come.

MARGARET RUSSELL: *'I was reading the Irish Times coming across from the shop, looking at Tom Humphries' interview with Charlie Redmond. The hurt and shock that I felt were unbelievable. They were making a skit of Paddy. It was an interview, so it was bound to be one-sided, but I felt as if Charlie had taken the opportunity to say what he liked, without Paddy having a chance to refute some of the things he said. It is the one article from all of the newspaper cuttings that really hurt me. I didn't realise how anybody could be stripped and destroyed by the media, but now we were living it. That piece of journalism will stay with me until the day I go to the grave. It seemed that, as far as that article was concerned, what Charlie said was the truth and that was it. There were two people in this, but the other man was not asked to give a word.'*

'Charlie's On and Off All-Ireland Day' was the main headline on the article, and above that it read: 'Tom Humphries finds Charlie Redmond insistent that his sending-off was bungled by the referee.' Humphries portrayed Redmond as a hero who had finally reached the Promised Land after some hard luck in previous years. As for the sending-off, Humphries wrote that I 'gave an impression of a man who had just lost control of the horse he was riding'. He then quoted Redmond:

> He sent me off and then he changed his mind and told me to stay on and then he re-changed his mind two minutes later and put me off. A great man to have at an All-Ireland, isn't he, a great man to have reffing an All-Ireland. I said to him, 'Watch it on the telly tonight; you've made the same mistake as Tommy Howard with Tony Davis two years ago.' He said to me: 'I'll take me chances.' I said to him, 'Well, enjoy this All-Ireland, Paddy, because it's the last one you'll ever referee.'

Davis was the Cork player controversially sent off in the 1993 All-Ireland football final by referee Tommy Howard. But I can state categorically that Charlie Redmond did not mention this when I sent him off. Redmond also told Humphries:

He's an experienced referee and he showed today how immature of a referee he is. Dublin should put in an objection if we ever have to play with him again. He was a disgrace today . . . I thought it was a terrible decision. The linesman said to me that I wasn't going off. The linesman was sticking up for me; the linesman says, 'No, he didn't do anything.'

CHARLIE REDMOND: *'No offence was meant by that article whatsoever. Things were said in the heat of the moment, but emotions were running high after the game. When we received the trophy, we weren't allowed back onto the field, which we were thick about. We were brought out through the back of the stand and thrown into the dressing-rooms. We didn't get to go back onto the pitch, for safety reasons, obviously. We actually weren't allowed into our own dressing-room. We were sent into another one, where there were reporters. Somebody said something to me, and I was a bit thick. What I recall saying, and I can't remember everything, was that the linesman had said that I wasn't to be sent off. And if Paddy hadn't seen the incident with Fergal Logan, then why was he sending me off?'*

Margaret has serious issues with that article in its entirety, but the part where Redmond mentions Tommy Howard and Tony Davis annoyed me the most. I swear on my children's lives that Redmond did not say those words to me on the pitch. He was spinning a yarn, looking to deflect some of the attention from himself while at the same time ensuring that I would take the blame for what had happened.

CHARLIE REDMOND: *'Thirteen years on, I don't recall saying those words, but I have total faith in Tom Humphries, and if he wrote that I said those things after the game, well, then I did.'*

It's like when an argument develops with somebody. One word borrows another, and, before you know it, it's out of control. I felt that Charlie got a right laugh out of the situation on the TV and in the newspapers, and that really upset me. He stayed on the field after he was sent off and I didn't see him. So what? I can live with that. But some of the other stuff, I can't live with, because it's simply not true.

MARGARET RUSSELL: '*I can see what Charlie Redmond was doing. He was hurting after being sent off in the All-Ireland final. Of course he was – anybody would be. So he decided to turn it around by making a skit of the situation, thereby deflecting the media glare from himself. It annoyed me. Tom Humphries got the big, funny story and the laugh was on Paddy Russell.*'

9

....

THE BURLINGTON

You gain strength, courage, and confidence by every experience
in which you really stop to look fear in the face . . . The danger
lies in refusing to face the fear, in not daring to come to grips
with it . . . You must make yourself succeed every time. You
must do the thing you think you cannot do.

Eleanor Roosevelt

*A GAA tradition, dispensed with in recent years, saw the four
competing finalists in the minor and senior deciders meet for lunch
at Dublin's Burlington Hotel on the Monday after the All-Ireland
finals. Leading figures from the GAA were present at this event,
along with the match officials from the two games.*

* * *

The Burlington Hotel was the last place I wanted to go on the
Monday afternoon. My hotel room had become a safe haven
to me, a place of asylum. I picked up the phone and called John
Moloney, the referee who had had such a huge influence on my
career from the very start. At my lowest, John was a man I could
confide in, and I felt that he would be able to identify with the
feelings that I was experiencing.

John was one of the greatest referees in GAA history, but in
Cork he will always be remembered for the two controversial
decisions he made in the 1976 Munster football final replay
between Cork and Kerry at Páirc Uí Chaoimh. There was the

awarding of a goal against Cork in controversial circumstances and the disallowing of one they scored against Kerry. On both occasions, John endorsed calls by his umpires, but the buck always stops with the referee. The public at large will also associate John with an infamous tackle on Kerry player Mickey 'Ned' O'Sullivan that went unpunished in the 1975 All-Ireland final against Dublin. In later times, John always cringed when he saw that incident on TV.

He was straight up. 'You have to go to the Burlington.' He said that he had been loath to attend the function in '75 but had gone and that he felt sure that he would have regretted it now if he hadn't. John and I often shared lengthy conversations on the phone, and I rarely, if ever, ignored his advice. So it was time to face the fear.

MARGARET RUSSELL: *'I wanted to come home, I really did. I couldn't wait to leave Dublin that day. I was in tears before the function, couldn't stop crying. I probably made a show of myself, but I was so caught up in the whole thing and Paddy's feelings. Walking into the Burlington Hotel, and you might find this hard to believe, it was like walking in with somebody who was after committing murder. I felt like everybody was staring and, under their breaths, muttering and whispering. "Look, here's Paddy Russell." Here we were, back in the eye of the storm. Paddy was talking to Danny Lynch from the GAA and I was wondering what was being said.'*

Lynch, the Association's public-relations officer, confirmed that I had the full backing of the GAA. Photographers followed me, looking for the perfect shot. Reporters asked if I wanted to comment, but they didn't press me. I think they could see how uncomfortable I was feeling, and, besides, under GAA rules governing referees in situations like this, I couldn't respond. I just wanted to go away and hide.

CHARLIE REDMOND: *'The county secretary, John Costello, came over to me and told me not to give any interviews to the press. And that word apparently came from the president of the Association. That's what was said to me. I was asked not to talk and I didn't.'*

Support arrived in the form of Tyrone captain Ciarán Corr, and I will never forget his words of encouragement. Ciarán told me that the Tyrone players had met the night before and that they were not blaming me for their defeat. Before everybody dispersed later in the afternoon, Ciarán reiterated his earlier comments. They meant an awful lot. 'Hold your head up high, Paddy,' he said.

He told reporters: 'When you're beaten, you're beaten. I've never been one to blame the referee . . . The man was devastated. I could see the way he was looking at me. His eyes were just a blank. The media got to him this morning a wee bit, I think. I just said to him, on behalf of the players, we have no gripes with you. I'm only letting you know that we have no problems.'

CIARÁN CORR: *'I can't recall now exactly what I said, but I do remember talking to Paddy. It's not in my nature to be nasty, and we had to accept what had happened. The man had made his decision, and you move on. I saw that Paddy wasn't feeling the best, and human nature took over. I could see by his expression that he was torn, and I thought that I would say a wee bit to him. A lot of people would say to me that I'm a bit too soft, but that's just my make-up. Paddy had to go to work the following morning, and so did I.*

'As far as I was concerned, and the Tyrone team spoke about this, we should have had Dublin beaten anyway, regardless of the late call against Peter Canavan. We knew we were the better team, but we didn't perform in the second half. It would have been unfair to turn around and blame the ref when we should have beaten Dublin by four or five points. The players knew that themselves. Paddy had a vacant look. He was dejected. This was one man out on his own on the field the previous day, in among 30 players. He will make right and wrong decisions, but you've got to respect a man who goes out there at that level to control a game. We just didn't perform on the day. And that was a bigger issue than Paddy Russell.'

Coming from the captain of the Tyrone team, Ciarán's comments were something else. It showed the character of the fella. I wonder, would I have done the same thing if I was Corr that day, or if I was captain of a Tipperary team in a similar situation? Would I go and speak to the referee and tell him that he was not to blame? Would I have come forward or continued to feel sorry for myself? I'll never forget Ciarán Corr. Some day, I would like to meet him face to face again and thank him.

MARGARET RUSSELL: *'I couldn't begin to describe how important Ciarán Corr was that day. "Hold your head up," he said. I think he stopped Paddy from going mental.*

'We were sitting down for the meal when Dublin player Keith Barr came and shook hands with Paddy. I noticed the bit of banter between the Dublin players. We were sat with officials, overlooking the minor and senior teams, who were seated on a level below. "Mooching" is the word I would use to describe Charlie Redmond making his way towards us. I got the feeling that there was a bit of pressure put on him: "Look, go up and get it over with."'

Charlie was chatting at each table as he made his way towards us. We had a good view of what was going on below. He offered up his hand, and I shook it. No words were spoken. That was it.

CHARLIE REDMOND: *'The day we were at the Burlington with the Tyrone team really stays with me. A reference was made to the refereeing, and I remember looking up at Paddy and his wife, who looked a little bit upset. At that moment, I really felt terrible, because it had gone past football at that stage. It was now affecting somebody who wasn't even on the pitch. It's something that if I could change, I would love to, and I think Paddy might like to change it, too. But it happened, we live with it, we get on with it, and it's not the most important thing that happened in our lives.'*

WILLIE O'MAHONY: *'I didn't go to that banquet. I could have, and, looking back, I should have, but I was back home in Oola. I could have been a support to Paddy and his wife. I was worried. I was down here, and Paddy was above. I wondered what he and the wife were thinking.'*

MARGARET RUSSELL: *'It felt like everybody was talking about Paddy, and they probably were. It was on the front page of the* Evening Herald *that day. We were just picking at the food, couldn't wait to get the* thing over and done with. The GAA president, Jack Boothman, spoke very nicely on the day and said that Paddy did a good job. Jack thanked Paddy, and then it was a case of "get me out of here". John Bailey's wife said to us, "I know you're upset but we've been there too."'

JOHN BAILEY (FORMER DUBLIN COUNTY BOARD CHAIRMAN): 'In 1986, after I had refereed the Cork v. Galway All-Ireland hurling final, a certain individual from Galway, a well-known member of the party, verbally abused my wife and I at the function in the Burlington Hotel on the Monday. This took place in front of the GAA president at the time, Mick Loftus, and the director general, Liam Mulvihill. It left a sour taste in my mouth for the entire day. It happened before the meal, and then I had to go and sit at the top table after being told that I was a bollocks, etc. That was unnecessary stuff, but you rise above it.

'I had refereed with Paddy over a number of years and had a lot of respect for him. I still have. He was one of the top referees in the country, and, as chairman of the Dublin county board in 1995, I congratulated Paddy for the time he had put into refereeing. No matter what game you go to, people will have different opinions. You have 80,000 people in the ground and they're all blinkered, favouring their own team. When the match is over, it should be left at that, but what happened to Paddy from a media perspective was unprecedented. I went to Paddy before, during and after the reception and told him to rise above it. Monday should be the day when a referee can unwind after a final and spend a bit of time with his wife and family, but there was huge hype. I just hope that what we did helped him on the day. The fact that I had been in that position myself nine years before might have helped him too.'

MARGARET RUSSELL: 'I've never forgotten that day in the Burlington. I was back there in December 2007, attending an ICA [Irish Countrywomen's Association] function. I walked through the revolving door and looked towards the corner where you enter the bar. I remembered standing there all those years ago and feeling so alone. We went into the room where Paddy had spoken with Danny Lynch. And the room in which the ICA meeting was held was the room where the post-match reception took place. It sent a shiver down my spine. I could picture it all again. I maintain to this day that it would not *have become such a huge issue had Dublin not been involved. The hype surrounding that team was just phenomenal.'*

Speculation was rife that Tyrone would lodge an appeal because Redmond had stayed on the field when he was sent off. In the end, they didn't go through with it.

CIARÁN CORR: *'The county board was coming at it from a different angle, but we wanted to win the All-Ireland properly, on the field of play. Sure, there were two or three incidents, including the man sent off staying on, but that actually reinforced my opinion that we should go home with a bit of respect rather than creating a hoo-ha about the whole thing.'*

PETER CANAVAN: *'There was some talk at the time that Tyrone had grounds to put in a complaint. There would have been legitimate enough reasons, because a player was sent off but didn't go. However, if Tyrone were going to win the All-Ireland, we didn't want to win it in the boardroom. The players didn't entertain that prospect for one second.'*

CHARLIE REDMOND: *'I often wonder, if I hadn't touched the ball for six or seven minutes, would Paddy have thought that he'd sent off somebody else? What would have happened if the game had gone on and Paddy hadn't realised that I was still on the field until later? The shit would really have hit the fan then. In some ways, Paddy did Dublin a favour sending me off so quickly the second time, because if he hadn't done, Tyrone would have had a legitimate case. I've often thought about that.'*

DOMINIC MCCAUGHEY (TYRONE COUNTY BOARD SECRETARY): *'It was one of those things. There was huge disappointment at the time, but challenging the result was never even discussed formally at any level. Aye, there was talk of it, surely, but a lot of reports about our plans were unfounded. The general opinion was that whatever happened on the pitch should stay on the pitch. End of story.'*

If only it were that simple.

10

···

PICKING UP THE PIECES

> There is not enough darkness in all the world to put out
> the light of even one small candle.
>
> Robert Alden

I'm particularly fond of the old saying that the night is always darkest just before the dawn. It has a deep personal resonance.

We arrived home from Dublin on Monday evening, having listened to more 'expert' analysis on the radio. Lying on the floor inside the front door was a card from our good friend, local man Pat O'Halloran, known as 'Spudy'.

Dear Paddy,

Just a short note urging you to forget about any criticism you are receiving. You are still an outstanding referee and I hope you will continue to be for many a year. Remember, the media are vultures, most of whom would have no idea of what the game is like to play but still consider themselves 'experts'. Your outstanding decision at the end of the game proves to me how courageous a man you are. Keep the head up. My best

wishes to Margaret and yourself and family. Looking forward
to seeing you refereeing Lattin's games again.

Yours,
Pat O'Halloran, Lattin.

It was the only post we received that day, and it meant the
world to us.

Pat McCarthy, a detective in Tipperary town, arrived to the
house soon after, along with Willie O'Mahony. Charlie Redmond
had told reporters that Willie had said it was OK for him to
return to the field of play, but I did not even need to ask Willie
if this was true. A linesman doesn't have that authority. If I am
running the line for a referee and he sends a player off, I can't
tell the offending player that he is all right to continue. It would
be ludicrous. Willie was upset by the reporting of the final, and
an irate McCarthy wanted my permission to write to RTÉ to
complain about the way I had been treated on TV and radio.

WILLIE O'MAHONY: '*People had been talking about it all day. It was a
major controversy. I think there was a funeral in Oola on the Monday
evening, and Pat McCarthy was at it. I went into Tipperary town
with Pat, and we had a pint. We went out to Paddy's then and gave
an hour out there. Paddy was in a bad state. I told him that I had said
nothing at all to Redmond, that he was spinning yarns. To this day,
I don't know what Redmond's game was. I still get slagged over the
thing. I remember meeting John Moloney after the game. He had been
sitting in the Cusack Stand and saw the Redmond incident. He had
thought at first that Redmond had got off, and he couldn't believe that
we were after leaving him on.*'

MARGARET RUSSELL: '*The phone never stopped ringing. Even though
our heads were wrecked, we really appreciated it. All the calls and
messages were supportive. It was as if there had been a funeral in the
family, really. It was as if we had lost something. Paddy was really
down.*'

On the Tuesday morning after the 1995 All-Ireland senior
football final, an incredibly fearful Paddy Russell returned

to work. I was based in Limerick with Connacht Minerals at the time, and walking in there was a hellish experience. Some colleagues wanted to talk to me about the match, the usual banter, but I wasn't in the form for it. Others could probably see how I was feeling and respected that I didn't want to rake over the hot ashes. Reporters rang work looking for me, but colleagues threw them off the scent.

That same day, I compiled my official match report for submission to Croke Park. An addendum read:

> I wish to add these further details to my report. During the course of the second half of the game, I had to send Charlie Redmond (Dublin) off for attempting to head-butt an opponent and as far as I was aware he had left the field of play. But after the game continued I noticed he was still on the field and involved in play. I checked with my linesman, who felt sure Charlie Redmond had gone off, but when I drew his attention to the presence of Charlie Redmond on the field, my linesman was quite amazed. I then went to Charlie Redmond and told him once more to leave the playing field, which he did after pleading with me not to send him off. I then continued with the game.

MARGARET RUSSELL: *'What is included in the report, and I always say this to Paddy, should have nothing to do with what the newspapers say. It's about what he did, and so the quicker he writes it up, the less chance there is that his thoughts will be coloured by the coverage.'*

My stomach was badly affected. I ate food, but I still felt empty. The world weighed heavily on my shoulders. Paddy Russell was in the papers every day. Russell this, Russell that. But for Margaret and the family, I would not have survived. If I had been on my own, I believe the unthinkable would have become a live prospect. Everything bubbles to the surface when I talk about it. I was in a truly sad state of mind. I felt so alone. But Margaret, my mother and father, Margaret's mother and sisters, they were the people who helped me out.

MARGARET RUSSELL: '*Paddy's parents were very upset too. His father is a very quiet man, a man of few words, but his mother was clearly very distressed. She lights candles at Mass on the morning of a game, praying that Paddy will have a good game. And she will ask me to ring her later to let her know how Paddy is after the match. She was reduced to tears by the whole thing. The words "Pat" and "Spillane" are bad words in her house. We have moved on since, but Paddy's mother never quite got over it. My own sisters, Lena and Teresa, were very upset over it too.*'

My mother was always anxious to see me after a game, and she was always a 'one-paper woman' – the *Examiner* on a Monday, just to see what was written about me. She might not say a terrible amount about a particular game or episode, but I would know when she was hurt.

If I didn't love refereeing the way I do, there's no way that I would have returned to it after 1995, because that All-Ireland final left me in the pits of despair. You hear about people destroyed from drink and drug addiction, but that game had a similar effect on me. It stripped me bare. People were trying to be nice to me, saying the right things, but they had read about the game in the newspapers, and their opinions were already formed. My experience told me that a journalist's word is almost always taken at face value and noted as the whole truth.

MARGARET RUSSELL: '*I gave all of Tuesday answering the phone again. I was on maternity leave after having our son Mark. It was the same again on Wednesday, the day of the GOAL charity match.*'

Newly crowned champions Dublin were due to play a Rest of Ireland selection in the annual GOAL match at Croke Park on the Wednesday night. As All-Ireland final referee, I was entitled to take charge of the charity game, but I seriously considered not travelling. However, after much consideration, I eventually decided to return to the scene of my very public humiliation.

I remember meeting Margaret before heading for Dublin. She suggested lunch at Kiely's in Tipperary town. No chance. It was like she'd hit me with a brick. I knew going there meant facing people. I was ducking just walking up the street in case I met anybody I knew.

MARGARET RUSSELL: *'People will read this and say that refereeing for the GAA is madness. And, really, what went on was madness.'*

Incredibly, when I returned to Croke Park for that GOAL match, I felt very much at home. The Dublin supporters were not aggressive in any way, and there was a carnival atmosphere at the ground – a far cry from the previous Sunday.

The exercise was brought to a finish 13 minutes into the second half when swarms of children invaded the pitch in search of Dublin hero Jason Sherlock, very much the pin-up boy of the time. Appeals from Micheál O'Muircheartaigh to clear the field fell on deaf ears as 'Jayo' ran for the dressing-room at high speed!

CHARLIE REDMOND: *'I didn't realise that Paddy was the ref that evening. I was suspended, and the guys who knew they wouldn't be playing, like me, had a few pints that day. I think the players wanted the game to be abandoned so they could go on the piss!'*

Then something quite amazing happened. As I looked around the field, people were running towards me with pieces of paper clasped in their hands. They wanted my autograph! If the stewards had not taken me in off the field, I could have stayed out there for hours. It was such a wonderful feeling, and I travelled home revitalised.

MARGARET RUSSELL: *'There were no mobile phones then. I've always felt that they are such a great invention, because if I don't attend a match, I can always ring Paddy afterwards to see how it went. But I was in limbo that night as I waited for him to come home. I hadn't a clue what had happened until he arrived in the early hours of Thursday morning. I was wide awake when he pulled into the driveway.*

'"Well? Who won? How did you get on?" I asked.

'"It was called off, they invaded the pitch."

'My heart skipped a beat. "Oh, God, no!"

'"No, all good! Everything went well. It was fun!"

'I was thrilled for him.'

The healing process began that evening. What an emotional roller-coaster ride those few days had been. On the Monday, I couldn't wait to get out of Dublin, but two days later I was signing autographs until my fingers ached.

11

···

THE LETTERS

What a lot we lost when we stopped writing letters.
You can't reread a phone call.

Liz Carpenter

When I received the assessment of my performance in the 1995 final, by former Ulster council chairman Micheál Greenan, it stated that I had 'lost it' after the Redmond sending-off. That didn't bother me at the time. It didn't matter what anybody said at that stage. I was already hammered into the dust.

It was the countless phone calls, letters, messages and, above all, the support of my family that dragged me out of the abyss. To everybody who wrote and picked up the phone, a heartfelt thanks. You don't know how much that meant. Some of the letters were simply addressed to 'Paddy Russell, Referee, Tipperary'.

A refereeing friend from Waterford sent this kind note:

How are you, Paddy? Hope you are keeping the head up – not easy with some of the so-called experts around. Dig in and get the hell on with your games. Last week's game says more about others than about yourself. Some of them haven't a clue. Jim O'Sullivan of the *Cork Examiner* was honest and fair. Hoping to meet you soon, Paddy, and thinking of you these days.

God bless,
Pat Moore, Ballinamuck

One of the letters was from Galtee Rovers player Séamus McCarthy, who had been so badly injured against Solohead:

Dear Paddy,

Just a note to express my support for you in what has been a difficult week. You are the best in the business and don't let Sunday get you down. Stick with it and keep your chin up.

Séamus McCarthy

Tony Jordan, a former referee and current assessor, compiled a lengthy letter. I've always got on well with Tony, who has a liking for my style of refereeing. He's always been kind to me in assessments. Tony wrote from his home in Clondalkin, Dublin, two days after the game:

Dear Paddy,

This letter will not take away the hurt you must feel because of the unfair criticism to which you were subjected because of the Charlie Redmond sending-off.

I believe it is bordering on the unbelievable that a player who is ordered off in an All-Ireland final by a referee who (a) takes his name for a serious offence, (b) tells him verbally that he is ordering him off and (c) clearly points to the sideline could have any doubt whatever about the decision of the referee. Of course, it is easy to say you should have ensured that he went off. Looking at the steps taken by you, you did what every other referee would have done in similar circumstances. You . . .

1. took his name and told him he was sent off;
2. pointed to the sideline to indicate your decision.

Isn't it strange how so many want to blame you for the subsequent confusion? Charlie was clearly ordered off. As a spectator, I knew he had been ordered off, and to me it is inconceivable that Charlie could have any other opinion. Was he hoping that somehow you would decide you had erred and leave him on or did he genuinely rationalise the situation and convince himself he had not been ordered off? Charlie and only Charlie knows the real truth as to why he stayed on the pitch. He made the error, not you, and it is totally unfair, in my view, to blame you.

Willie O'Mahony drew your attention to the fact that Charlie had remained on the field of play. Despite Charlie's protestations it was clear that Willie O'Mahony had no doubt about your decision and that was why he drew your attention to Charlie's continuing presence on the field.

Your final decision was also a very brave one. I do not know whether the ball was hopping or not and, having watched it a number of times on TV, I still do not know. What is clear is that (a) your positioning is perfect, (b) you blew immediately for the foul and (c) you clearly indicated a pick-up. Consequently, I fully accept your decision to be in accordance with what you saw.

It is a pity that your enjoyment of the game and the post-match celebrations are both tinged by this controversy. John O'Leary, in his comments on television at the post-match dinner, said that it was 'not an entertaining game but that the cup was at the end of the room'. Does that mean that, in the view of players, entertainment is something that might follow but is not a priority? Can it be construed as meaning that the end result, however achieved, is all that matters and the process is irrelevant?

Maybe it is time that referees just referee the games in accordance with the rules and refuse to take on the responsibility of players whose obligation it is to ensure that the game flows. My firm view is that we must be much more proactive in defending our referees and must endeavour to create a climate whereby they feel assured of administrative backing at all levels if they are to take on what looks like a win-at-all-costs mentality.

Keep up the good work of refereeing and try to put the unfair criticism behind you.

With every good wish,
Tony Jordan

A few days later, a letter arrived from the Tipperary football board, signed by long-serving secretary Eddie Lonergan. His words were a real tonic.

A Chara,

I have been requested by the Tipperary football board to write to you to congratulate you on your performance in refereeing the All-Ireland football final.

The board strongly condemned the media in general and Radio Éireann in particular, which it felt did not behave responsibly as a national station should.

The board will be waiting anxiously to see how the authorities deal with the matter, particularly as at the time of the sending-off there appeared to be an attempt to intimidate you by the player concerned and by the Dublin manager.

In conclusion I wish to thank you for your service to this board and trust that you will be available for some time to come.

Mise le Meas,
Eamon Ó Lonargain

The support didn't just come from my own county. My neighbours just across the border in Limerick also took the time to write. On behalf of the Limerick Referees Association, secretary Ben Mullane said:

A Chara,

Further to a meeting of the Limerick Referees Association which took place on Wednesday, 20 September, it was unanimously agreed that I write to you and inform you of our association's full support of your handling of the All-Ireland football final.

The meeting felt that you were very much mistreated and misinterpreted by all aspects of the media plus Dublin team members and all this was very unfair on yourself and family. The meeting felt very strongly that no referee should have to put up with that kind of behaviour.

Wishing you continued success in the future.
Mise le Meas,
Ben Mullane

Incredibly, a letter arrived from Tyrone, and I opened it with a natural sense of trepidation. I need not have worried, as Declan McCullagh from Omagh wrote:

Dear Paddy,

Just a little note to say how sorry I felt when I heard and read some of the comments about your handling of the All-Ireland final. Such comments were quite honestly unwarranted and disgraceful and were issued by these self-styled 'experts' in our national media. I often wonder how many of them graced the fields of Croke Park!

Anyhow, as a dedicated Tyrone supporter I was naturally heartbroken at the result but quite honestly we didn't deserve any better – on the day, we played terrible.

I hope that Sunday's match has not dented your enthusiasm for the game and that in years to come we'll see you officiating at the top-level games in Croke Park. Wishing you and your family well.

Yours sincerely,
Declan McCullagh
PS Sure there's always 1996!

And that wasn't the only correspondence I received from Tyrone. Father Peter O'Neill, from the Columban Fathers, wrote from Dungannon:

Dear Paddy,

Greetings from Tyrone.

We are all feeling a bit sad up here but we are not down. I have talked to a lot of people here and I want you to know we appreciate the very difficult situation you found yourself in on Sunday. It clarified once and for all that it is impossible for one referee to do all the things demanded of him in today's game. Keep your chin up and so will we. Hopefully Tyrone will some day win Sam and we hope we can entertain and give joy to the people in doing it.

Give my kindest regards to your wife, who, like many a wife and girlfriend in Tyrone, has felt the pain of it all.

There is always sunshine somewhere. God bless always.

A very interesting letter arrived from John Gough, who took charge of the ill-tempered 1983 All-Ireland final, when Dublin finished the game with 12 men and Galway with 14. He wrote:

A Pádraig, a Chara,

I would like to congratulate you on your performance in the All-Ireland final. I thought you had an excellent game and I have on occasion been very critical of some referees. It says a great deal for your handling of the game that there were only two incidents which caused any problem. At the end of the game you made your decision that Canavan struck the ball on the ground from only three yards. You were closer than anyone else in the ground and after watching the incident about four times on video I could not say you were wrong, even though I would have loved Tyrone to equalise.

On the Redmond incident you clearly put him off the pitch and clearly indicated your intentions – absolutely the correct decision. Your actions in ensuring that he left the pitch were courageous. No referee could have done better in the circumstances. The actions of Redmond and O'Neill, the Dublin manager, deserve the highest condemnation.

I sincerely hope you continue to referee as you have a great deal to offer the game in terms of honesty and integrity, along with your undoubted fitness and knowledge of the rules.

Please take heart from the fact that you only put one player off in the All-Ireland final. I had to put four off and if I had been able to identify the Galway centre-half it would have been five.

I am still refereeing and enjoying it. I hope you do the same. Don't let the hacks get you down. Remember, to sell papers they can be less than honest . . .

Once again, take heart from a game well done. I hope your county backs you, I hope your province backs you and I hope Games Administration and the Association support you.

Sorry I didn't write sooner.

Is mise le meas mór . . .

It's true what they say. At your lowest, you discover who your real friends are. And sometimes you discover friends you never knew you had.

12

THE VIDEO

> Wouldn't it be nice if our lives were like VCRs and we
> could fast-forward through the crummy times?
>
> *Peanuts*, Charles M. Schulz

I lived with the events of that fateful All-Ireland final day for more than 12 years before finally deciding I needed closure. To say that I was pilloried afterwards would be no exaggeration, but on Sunday, 13 January 2008, the 1995 All-Ireland football final was finally exhumed and dealt with. The videotape of *The Sunday Game* had always been in the family home, a private Pandora's box that I thought I would never open.

My decision not to look at the tape for so many years was based on fear, much of it irrational. Fear that perhaps, on a second viewing, things would look desperately bad, that the footage would indicate that I had made incorrect calls. Maybe Charlie Redmond did not deserve to be sent off. Maybe the ball was slightly above the ground when Peter Canavan fisted it left to Seán McLaughlin. Were Tyrone really robbed of a replay? I would hate to have that on my conscience. Perhaps it was better to let sleeping dogs lie. But, no, this was something I had to do.

CHARLIE REDMOND: *'I didn't watch the game until a year afterwards. If I don't see it on the night, I generally don't watch it. In fact, I've only seen the match twice since. Thanks to TG4, you see some of the old classic games on TV. It came on one night, and the kids were watching. I walked out of the room and went out digging in the garden. I'm not comfortable with it, and I don't like the kids watching it either, seeing me getting sent off. They're very young – eight, ten and thirteen.'*

CIARÁN CORR: *'I've never actually watched the game in all these years. TV stations and other people have sent the DVD, but I have never looked at it. My son asked me two or three times to watch it, but I put it on in a different room and let him at it. It's one of those things. I had sacrificed myself for a number of years, I was coming near the end of my career, and I was team captain. It knocked me back a wee bit. Maybe I'll open a bottle of Jameson and watch it some day. I might blame Paddy then! I must be mentally scarred from the whole thing, because if I'm not, then why haven't I watched it? It gets me thinking a wee bit. Anything bad that happens in life, you tend to put it to the back of your mind.'*

I never wanted to watch anything to do with that game ever again until I realised that I had to when I sat down to recount my career. If it came on the TV by chance some night, I would probably walk out of the room. There's hurt there still.

I chose my moment carefully. Margaret was out, my eldest son Shane was away training and Mark was watching TV in another room. At 8.30 p.m., I picked up 'Exhibit A', the tape a sickly green in colour, before slotting it into the VCR. Finally, I was ready to have a peek.

'It would be fitting, I think, if, among the last man-made tracks on Earth, would be found the huge footprints of the great brown bear.' I find myself watching the closing moments of a nature documentary dedicated to the grizzly bear, and the narrator informs me that the above comment was uttered by Earl Fleming, the American naturalist, in 1958. I'm sure he's right, but I don't care much right now.

The *Survivor Special* ends and RTÉ's continuity announcer tells viewers, 'Stay with us for *The Sunday Game*, after the break.' I'm not going anywhere. It's taken almost twelve and a half years for me to pluck up the courage to watch what's coming next.

Advertisements follow for a host of products, ranging from energy-efficient light bulbs and Castrol motor oil to Head & Shoulders shampoo and Chan Broad Spec, 'the all-year-round wormer and flukicide for sheep and cattle'. All-Ireland final day wouldn't be complete without those ads for animal treatments. Then there's a quick look ahead to Monday evening on Network 2, including *Blackboard Jungle*, the old quiz show for secondary schools hosted by Ray Darcy, *Top 30 Hits*, *Cybill* and *Black Box*.

The continuity announcer returns: 'Back to this evening, and it was a game of two halves with a breath-taking finish – and it features in the final *Sunday Game*.' That famous theme tune, which made a welcome return this year, blasts out from the TV set and my heart begins to race even faster, if that's possible.

A gleaming Sam Maguire Cup is the first shot following the opening credits, with presenter Michael Lyster setting the scene in the background. 'Pride of place for Sam Maguire at the All-Ireland football champions' victory banquet on Dublin's Southside,' he proclaims. Soon, a fresh-faced Lyster fills the screen before Marty Morrissey gets the word on the street before the game.

Beginning the sequence of vox-pops, former Kerry player and manager Páidí Ó Sé says that, in the days leading up to the game, he's felt sure that Dublin will win, but now he warns that it's not going to be easy. 'It's our time!' roar Tyrone supporters, but a Dublin fan insists, 'Sam is coming back to the capital. We're taking it home. It's up in the North too long.' (Ulster counties had won the four previous All-Ireland senior football titles. Down (1991 and 1994), Donegal (1992) and Derry (1993) had all prevailed, and Ulster cast a long shadow across the Gaelic football landscape.) Kerry native and former Ireland rugby international Mick Galwey tips the Dubs before two Tyrone supporters, each sporting 'God 14' on the back of their replica jerseys, chant, 'Peter Canavan walks on water!' In one of the local boozers, a Dublin fan predicts that with golden boy Jason Sherlock a marked man, Jack Sheedy will steal in for a vital goal. 'Sheedy's not even playing!' Marty Morrissey reminds him.

Back to the studio and Michael Lyster. 'As the game progressed, it was clear that this was also destined to be a day of strange events, debatable decisions and downright bizarre incidents.'

And suddenly, there it is. The incident that, in so many ways, has defined me. The clock on the top left-hand corner of the screen shows that 10 minutes and 12 seconds of the second half have elapsed. Match commentator Ger Canning is animated. 'And the referee . . . now, what's he doing?' I am sending Redmond off for aiming a head-butt at Fergal Logan. 'He's sending him off, I think . . . Charlie Redmond's being sent off, the goal-scorer early on in the game, for that head-butt there on Fergal Logan. Dublin are down to 14 men. I think that's what the referee's decided.'

Back to Lyster again, who has come over all Shakespearean. He declares, 'To go or not to go? That was the question for Charlie Redmond this afternoon. That will be one of the many talking points on *The Sunday Game* tonight. And we'll be taking up those points later on with our panel. As usual, our panel is Colm O'Rourke, who, of course, was a member of the Meath team beaten by Dublin on their way to the final, and Pat Spillane, who scored a vital goal for Kerry when they beat Tyrone in the All-Ireland final of 1986.'

I settle down, as best I can, to watch the highlights of the 1995 All-Ireland senior football final. The first half went well but all hell broke loose minutes after the restart. 'I think,' says Ger Canning, 'that's what the referee's decided. Charlie collided there initially with Fergal Logan, then an attempted head-butt . . .'

Mick O'Dwyer, Kerry's legendary former manager, is co-commentator alongside Canning. He says, 'Charlie had got the free at that stage and there was no need whatsoever.'

'Well, he's not sent him off, has he? Charlie's still on the park.'

'Very lucky to remain on the park, I can tell you there, Ger. Very, very lucky.'

'He's had the name taken. He's had so much misfortune in All-Ireland finals. It would have been a dreadful way for him to finish up this match. So, correction then. Both sides at full strength still. Fifteen against fifteen.'

I'm on my way to Willie O'Mahony before I return to send Redmond off – for a second time.

Ger Canning comments, 'He's gone back to talk to Charlie Redmond again. Did he in fact send him off a few minutes ago and Charlie continued? This is all very confusing. I've certainly never seen anything like this in an All-Ireland final. I think he has sent him off. So Dublin are indeed down to 14 players.'

After watching the video, I do have one major regret, which has nothing whatsoever to with Charlie Redmond or Peter Canavan. Tyrone centre-forward Pascal Canavan, Peter's older brother, should have been sent off seconds after half-time for a wild swipe at Dublin player Brian Stynes. Midfielder Stynes collected possession from the throw-in, and, as he surged forward, he was surrounded by three Tyrone players, one of them Canavan. From the side, Canavan connects with a punch on Stynes. On the pitch, I was blind-sided and unaware of what had happened. But it looks bad on the video, and it irks me. I thought that Canavan was flicking the ball away when he was actually hitting his opponent in the face. The Redmond and Peter Canavan incidents were analysed to death afterwards, but there was no mention of Pascal Canavan.

Mark had come in and joined me in front of the TV, watching the footage for the very first time. Thank God my two boys were too young to understand back then. At the time, Shane was five years old and Mark was newly born. His response now was, 'You did well, Dad.' That meant a lot. He's not afraid to speak his mind, and I value his opinion.

I can identify so much with the former Premier League soccer referee Graham Poll. In his autobiography, he wrote about the embarrassment he felt after the 2006 World Cup finals, during which he gave a Croatian player three yellow cards before he was sent off. Poll's wife collected him at the airport when he arrived home from Germany, but he didn't want the children there because the media attention had been so intense. Shane and Mark are hugely interested in the GAA. Shane was a member of the Tipperary minor football team in 2008. If something like the Redmond incident occurred now, the boys would be hugely affected, I'm sure. I would hate that.

When Margaret arrived home, I told her that I had watched the tape and that I felt relieved. I was expecting it to be a lot worse because I had it built up as something huge in my own head. I recalled the way people described the game back then, the newspapers the following day, the radio shows, the aftermath.

On the night of the game itself, the footage of the actual match in *The Sunday Game* barely registered. I was in a daze. The consensus seemed to be that the game was a disaster. I had performed desperately. I was the root cause of the controversy. That wasn't how I had felt leaving the pitch, but in the hours that followed it was evident that I was in for some heavy criticism.

Looking back on the decisions I made during the game, I didn't cop out. Sending Redmond off for a second time was a big call on my part. At that moment, my reputation could have been ruined. If Charlie had stayed on, the entire incident might well have blown over without any fuss. At that time yellow and red cards were not in use. 'He only booked him,' they would have said. Who would have known? Well, I would.

Nobody likes to make mistakes, but just two aspects of the game disappointed me. The Pascal Canavan challenge made me cringe, and Fergal Logan would have been sent off, too, had we identified him in the Redmond incident. The rest? Spot on. I sent off Charlie Redmond for an attempted head-butt. Right call. Back over to Charlie Redmond. Right call. If I had lied afterwards and claimed, for the sake of peace, that I had not sent off Redmond in the first place? Wrong call. Peter Canavan touched the ball on the ground. Right call.

In the rest of the programme, representatives from both teams were interviewed at their hotels after the game. Tyrone manager Eugene McKenna said, 'I wouldn't like it to be sour grapes but the referee probably would realise that he didn't have as good a game as he could have had. And he probably won't include it in his CV application for the next All-Ireland final.' McKenna was visibly hurting. If Tipperary were playing and something similar happened, I would probably feel the same way myself. We only see our own team. We don't acknowledge the frees that should be given to the opposition. Very few people are able to be objective in such an emotive situation.

Peter Canavan was more diplomatic. 'We still didn't get the point and that's all that matters now,' he said. 'At the time, I'm not too sure, I thought maybe the ball was bouncing, and when Seán kicked it over, I thought the point would stand. I couldn't really believe it when the ref gave a free-out.' I had no other option.

Over to the Dublin team hotel, and he looks rather sheepish, does Charlie. Nervous, shaking his head from side to side, almost as if he's afraid to look RTÉ's Ger Canning straight in the eye. The venue is Jury's Hotel on Dublin's Southside.

Redmond told Canning, 'I was fouled by . . . I think it was Paul Devlin. And Fergal Logan had no part in the incident, and he came in and tried to injure me. I took exception to that and made a very rash challenge on him, a challenge which let down my fellow players. I feel very sorry for that. I felt that the referee's actions after that were unwarranted. I didn't deserve to get sent off. If anybody deserved to get sent off, it was Fergal Logan.'

Canning responded, 'Did the referee send you off at that point? What did he say to you?'

'The referee told [stammers] . . . didn't say anything to me; he just pointed to the sideline. And then he's had a conference with the linesman, and the ball was thrown up again, and I was still playing on the field. I was right in front of him, as Colm O'Rourke says, and he said nothing to me. I assumed that I was still playing in the game.'

'Originally, it seemed like there was a free to you, and then there was the hop ball. Did that, in your mind, say to you that the referee had changed his decision?'

'I thought the referee had changed his mind. I heard a conversation between the linesman and the referee in which the linesman spoke up for me and said that I didn't head-butt him, that I went into him. And I didn't head-butt Fergal Logan. I think Fergal Logan might back me up on that one. The referee made a decision and I can't change that.'

'You continued playing for about three minutes. What do you remember next?'

Redmond laughed. 'Getting sent off.'

'That's the simplistic way. What happened? The referee came right across the field to identify you . . .'

'He came over to me and he, eh [puffs], he said, "You shouldn't be here." I said, "I know, I failed a fitness test yesterday. I shouldn't be here!"'

Cue laughter and sustained applause.

That was the moment I officially became a laughing stock.

But, then again, I shouldn't have been tuning in at all; Pat Spillane had advised earlier that, if I was watching, I should switch off. He described the game as 'GUBU – grotesque, unbelievable, bizarre and unprecedented'. In Spillane's view, it was 'grotesque' because it was an error-ridden game with 56 frees. 'Paddy Russell did not contribute to this being a good game. He had a very, very poor game, and I would suggest, Paddy, for the rest of the programme, maybe you might switch off your television. He was very poor.'

I've come to expect that type of stuff from Pat Spillane. He has strong views, and, of course, he's entitled to these – but it so happens that they are broadcast all over Ireland. He's criticised people harshly on numerous occasions, and I feel sure from my own experience that I am not the only person to have found his remarks humiliating. What he said that night was very hurtful.

He continued, saying that the final was 'unbelievable' in terms of the high fitness levels on show, particularly from Dublin and that it was 'bizarre' when, after the sending off, 'both the referee and the linesman actually forgot that [Redmond] had gone off the field'. It was 'unprecedented' because, as far as he could remember, a team had never won an All-Ireland final having scored just two points in the second half.

In his interview with Ger Canning, Dublin manager Pat O'Neill reflected: 'There seemed to be controversy. I really didn't understand what was going on. My own impression when [Redmond] came across from the far side of the field was that there had been a second incident, but it doesn't appear that way now.'

So, there were some harsh words throughout. Deep down, though, I was pleased, because watching the tape reinforced what I was already quite sure of: I made massive, brave calls in that game, and they were 100 per cent correct.

Watching the videotape really did bring closure for me. Many, many people have questioned my refereeing down through the years, but family and close friends will verify that my integrity and, above all, my honesty can never be called into question.

Yellow and red cards, which clearly show whether a player has been booked or sent off, would have been a major help, but they were not in force at the time. In those days, a referee signalled towards the touchline when he was sending off a player. Maybe Charlie didn't understand my culchie voice. Still, 'You're off' is a pretty clear statement in my view. People hear what they want to hear sometimes, but I'm convinced Charlie knew. And he played the media game to perfection.

13

··

REFLECTIONS

This is not the end. It is not even the beginning of the end.
But it is, perhaps, the end of the beginning.

Winston Churchill

O n Wednesday evening, 4 October 1995, Charlie Redmond
walked away from a meeting of the GAA's Games
Administration Committee with a three-month ban. The GAC,
after deliberating for forty minutes, imposed the minimum three-
month suspension on Redmond for his attempted head-butt on
Fergal Logan.

'Redmond Relief' screamed the back-page headline of *The Star*
newspaper. *The Star* carried the news as the lead sports story
on the Thursday morning. Roy Keane being ruled out of the
Republic of Ireland's European Championship tie with Latvia
was relegated to the secondary story. It was that big.

The suspension took effect from 17 September, the day of
the All-Ireland final, and as he left the GAC meeting, flanked
by Dublin county board secretary John Costello, Redmond
immediately issued an apology to me.

CHARLIE REDMOND: *'When I got the suspension, I said that I hoped
Paddy and I could put it all to bed and that we could share a pint. It
was a comment that Des Cahill picked up on: "Typical Redmond! He
wouldn't buy a pint, he wanted to share one!"*

'To this day, it's still a much talked-about incident. I still get ribbed about it all the time, everywhere I go: "There's the man who got sent off twice in an All-Ireland final." It's something that's going to live with me until the day I die. While I'm comfortable with it, it's something that I wish had never occurred. It would have been terrible had we lost the game. I've said many times since that when I woke up on that Sunday morning, my goal for the day was to win an All-Ireland final, and I went back to bed that night having achieved it. I've always regarded myself as being a team player, not an individual, and the fact that I wasn't on the field at the end is immaterial. Once Dublin won, that was all that mattered.'

CIARÁN CORR: 'I've never held a grudge against Paddy. I've seen him refereeing the odd game since here and there, and I've recognised his face in the newspapers and on TV, but we've never met since. I retired two years after that All-Ireland final. I was twenty-seven with three prolapsed discs in my back. When somebody tells you that if you keep playing, you'll end up in a wheelchair, you tend to listen. At the time, I was already losing the power in my left leg.'

During the week after the final, former Kerry goalkeeper Charlie Nelligan rang wishing to distance himself from the remarks of a former teammate, Pat Spillane. Pat McEnaney was in touch, too; he's always great to call when I feel I need the opinion of another referee.

PAT MCENANEY: 'I attended the 1995 final. I didn't pass many remarks at the match. I felt that Redmond was on the pitch for a couple of minutes, but it was corrected, and I didn't read too much into it. But this was Dublin and when Dublin are involved, there is a massive media presence, and that was true back then, too. Paddy took it all very personally. That's a fault I would see in Paddy. Sometimes you have to let it go over your head. It hurt him for a long, long time. I often wonder what kept him going. I know there have been times when he felt like walking away from it all, but it just shows that, while he's a quiet man, he's got great inner strength.'

I would hope that I too could be a help to other referees when things go wrong for them. After all, we're all in this unique club together. Sometimes I don't think that we support each other enough, and this rings true in all walks of life. I remember, during his career, the great Tipperary hurler Nicky English was a god one day, castigated the next. Some people even wrote off the current Tipp hurler Eoin Kelly after one below-par year in 2007. A man who had won five All Star awards. People can be so fickle.

MARGARET RUSSELL: *'I think that support is even more important for a referee. Players at least have the support of their teammates. A simple phone call can make all the difference for a referee.'*

I felt huge nerves when I returned to refereeing, tentatively, at club level. I could hear the wisecracks on a still autumn evening. It's difficult not to in that environment. When you're in the midst of thousands of people, at least the catcalls are drowned out. But I was just happy to be back out there. I had been refereeing for so many years. This was all I knew. If I didn't have this, what would I do? If you had been doing something all of your adult life and you suddenly had to contemplate giving it up, how would you react?

I have noticed in old photographs and TV footage that I had black hair before the 1995 final. It began to turn grey shortly afterwards. The stress really got to me. I think it affected me so badly because I'm a perfectionist in a lot of ways. Sometimes I think I suffer from a mild form of OCD, because even if, for example, a chair in my sitting room is positioned in a certain way that doesn't seem right, I'll have to move it to a place that seems right to me.

In a way, because GAA rules precluded me from speaking publicly on the matter, I was the silent victim of that All-Ireland final and the fallout from it. The reason the GAA do not allow referees to talk about matches they've been in charge of is quite simple. When a suspension is hanging over a player, a referee has to keep his mouth shut, as anything he might say about a particular incident could prejudice the case against the player, who could use the referee's comments to escape on a technicality.

You will notice that in the English Premier League some referees appear on TV after games to explain controversial decisions they have made. There are pros and cons to dealing with the media, in my view. From my limited experience of talking to the press, it is apparent that they can put their own twist on the story. If you speak to a reporter, it's out of your hands, because newspapers decide the headlines and the slant for the story. If I had had the chance, I think, particularly when I look back on some of the coverage, maybe I would have spoken out in the aftermath of the 1995 final. I would not have discussed the match as such, but I could have contradicted some of the things Charlie Redmond said in his interview immediately afterwards.

Referees have to be able to trust a reporter, because they can see the headlines steaming down the tracks. And, having been burned in the past, I'm always reluctant to speak to journalists, even off the record. Jim O'Sullivan from the *Irish Examiner* and Seán Moran of the *Irish Times* would be two guys I would trust. I have good time for Jim, but I would always ask him not to quote me if he has asked me a few questions. But being splashed all over the front and back pages of the newspapers? I never asked for that during my career.

Out of the entire affair, there is one thing that I am thankful for. I never received one abusive phone call or threatening letter. I have heard former and current referees speaking about how, at times, they've felt really threatened or abused, but, although you might find it hard to believe, I can honestly say that that never once happened to me. Sure, you'll get the letters from the 'anoraks' picking you up on decisions at local matches, but that's good, constructive stuff, telling me that I didn't realise what was going on with the full-back, for example, or how an umpire might have let me down. Things were bad in 1995, and the media coverage did get me down, but I knew even then that others had experienced worse. Séamus Aldridge has told me that he received threats after allowing Mikey Sheehy's controversial and famous chipped goal over Paddy Cullen to stand when Kerry beat Dublin in the 1978 All-Ireland senior football final. And a Tipperary referee, Séamus Roche, has spoken on local radio about how he has felt in real danger on more than one occasion.

SÉAMUS ROCHE (2005 ALL-IRELAND HURLING FINAL REFEREE): '*After one intercounty game, an official from one of the competing counties approached me, to be seen shaking my hand, and proceeded to say to my face, "You fucking rode us." But you wouldn't hurt my feelings too easily. If that had happened to me a few years earlier, it might have affected me differently, I don't know. Paddy had been around a long time when he had the mishaps. But I wonder if some of the younger fellas coming through would be able to handle it. Paddy is a very strong character and has proven it. He doesn't get involved in altercations with players; he just calls it as he sees it.*

'*In May 2004, I made headline news after a match between Holycross-Ballycahill and Boherlahan at Semple Stadium in Thurles. I think the incident was blown up to be bigger than it actually was. Somebody grabbed my shoulder to spin me around and, with evening dew on the surface, I slipped. On the ground, I saw feet and felt that I should get up quickly in case someone put the boot in. A crowd had come down out of the stand by then, and there were heated words. I was not struck by anybody, but I got a massive fright, particularly when I looked up and saw all of these people shouting down abuse at me. I had to get up and back away to the other side of the field.*

'*I also recall an incident after an Under-16 match when I was grabbed by the throat by a woman. She was an aunt of one of the players, and she had an English accent. They had lost, and, of course, she blamed me. That was a funny experience. I couldn't do anything because it was a woman. She had a lovely, polished accent and told me that she was going back to London the next day but not before warning me, "I'll be going to Croke Park about you!"*

'*Things like that didn't bother me, but I did get a horrible letter once, and that wasn't pleasant. The writer expressed a hope that my family and I would never experience another day of good luck. I was also advised to hang up my boots.*'

The Kildare referee Mick Monahan, now retired from the

intercounty scene, received a death threat after a game between Ulster rivals Donegal and Armagh.

MICK MONAHAN: *'It was the 2003 All-Ireland semi-final. Tyrone had famously swarmed all over Kerry the previous week. The game went well up until the point when Armagh's John McEntee swung an elbow at one of the Donegal players. I was two yards away, but I didn't see it. It blew up on the TV that night, and the Garda made me aware of a death threat. It turned out to be a hoax, but it had to be taken seriously, and I was given an armed escort from Croke Park. The worst part was that I didn't tell my family about it that night – I didn't want them worrying about it – but* The Star *got wind of it.*

'The threatening call originated in Dublin and was made to Leixlip GAA club in Kildare, who then contacted the Garda. It was some guy who was after having a few drinks. The Garda rang me back six months later and told me that it had been a wind-up. There was such a hullabaloo over the McEntee incident, and some of the comments made on TV that night were way over the top. One of my lads was very young at the time, and he walked out of the room when we were watching the coverage. That's the way it can affect families. I wasn't getting paid to referee, and I started to question why I was doing it then. My hobby was impacting on other people's lives. I wasn't scared at the time, though. If anything, I felt more hurt by the personal comments on TV than by the death threat.'

It's rare that people will go out of their way to comment on positive feedback a referee has received. I've never had a case where somebody said, 'Hey, Paddy, the papers said you did a fine job on last Sunday's game. Well done.' But if a game goes badly, there are plenty of people out there who will let me know all about it. People are reluctant to praise each other these days. It's a poor reflection on modern-day society.

I rarely looked back on 1995 until I sat down to write this book. I wish it had never happened, but it did, and even though it was extremely difficult, I had to move on. I wouldn't wish what I went through on my worst enemy. My second All-Ireland senior football final should have been the pinnacle of my career, but the way it panned out, I wished I had never been appointed to do that game.

I first spoke publicly about the 1995 final to Jim O'Sullivan for his book on GAA referees, *Men in Black*, which was published in 2002. A few months after the book came out, a poignant letter dropped through my door, and I am most grateful to the writer for allowing it to be reproduced here:

28 March 2003

Dear Paddy,

I have just finished reading Jim O'Sullivan's publication *Men in Black*. I was particularly interested in reading your account of the 1995 All-Ireland football final.

Paddy, you had an excellent match and I am not saying that just because I am a Dublin man. You made two excellent and courageous decisions on the day.

Firstly, Charlie Redmond deserved to be sent off in the second half. He should have left the field of play immediately. When you realised that he hadn't gone off, you immediately reordered him off . . .

Your second decision was also correct and very courageous given the circumstances and closeness of the game. Referees are sometimes accused of playing for a draw if the occasion arises. Peter Canavan had a terrific game and would have easily won man of the match had Tyrone won. However, he made one costly error. When the ball dropped to him late in the game he fumbled the ball and it hit the ground. He put his hand on the ball, which was on the ground. A foul. You saw and called it. I also had a good view of it because I was at pitch level in the Dublin dugout. The rest, as they say, is history . . .

Paddy, we should have met on that fateful Sunday in September 1995 but injury prevented me from taking part. That is something I have to live with. I have long admired you as a referee and I am just starting out on this new chapter of my sporting life. I would welcome any advice from a maestro.

Again, many thanks for making that correct and courageous call in 1995. I have an All-Ireland winner's medal down to your integrity and sheer professionalism as a result.

Yours in sport,
Dermot Deasy

In February 2008, I rang the mobile phone number at the bottom of the letter to ask Dermot's permission for his letter to be included here. I thoroughly enjoyed our phone conversation. Dermot spoke to me about his own refereeing career and how it is progressing. I wished him the best of luck and expressed my wish that some day soon, I would see him officiating in a big match at Croke Park. What a story that would be.

14

THE REAWAKENING

We must learn to reawaken and keep ourselves awake,
not by mechanical aids, but by an infinite
expectation of the dawn.

Henry David Thoreau

Time, and no little support, did the trick, and the 1995 All-Ireland senior football final slowly began to work its way out of my system. The GAA, privately and publicly, were pretty supportive during the entire affair, but what meant the most to me was the opening round of the 1995–96 National Football League. The country's leading referees were notified of their fixtures, and I felt sure I would pack it all in if I had been consigned to the depths of Division 4. I began to envisage worst case scenarios. The GAA had the perfect opportunity here, if the Association's bigwigs so wished, to end my refereeing career.

I need not have worried. Just weeks after the final, I was handed a glamour opening-round league fixture: Kerry v. Kildare in Tralee. It was concrete proof that I was still very much in the game.

When my name was announced over the PA system, polite applause broke out amongst the spectators. More healing. I heard that lovely sound but could barely believe it. Surely this could not be true. One of my umpires that day, Nicholas Lonergan, assured me that it wasn't a dream. Those spectators were applauding me.

The season went well – so well, in fact, that, remarkably, I found myself in the shake-up for the 1996 All-Ireland final between Mayo and Meath. I believe that it came down to a straight vote, for Pat McEnaney or myself, and, after a split decision, Dan McCartan from Down held the casting vote. Dan, chairman of the Games Administration Committee then, voted for his fellow Ulsterman Pat.

P.J. MCGRATH: *'It's a fairer system now, I think. The CRAC, the Central Referees Appointments Committee, selects the referees for all games and for the All-Ireland finals. It's a three-man committee, made up of Jimmy Dunne, chairman of the GAA's Central Competitions Control Committee; myself, as chairman of the National Referees Association; and a third man, Tyrone county board secretary Dominic McCaughey, who is the presidential nominee. I think that a referee coming up now has a far better chance of getting to a final, because his faults are pointed out, and he can work on them. Referees are a better, more competent bunch because there is a huge educational aspect involved these days.'*

I recall that Mayo were quite unhappy with Pat's appointment. The Connacht champions would have preferred me to take charge of the game.

PAT MCENANEY: *'I was working as an area rep, and Meath was one of my patches. And then there was a rumour that I was a member of Trim Golf Club. That was checked out by people from the media. I never even played golf in my life. Those are the things you have to live with. There was an awful lot of media attention around that game. I met both camps, too, beforehand. The GAA's selection committee wasn't very happy with that move. It was a break in protocol. I met the managers and players of both teams. It's easier now. People know my style and my refereeing.'*

I was thrilled for Pat. Sure, it would have been nice to get a third final, and it would have capped a remarkable turnaround from 12 months before, but I was happy enough just being considered again. My consolation prize was the role of standby referee, doubling up as linesman, with Clare's Kevin Walsh on the other touchline.

It was very much bonus territory, as the first game between Meath and Mayo finished in a draw. Mayo were on course for a long-overdue title, but a late Meath point broke their hearts and ensured that we would be back for part two. Meath were like that back then. They could always dig themselves out of a hole. They were no slouches in the physical stakes either, but there was nothing in the drawn match to suggest that trouble would erupt in the replay.

But erupt it did, in the form of a mass brawl that left Pat with some difficult decisions to make. Numerous players could have walked, but Meath's Colm Coyle and Liam McHale from Mayo were the players sent off. Normally, a referee will look for the first two guys involved in a melee, or for a player who has come a long way to get involved when he had no business being there.

PAT MCENANEY: *'Myself and my umpires did a lot of talking that day, down at the Hill 16 end. We picked out two. Paddy and Kevin didn't disagree. We could have picked ten out of there. You'd go from taking a 14-inch neck of a shirt to a 16 after stuff like that. It makes you a much stronger person. Paddy's experiences have done likewise for him. When something like that happens, you don't think about what other refs have gone through. You think about yourself.'*

I envy Pat sometimes because he comes across as so confident in himself, but he is no different from the rest of us, and that experience left him shaken. If a game goes badly for me, I'm down in the dumps, and visibly so. I struggle pulling on the jolly mask. I'm sure it's low self-esteem, and that's why the assessments mean so much to me. I can't rest until an assessor verifies that I've had a good game, even if plenty of people have told me that I did.

PAT MCENANEY: *'My dad died in November 1996, so the final was soon relegated from my mind. It took me four years to get another final; I think I was thought of as the bad cop for three years afterwards. But it wasn't the worst match I ever refereed. That was in 1998. It was the Munster championship, Kerry and Cork. I went to Cork on the Saturday, a beautiful day, and on the Sunday I had the attitude that I would stand back and let the two teams play football. It lashed rain two hours before the throw-in, but my attitude didn't change. And the teams did everything bar play football.'*

Pat was shaken after that Munster championship match, very shaken. That got to him more than 1996, I think. My old mentor John Moloney often said to me that Cork v. Kerry is a different ball game entirely. I refereed those two teams so many times and knew what to expect after a while. You just can't let anything go. Perhaps the players knew that was my attitude, because they were inclined to behave when I was in charge. They probably felt they could push the boundaries a bit more with a referee from another province. It must be the same when I referee two Ulster teams. Coming in from outside can work for or against you. The likes of Pat or Brian Crowe would know the players better up in Ulster. The rule whereby a referee could not take charge of a championship match outside his own province was still in place less than 15 years ago but has since been changed.

P.J. MCGRATH: *'Now we make sure that we go the opposite way and appoint outside of the province. Paddy has done all four provincial finals, but in my career I only took charge of one Connacht final, because my native Mayo were involved almost every year. That provincial system limited my opportunities, but that's life.'*

PAT MCENANEY: *'That 1996 All-Ireland final was my first time experiencing real controversy. It's a strange thing to suddenly find yourself at the centre of a media whirlwind. I thought of it this year when Ray Boyne, part of the backroom team with Dublin, was in a similar position. He just lost the plot for a split second after the league game with Monaghan this year and head-butted a player. Ray's a very respectable man, a bank manager with three young kids. All at once, there he was on the front pages of the newspapers, and he didn't sleep for four days. Nobody thinks how it affects people. Having said that, if I'm on the front page of the* Independent *in the morning, I don't give a damn. You just have to go through it. If somebody has a cut about my refereeing, it doesn't bother me. You become immune to it. You adjust. It's a bit like suffering a toothache that won't go away – you just take Anadin and get on with it. After Mick Monahan got the death threat a few years ago, I picked the phone up because I knew what he was going through. Mick was going to quit. I'm not saying I was the cause of him staying on, but I played a part in him coming back, and he went on to referee an All-Ireland final.*

'From day one, Paddy had the height of respect for me, and the feeling was mutual. I watched the 1982 All-Ireland final on TV this year and noticed that he was the linesman. I couldn't believe it was him. We'd chat on the phone maybe five times a year. But I'd ring him. Paddy might ring me looking for directions, but otherwise he's a private sort of fella. He's an absolute gentleman and a man who you could go to war with and know that he would never let you down. When he was a linesman and I was the ref, he was always looking out for me. Some referees might feel they were above running the line, but when he was linesman for me and me for him, we were working with each other. I knew that I could trust him. We know each other much better now. Three or four times early in my career, Paddy was an amazing help. He was an established referee, but he did whatever he could do to help. It was never the case that I was this young buck coming through onto his patch. He never felt envious or threatened.'

Pat always said that he wanted to go back to Croke Park and referee another All-Ireland final after 1996 to prove himself. He didn't want to be noted for that one. He's done two more, in 2000 and 2004, and those went well. Sadly, the same chance never came my way after 1995. I would have loved to have had that opportunity.

15

....

RED HAND RULE

The wheel is come full circle.

King Lear, William Shakespeare

The 2003 All-Ireland senior football final. Tyrone on the cusp of history. Manager Mickey Harte finalising a tactical masterstroke. Here we are again, Peter Canavan and I. Peter is preparing to come back on the field with ten minutes of a gripping final against Armagh remaining. Harte had brought him off earlier to conserve his energy, but now the captain is ready to come back on and lead the team home.

Peter's straining at the leash to get back on, but I can't let him. The Tyrone county board secretary has not yet completed the necessary paperwork. As a linesman, I need confirmation from the fourth official on the sideline that Peter is free to run back onto the field of play. He's anxious to get on, Tyrone's supporters aren't best pleased, but there's nothing I can do.

PETER CANAVAN: *'I asked Paddy to let me on the pitch, but I gathered he was waiting on the fourth official. There was a panic to get me on, and I was dying to get in there. I didn't say it but it was in the back of my mind: Jesus, you denied us an All-Ireland final in 1995, and you're not going to do it again. Thankfully, I didn't say that. What happened on the touchline may have been highlighted later, with people insinuating that Paddy was anti-Tyrone and whatnot, but he was genuinely waiting on the nod from the fourth official before he could let me go on. When you're captain of a team trying to win a first All-Ireland, you kind of disregard those technicalities, but it was no big deal later as far as we were concerned.'*

I had never seen a player as hyped up for a match as Armagh's captain Kieran McGeeney was that day. I couldn't really blame him, either, as here you had two neighbouring Ulster counties pitted against one another in an All-Ireland final for the very first time. As McGeeney arrived at the centre circle to meet referee Brian White and Canavan, I could see how psyched he was. There were no words spoken. McGeeney won the toss, shook hands with Canavan and moved away.

McGeeney played well that day but I felt he was too uptight and I saw a different side to him. On other occasions, he'd seemed genial and more relaxed. But then again, Kieran's a very serious individual, and this was a very serious game.

I'm sure the fanaticism in Ulster about the GAA stems from what they have gone through during the Troubles. I've heard stories from guys up there about being pulled over at British Army checkpoints and asked where they were going; if they replied that they were on their way to a GAA match, they would be made to stew on the side of the road until the game was over.

Tyrone defeated their great rivals from Armagh in the 2003 final by 0–12 to 0–9, and Peter Canavan had his All-Ireland medal. Two years later, the Red Hands were on the march again, and fate decreed that they would do battle again with Armagh, this time at the All-Ireland semi-final stage. The scene was set for the mother and father of all battles between Armagh, champions of 2002, and 2003 winners Tyrone.

Tensions had been running high since a controversial Ulster final replay between the two counties earlier in the summer. Tyrone's Stephen O'Neill, Canavan and Armagh's Kieran McKeever were dismissed by referee Michael Collins. The ref later admitted that he had sent off O'Neill in error, while Canavan was cleared on appeal.

Both counties were very concerned about who was going to referee the All-Ireland semi-final. The stakes were unbelievably high; it was winner-takes-all stuff. There was a clamour for Pat McEnaney, who had refereed the drawn Ulster final, but the GAA ignored behind-the-scenes overtures from Tyrone and Armagh.

Croke Park plumped for yours truly, and I felt deeply honoured. The GAA placed its faith in me to take charge of a game that some thought might spiral out of control. It was a huge vote of confidence in me, an acknowledgement that I was on top of my game again. Players crave big occasions like this, but referees relish them too.

It can be hard to while away the hours and minutes before a game of massive importance. If there's a minor match on beforehand, I'll watch some of that, but waiting for the big one is a fierce long drag. It's difficult to enjoy the occasion. However, I don't think I was ever as relaxed before a game as I was before Armagh v. Tyrone. I remember looking skywards and feeling incredibly calm, ready to stamp my authority on this titanic encounter.

PAT MCENANEY: *'Paddy always made great recoveries from being kicked in the teeth. It's very true that both Tyrone and Armagh wanted me, but I think the committee made the right choice with Paddy. He was refereeing very well and went on to produce a very, very good performance. I would be classed as a bigger risk-taker than Paddy Russell. But I admire his style absolutely. If you want a safe pair of hands in a match, he's the man.'*

PETER CANAVAN: *'It was one of the best games we ever played: hard-hitting, close and physical, with great scores. And it was ironic that there was a twist of fate at the end.'*

MICHEÁL O'DWYER (MATCH UMPIRE): *'The atmosphere at that game is something that I will never experience again. The colour around the ground was unbelievable – the red and white mixed with the orange and white. The match was the equivalent of an All-Ireland final, and the way Tyrone won it was as good as winning that year's final.'*

STEVIE O'DONNELL (MATCH UMPIRE): *'It was a great occasion. We* travelled up by train that day, the first time we'd used that mode of transport for an All-Ireland semi-final. Normally we would drive up and park at Croke Park. We met Maebh Lowry on the way up, an Armagh woman living in Tipperary town, and the craic was good. But we were wary of a dogfight, a typical Armagh v. Tyrone game – a stop–start affair with nothing but pulling and dragging. It ended up being one of the best championship games that I was ever involved in.'

Late in the day, and with the scores locked together at 1–12 apiece, I awarded Tyrone a free-in, halfway between the Hill 16 goal and the Hogan Stand. It was on the 20-metre line, and the angle was pretty acute for the free-taker. It seemed as though Eoin Mulligan would step up to the crucial kick, but after a discussion between Mulligan and his former schoolteacher Canavan, the master took the ball in his hands.

MICHEÁL O'DWYER: 'When Peter Canavan was taking that free, Tyrone's goalkeeper, Pascal McConnell, was in front of me. He was crouched on his knees, head in his hands, unable to look. Time stood still. I was watching the clock on the big screen. I knew there wasn't much time left. I glanced at my own watch. "Kick-out at the other end and we're out of here," I thought. When the ball went over the bar, Pascal put Michael Flatley to shame jumping around the field! And Stevie O'Donnell ran away with the ball!'

STEVIE O'DONNELL: 'I remember the free that Canavan stuck over the bar. I was at the Hill 16 end, and I'll always remember Eoin Mulligan picking up the ball with one hand and showing it to Canavan. The pupil said to the teacher, "You take it." In my mind's eye, I'm looking at Peter. He turned to the side, and I could see his sharp look for the black spot. Paul Hearty was in goal for Armagh and he was roaring, "We're clearing this! It's going wide! It's going wide!" They tried everything to put Peter off, but he was so perfect with his kick. It cleared the crossbar right in the centre, and I caught the ball when it dropped behind the goal. I have that ball at home with me – a souvenir from a classic match.'

PETER CANAVAN: 'It was never set in stone that I was hitting that free. There was a real doubt. Eoin was hitting them closer to goal.

This is the way it happened: I had been involved in a passage of play, and when I was catching my breath, Seán Cavanagh came over to me and said, "You're hitting that." Brian McGuigan was the same. I had no intention of taking it, because I had full confidence that if Mugsy had hit it, he would have scored as well. He was playing on top of his game. But, bearing in mind what the two boys had said, they put me on the spot, and I wasn't left with much choice. Out of politeness, I asked Eoin if he wanted to take it. If he'd said yes, I would have stepped aside and let him have it but he said, "I don't mind." That made up my mind. I had to hit this.'

I spoke with Peter before he stepped up to take that kick, and people often wonder what was said between us. I told him to go back to a certain point, because some free-takers are clever at stealing a few yards, particularly when they're kicking from the hand. I always inform a free-taker of where his mark is – 'You'll be taking the free from there, and don't come back further than that' – because I would hate to penalise him for straying beyond it. In such a case, the referee is obliged to throw the ball in between two players, one from each team.

PETER CANAVAN: *'The free didn't go our way against Dublin in 1995, but now we had that chance. I recall asking Paddy how long was left. I knew that it was probably one of the most important kicks of my life. He just said there wasn't long left – there was no definitive answer. Then he told me to go back to a certain point. If I'd kicked it and it had gone wide, I know what people would have said and written. They would have been right, too. But it went over, and I got the credit.'*

There was never any doubt. Peter's kick secured a precious 1–13 to 1–12 victory for Tyrone, and the maestro went on to score a crucial goal in the final against Kerry as a second All-Ireland crown in three seasons was secured.

The Monday morning newspapers after the semi-final focused on the history between Peter, Tyrone and me. The shadow of 1995 will never fully disappear, I suppose. That All-Ireland semi-final in 2005 was extremely dramatic, Tyrone winning by a point ten years after losing the 1995 final by the same margin. A late point disallowed in '95, a late free awarded in their favour a decade later. There was an ironic symmetry to the whole thing.

And those were the two prime opportunities in my career to 'make a draw out of the game', that phrase so many GAA people seem to be fond of. If anything, the situation in 2005 was even more amenable to creating a draw. Teams level late on, classic game, bumper replay on the cards: make a draw out of it. But that's never once entered my head, and never has during a match. My refereeing philosophy is quite straightforward. I read the rule book and try to implement those rules as best I can. I'm a stickler for that. In fact, I'll always read the major rules of the game as a refresher before I take the field of play.

PETER CANAVAN: *'The history with Paddy and Tyrone would have been a bigger thing with the supporters and the press than with us. I know that when Tyrone teams played and Paddy was refereeing, it was never brought up by the players and the management. It was never considered an issue.*

'Being awarded that free in 2005 didn't make losing the 1995 final any easier, but I was very much aware that I was part of something special. It was the third time we had played Armagh that year en route to winning the All-Ireland. I hadn't lasted too long in the replayed Ulster final, and I was so aware of the importance and the sense of occasion surrounding that kick in the All-Ireland semi-final. It was certainly ironic that Paddy Russell was the man blowing the final whistle that day.'

I must thank Brian McGuigan here for protecting me after the game. An irate Armagh supporter had entered the field of play from the Cusack Stand, but Tyrone's centre-forward held the man back as he raced towards me.

I noticed that the Armagh players were absolutely devastated as they trooped off the pitch. If another team had beaten them, perhaps they might not have taken it as badly. For them, losing to Tyrone was different.

That day, Armagh manager Joe Kernan decided to withdraw the inspirational McGeeney towards the end of the game. I have to admit that I was surprised. Even though he had not performed particularly well on the day, McGeeney was renowned as Armagh's driving force and spiritual leader. It was a big talking point after the game, but, of course, it's easy to be wise after the event. If McGeeney had stayed on and Armagh had still lost, Kernan might have been criticised for not taking him off.

It was a simply incredible afternoon, and it proved once again that sport can be the greatest scriptwriter of them all.

16

OMAGH

Disappointment to a noble soul is what cold water
is to burning metal; it strengthens, tempers, intensifies,
but never destroys it.

Eliza Tabor

'The most disappointing and upsetting day of my years
refereeing': a telling line from the attachment to my match
report on the National Football League tie between Tyrone and
Dublin played at Healy Park in Omagh on Sunday, 5 February
2006.

The match became known as 'The Battle of Omagh', and the
fallout left me on the brink of retirement from refereeing for
the second time in my career. I had been close to quitting after
the 1995 All-Ireland senior football final between the same two
counties, and what happened in Omagh dredged up some old
familiar feelings I had hoped were buried forever.

Call it coincidence or a cruel twist of fate, but, just like in
1995, I decided to sleep in an unfamiliar bed the night before
Healy Park. I had always vowed after 1995 that I would never
again be away from home on the night before a big game, not
unless it was absolutely necessary. However, this was a match
200 miles from home at a time of year when the road and the
driving conditions would be unpredictable. I had never refereed

at Healy Park before, so it made sense to travel up on the Saturday night.

I had spoken during the week to Pat McEnaney, whose brother Séamus owns the Westenra Arms Hotel in Monaghan town. We arrived around six o'clock.

PAT MCENANEY: *'It was such a long journey for Paddy. I organised for him to stay in the Westenra and gave him directions for the way up. The only thing I forgot to organise for Paddy that weekend was the police escort out of Omagh! I'd often be slagging Paddy: "Every time I see you on the television, there's a crowd around you!" It always gets a laugh. We would be bouncing off each other.'*

STEVIE O'DONNELL (MATCH UMPIRE): *'I'll never forget the night before the game. Paddy, Liam O'Dwyer and Seán Bradshaw decided that they would sleep in one room, but Seán is 6 ft 5 in. tall, and, naturally enough, he has two very long legs! Seán's legs were hanging out over the end of the bed, so the only way that he could get a good night's sleep was to face the bed for the window and rest his legs on the sill!'*

I remember going out onto the field in Omagh that afternoon as usual, ten minutes before throw-in. Dublin were warming up at one end, but they didn't return to their dressing-room until five minutes before the match was due to commence. As this was the first league game of the year for reigning All-Ireland champions Tyrone, it was expected that the Dublin players would form a guard of honour as the Tyrone team ran out onto the field, but this did not happen.

STEVIE O'DONNELL: *'When we arrived at the ground, some fans were saying that a right battle was in store. It dated back to the 2005 All-Ireland quarter-final between the two teams, which Tyrone won after a replay. There was serious needle, and it quickly became apparent that there was more than just football at stake here. Healy Park is a large complex, with the dressing-rooms off the main hallway. Tyrone emerged for their warm-up, and I could already detect tension. The Dublin players were agitated coming off the team bus – pumped up, really psyched. I was standing beside the Dublin dressing-room door before they came out, and they were roaring and shouting at each other.*

I mentioned it to Paddy: "They're niggling already. Dublin won't give Tyrone a guard of honour."'

It wasn't just the players who were on edge. The crowd also seemed geared up, and there was a worryingly bad atmosphere. The stewards were local and there was no police presence. That was frightening, and I didn't know what to expect. At matches down south, you have a Garda presence to help keep the peace, but it's different in Ulster. I remember refereeing Antrim v. Derry at Casement Park in the 2000 Ulster championship, and after the game it was literally every man for himself as we all left the ground and headed for the M1 motorway. If I had found myself involved in a flashpoint incident, there would not have been much in the way of protection.

STEPHEN MCGEEHAN (ULSTER COUNCIL): *'In the six counties in the North, we currently do not have legislation that requires us to have a PSNI presence at our fixtures. Legislation relating to the Northern and Southern jurisdictions is mostly similar but with some delicate differences. For Ulster championship matches, under the safe sports grounds legislation in the South, there is an expectation that we place a proper number of gardaí in the ground relative to the attendance. We would normally work on a ratio of one uniformed garda per thousand people. We would also use Frontline or another security agency to look after the more difficult elements of crowd control, as well as general stewards. So on the day of an Ulster final, when there might be 33,000 people in Clones, you would see 30 gardaí in place, along with 200 to 300 stewards and roughly 70 security guards. In the ever-improving climate of policing in the North, it would be expected that there will be continued and improving relations with the PSNI. That is already the case.*

'In a run-of-the-mill league match, the host county, under the control of the county board, must have an event plan. The Ulster championship is the responsibility of the Ulster council, whereas the National League is the responsibility of the host county. At Healy Park, health-and-safety requirements rested with the event promoter, so it was the duty of the Tyrone county board to put in place arrangements for safe event management.'

MICHAEL MCCARNEY (TYRONE COUNTY BOARD SAFETY OFFICER): *'We had 40 stewards that day at Healy Park. I was the event controller. We don't ever have police or security at the ground, just voluntary Tyrone stewards. You only see Frontline security at the Ulster council matches. A lot of the Dublin supporters came and stood on the Country End terraces. A Budweiser bottle was thrown at Pascal McConnell. I had to go down and stand at that end of the pitch for the entire second half because it was dangerous. There was the odd skirmish between Dublin and Tyrone supporters. I watched a lot of boys coming in before the game, and I was trying to stop them bringing in drink. It was a difficult job. At half-time, a Tyrone man from Coalisland collapsed in the toilets due to sheer excitement. There hasn't been a game like it at Healy Park since, that's for sure. But what happened that day was brought on by the actions of the players on the pitch; it had nothing to do with the crowd.'*

On the pitch, the ill will erupted into a skirmish as early as the fifth minute, when a free-for-all broke out close to the Tyrone goal. Dublin's Alan Brogan and Tyrone's Brian Meenan were yellow-carded. Some pundits commented afterwards that I should have laid down a marker by issuing a red card, but there was no sending-off offence there. Deep down, no referee ever wants to send a player off, and my umpire Seán Bradshaw was insistent that yellow cards were sufficient. Seán was upset later when it was suggested that red cards should have been given out, but I trust his judgement. He was closer than anybody to the incident, umpiring right beside it.

MARGARET RUSSELL: *'I wasn't in Omagh, but, of course, I later became aware of the enormity of the episode. Once you see a melee in the GAA, especially if it's televised, it's headline news. The game was on TV, and I'd always watch a match that Paddy was involved in when he was far away from home. I'd also let him know if there were any comments from the studio experts. At half-time, I felt that Paddy was doing fine. He got the ones he had to get, but after the match he was a bit concerned about whether or not he should have sent off somebody at the start.'*

As an altar boy. This photograph was taken at the grotto in Emly. The priest is Father Robert Mullally, who was a hugely popular figure in the parish. I'm the boy on the far right of the picture.

Here's my best superhero impersonation. One minute I'm a GAA referee . . .

. . . the next I'm proudly wearing the colours of my home club, Emly!

The Emly team pictured before the 1975 county minor football final against Clonmel Commercials. Losing that game is right up there among the biggest disappointments of my career. I'm kneeling at the far left of the front row.

Emly: intermediate county football champions, 1983. I'm pictured here fourth from the left in the front row.
(© Jerry Ring)

Emly: West senior football champions, 1987. I am second from left in the front row, with my brother Jimmy on the far right in the front row.
(© Jerry Ring)

Where it all began. Seven of the referees who completed a course taught by John Moloney and organised by the West Tipperary Bord na nÓg in 1976. Back row (left to right): Paddy Lonergan, Roger Kennedy and John Lonergan; front row: Nicholas Lonergan, Paddy Russell, Brother Michael O'Grady, Mickey Collins and Tom Meehan. The Bord presented each referee with a complete outfit at the end of the course.
(courtesy of *The Nationalist*)

Lining out with my first loyal team of umpires: (left to right) Mickey Collins, Lar O'Keeffe, me, Ailbe Burke (RIP) and Davy Crowe.

And with the men who have served alongside me in recent years: (left to right) Micheál O'Dwyer, Liam O'Dwyer, me, Stevie O'Donnell and John O'Brien.

One of my most treasured photographs captures the finest referees in West Tipperary together. Back row (left to right): Pat Moroney, Sammy Ryan (RIP), Nicholas Lonergan, Willie Morrissey, Paddy Lonergan and Tom Meehan; front row: Paddy Russell, Liam O'Dwyer, George Ryan, John Moloney (RIP) and Jerry Ring.

Receiving an 'up-and-coming' referee award in 1987. I'm on the left in the back row, beside Father Séamus Gardiner and Willie Barrett. Seated is GAA President Mick Loftus, flanked by my wife, Margaret (right), and Willie's wife, Joan.
(© Jim Connolly Photography)

Receiving the 1988 National Referee of the Year award from GAA president John Dowling (left) with Fr Séamus Gardiner on the right.
(© Jim Connolly Photography)

The 1990 All-Ireland final. I'm ready for my first All-Ireland senior football final as Cork captain Larry Tompkins (left) and Meath's Colm O'Rourke shake hands before the game. (© Sportsfile)

The 1995 All-Ireland senior football final. With me standing in the middle, Dublin captain John O'Leary (left) and Tyrone captain Ciarán Corr shake hands before the big game. Also in the picture are linesmen Willie O'Mahony (Limerick) and Francis Finan (Sligo). (© Sportsfile)

'You're off, Charlie.' Dublin's Charlie Redmond is sent off for the second time during the 1995 All-Ireland senior football final between Dublin and Tyrone. (© Sportsfile)

I am escorted from the pitch following the infamous 'Battle of Omagh', the National Football League encounter between Dublin and Tyrone played at Healy Park in February 2006. (© Inpho)

During the first half of the stormy National Football League match between Dublin and Meath at Parnell Park on Sunday, 20 April 2008, I send off four players: (left to right) Shane McAnarney, Paddy Andrews, Niall McKeigue and Bernard Brogan. (© Sportsfile)

Kerry captain Paul Galvin knocks my notebook to the ground before being sent off during the Munster senior football championship tie against Kerry at Fitzgerald Stadium, Killarney, on Sunday, 15 June 2008.
(© Sportsfile)

The team that keeps this referee in check: (left to right) Mark, Margaret, Paddy and Shane Russell.

By the time the game had finished, I had issued four red cards and twelve yellows, including double awards to Alan Brogan, Stephen O'Neill and Denis Bastic. In the second half, two more serious melees erupted, one of which spilled over onto the sideline. Dublin pair Brogan and Bastic, along with Tyrone forward O'Neill, were sent to the line, while my linesman Derek Fahy reported Tyrone's Colin Holmes for striking with the fist. After that, Dublin manager Paul Caffrey took his subs down from the stand for safety reasons.

STEVIE O'DONNELL: *'There were so many incidents during the game, a lot of them off the ball. I could have called Paddy for five or six, but, for that to happen, you have to wait for a break in play at your end of the field. The fans had paid £12 sterling that day, I think. It's a lot of money, and you don't want the game held up every two minutes. We were right not to pick up on every single off-the-ball incident. If we had done, we might as well have abandoned the match.'*

Dublin won the game but were booed off the park. I wasn't exactly spared either. It was a frightening experience. The lack of police presence made it scarier, but, at the same time, it was a blessing in some ways. The last people I want to see after I blow the final whistle are gardaí making their way across the pitch to escort me off. You might feel you have handled the game quite well, but the seeds of doubt are bound to be sown when the Garda arrive. They are there to protect you, but the impression that's created of you is not a flattering one. Those who have not attended the game, when they see TV footage or newspaper photographs of a Garda escort, will immediately assume that the referee has had a bad game.

MICHAEL MCCARNEY: *'I knew that the fences in the Omagh stand were at a low level, and anybody that really wanted to get over would have felt confident of making it. They didn't; the stewards held them back. It was a fiery day; I'll not forget it. Paddy and his umpires were collected off the field. There might have been a few boys spitting in the tunnel and firing a few verbals, but it would never have got to the stage where he'd have been attacked.'*

MICHEÁL O'DWYER: '*I missed Omagh because of a club function. But if I had gone that day, I wouldn't have umpired with Paddy any more. It would have shaken me to the core.*'

STEVIE O'DONNELL: '*As we were coming through the tunnel off the field, a lot of abuse was flying. We felt crowded. When you go through the tunnel at Healy Park, you have to go across a yard at the back of the stand to reach the dressing-rooms. We had to mingle with the crowd going out. There was a human chain on both sides of the yard to protect the teams and the officials. There was serious unease. The atmosphere in our dressing-room was the very same as if somebody had received terrible news.*

'*How did it all go wrong? Well, it didn't go wrong from the officials' point of view. Over and over again, I'll say it. The 30 players who went out on the field had no interest in playing football. They made life pure hell for us. Players have a responsibility to go out and behave themselves, but many won't. Some will do anything to get the better of their opponents. Driving home in the car, it was like there had been a death in the family. Paddy drove for a while, and then I took over for the rest of the way. On the radio, RTÉ's Micheál O'Muircheartaigh stated that he felt Paddy should have abandoned the match.*'

I thought about calling off the match, but that's the nuclear option, and I never truly considered it. There was no real security to speak of at the ground, and had I abandoned that game, all hell would have broken loose. Tyrone supporters sitting in the stand were irate already, to the point where the Dublin subs were moved out of there. I had to weigh up all these factors. Calling a halt could have caused a riot. It would have been far more dangerous to call off the game and leave 30 players behind me to their own devices as I trooped off home.

PETER CANAVAN (FORMER TYRONE CAPTAIN): '*I wasn't in Omagh, but obviously I saw the highlights on TV, and it was bad form. There was an undercurrent of real menace, something very similar to what happened at Parnell Park this year. I believe that former Dublin manager Tommy Carr hit the nail on the head when he said recently that Dublin are playing with a chip on their shoulder. They feel as if they have to prove themselves physically to others, that otherwise people will perceive them to be soft-centred. Tyrone beat them after a replay in 2005, and Dublin would have been criticised for folding when the going got tough. At Healy Park, they went out prepared to make a statement and to show that there was no lack of toughness on their part. It was a "one in, all in" approach. That happened with the 2008 Meath game as well. They felt that they had to prove something. It shouldn't be like that. It's not Dublin's natural game, because they have so many skilful, gifted footballers. Having played against them, you could not pick out one player that goes out to "do" an opponent or who is renowned as a dirty player. In my view, it's a mentality that they've developed. Whether they've arrived at that as a team or whether the management have an influence on it, only they can say.'*

Barely a word was spoken on the way home to Tipperary that evening. We stopped for food in Cavan and met the former Ulster council chairman and ex-referee Micheál Greenan. I couldn't eat. I was beginning to feel like I had done after the 1995 All-Ireland final. 'Time to get out,' I was thinking. And I really believed that I would.

17

....

HOLD THE BACK PAGE

Do not brood over your past mistakes and failures,
as this will only fill your mind with grief, regret and
depression. Do not repeat them in the future.

Swami Sivananda

Margaret was waiting for me when I arrived home, late. My first words were: 'That's it, no more.' I hate the media attention, and, from previous experience, I had a fair idea that Monday and the following days would be sticky.

I would prefer to be locked away in a dark room rather than face all of that stuff. It's a simple wish of mine before I take to the field: I want to referee the match and leave it at that. The only time I want to see my name in the newspapers is at the end of the match report: 'Referee: P Russell (Tipperary)'.

MARGARET RUSSELL: '*I had spoken to Paddy after the game, and I saw Mickey Harte's interview on TV. He'd been positive, and I told Paddy what he'd said. I really thought that might help. But Paddy was very down when he came home. He spoke about retirement again.*'

The fallout was very public, but I had support from the two managers, Dublin's Paul Caffrey and Tyrone's Mickey Harte. Reporters who went to them after the game wanted the pair to stick the boot in, to criticise me and say that I'd made a complete balls of it. Mickey didn't rise to the bait and neither did Paul, who was fulsome in his praise. Mickey said, 'If Paddy Russell had been God Almighty, he couldn't have refereed the game today.' Nice words, but, at the time, they were little consolation to me.

In championship games, players are more conscious of their behaviour and are afraid of getting sent off. But this was the opening round of the National League in Omagh and it seemed to me that some guys didn't mind if they were given their marching orders. It wasn't football they were interested in, it was settling scores and laying down markers for the year ahead.

I'm still sure that the previous season's All-Ireland quarter-final was the root cause of the trouble. Going in at half-time during the replay, there was a bust-up near the tunnel. Tyrone were perceived to have won that particular exchange, and perhaps Dublin felt that they had been pushed around once too often. What better place to flex the muscles than in Tyrone's back yard? Even before that, at Parnell Park in February 2004, I had sent off Tyrone's Stephen O'Neill and booked nine other players in a fiery game that Dublin won by a point. Dublin's Senan Connell was forced off very early after taking a frontal hit from a Tyrone player and Dublin were very fired up after that incident.

Despite these warning signs, I was disappointed that the game in Omagh had developed in the manner it did, and I was beginning to despair, wondering if this was the way it would be every time I stepped out to referee a match. It had been my first intercounty game of the new season, and I found myself slap bang in the middle of controversy again. And all of this just six short months after I had taken charge of the classic 2005 All-Ireland semi-final between Armagh and Tyrone at Croke Park. That had been a brilliant game for me to referee, and I had been on such a high afterwards. Those good memories quickly vanished at Healy Park.

On the Monday, I happened to be off work for the day and took the opportunity to submit my match report to Croke Park. Margaret phoned to see how I was doing, and she told me that

Mick Frawley, the former Tipperary football board chairman and an Emly clubmate of mine, had rung at 8.30 a.m. Mick had said not to worry and warned me not to speak to the media. Local people had been calling with messages of support. They said that they had been watching the game on TG4 and felt that I had done well. As far as they were concerned, there was nothing that I could have done to prevent the game getting out of hand.

Because there was not enough room on the report sheet for all of the information I wished to submit, I included an addendum clarifying that Alan Brogan had been sent off for a second yellow card and not a straight red, as many believed. As far as I knew, I had produced a yellow before I'd shown Brogan the red, but reporters and other eyewitnesses insisted otherwise. I had asked Derek Fahy and my umpires, who couldn't recall.

With heavy heart, I penned the first sentence:

> The following sheet is an addendum to my report on what I regret to say was the most disappointing and upsetting day of my years of refereeing.
>
> As far as I am aware the first incident that took place was approx. five minutes into the game, when I awarded a free to Dublin. For no apparent reason there was a melee on the 13-metre line which involved several players from both sides. I consulted with my umpire on that side and yellow-carded Alan Brogan (Dublin) and Brian Meenan (Tyrone). Play continued after that.
>
> The next occurrence took place approx. ten minutes into the second half and seemed to be the result of a Tyrone player being fouled by Alan Brogan (Dublin). I second-yellow-carded Alan Brogan, followed by a red card, and dismissed him. At this stage most of the players from both sides were involved in a mass brawl, which ended up out on the sideline. At this point I seriously considered calling off the match as tempers were at a very high level. I decided it might actually be better to try to continue and restore order rather than leaving both teams together on the field.

> The linesman reported Colin Holmes, Tyrone, for striking with the fist. Colin Holmes was red-carded and dismissed. Order was somehow restored and the game continued. Although a very tense atmosphere prevailed, the game ran to full time.

Three days after Omagh, I pulled out of a Sigerson Cup fixture, University College Cork against National University of Ireland Galway at the Mardyke in Cork. I was in no fit state to referee the game. I was sick. I was so paranoid, convinced that everybody was talking about me behind my back. That's where the real hurt is. It's especially difficult when you have to referee a juvenile game on the Monday night while, at the same time, you're the centre of attention in the newspapers, on the radio and on the TV sports bulletins. People ask questions. Some of them are genuine, but it's difficult to face them. Only time can heal the pain.

I was devastated. The match itself had been bad, but the media reaction knocked me for six. Admittedly, it didn't set a good example for young people watching on TV, but I've seen far worse at club level. Looking back, there was a lot of pushing and shoving, but I didn't see anybody getting a real slap of a fist. Pulling, dragging, players tumbling to the ground: it was childish stuff, but there was nothing really out of hand. Compared to that incredibly violent club match between Solohead and Galtee Rovers that I'd refereed back in 1983, the Battle of Omagh was not so shockingly bad. If the match had not been televised, it might never have become such a big issue, but the cameras added fuel to the fire. It was the same later with the Parnell Park match: even though a similar incident took place that very same day when Armagh met Cork, barely a word was spoken about it.

I got back up on the horse at Páirc Uí Rinn in Cork on the following Saturday night, running the line as the home side entertained old rivals Kerry in the National Football League. The reaction I got from the people I met, from both counties, was heartening. The Cork and Kerry folk were superb. 'You were right not to abandon that game,' Frank Murphy said to me. Frank is secretary of the Cork county board and one of the most respected officials in the GAA.

I was informed by the GAA's Central Disciplinary Committee (CDC) that they had a letter for me to sign. The previous year, players from Armagh and Tyrone, Ryan McMenamin, Paul McGrane and Kieran McKeever, had avoided suspensions because of a loophole relating to video evidence. The members of the CDC were anxious that the players charged following the Omagh debacle would serve their suspensions.

The letter read:

> I confirm that I did not see, nor did any of my match officials report to me, any incidents which would have involved me deciding to take or not to take disciplinary action involving the following players, other than what I reported in my official match report of the above game (Dublin v. Tyrone).
>
> Tyrone: Ryan McMenamin, Michael McGee, Eoin Mulligan, Kevin Hughes.
>
> Dublin: Bryan Cullen, Ciarán Whelan, Kevin Bonner, Alan Brogan, Peadar Andrews.

After poring over video evidence, the CDC had picked out these players, and I signed the letter stating that I had not dealt with these individuals. The way was now clear for the CDC to pursue them.

I was present a few weeks later when CDC chairman Con Hogan, a native of Tipperary, attended a seminar for intercounty referees in Athlone, as Omagh continued to tear me up inside. I was clearly rattled sitting among my peers, and Hogan's words reduced me to tears as he addressed the gathering. Reading aloud a statement issued on behalf of the CDC, he stated that I was not to blame for what had happened at Healy Park. I was deeply appreciative and outwardly moved, but despite this I still felt wounded by the whole episode.

CON HOGAN: '*At the time, Paddy came under fire from some in the media, but I felt that he had handled everything properly. There was no way that any one person could have handled the melee that occurred, and Paddy dealt with it as best he could. We did ask Paddy about the decisions he took, not to question his judgement but simply to ask him if he had considered any others. Our view was that no referee could have seen everything. We then went and dealt with the offenders. We suspended some people, but the suspensions didn't hold up. The Omagh case acted as a precursor to the rules that the Association used after the Parnell Park incident in 2008. They were strengthened considerably, to ensure proper use of video evidence. The committee in charge can now get back to the ref and ask him to look at video evidence again, to see whether or not he would change his opinion on certain matters.'*

P.J. MCGRATH: *'It was a hard game to handle. These things happen. It starts with handbags stuff but keeps going and going. Paddy was in a strange place, miles from home, hoping that it would stop, but it didn't. I remember talking to him after it. I have a habit of ringing refs when things haven't gone so well. He was down after Omagh, no doubt about it.'*

The hurt began to ease slowly, but the heat of the media spotlight was never too far away, and I was about to suffer another major burn, one that left a deep scar. On Thursday, 16 February, I was back-page news again. The *Irish Independent* carried a copy of the letter I had signed for Con, along with my original match report and the addendum that accompanied it. I could not believe my eyes. This was unprecedented, and I felt like I was being hung out to dry.

MARGARET RUSSELL: *'I can remember 1995 and all that went with it a lot more clearly, because it affected me a lot more than Omagh. But I was very hurt when Paddy's report was copied in the newspaper. The referee's report is supposed to be sacrosanct. But here, for everybody to see, was word for word what Paddy had written to the powers that be at Croke Park in the days after Omagh. Again, the phone started ringing non-stop, and it was pretty hectic. I thought to myself: "Here we go again."'*

As far as I can gather, somebody from the Dublin or Tyrone county board leaked the information to the media. The boards each receive a copy of the referee's report from every game, and I would be very surprised if the leak originated from Croke Park, especially with the cases against the charged players hanging on a knife-edge. I'm sure the thinking behind the leak was that if the information I had submitted to Croke Park was in the public domain, then it would be extremely difficult to suspend the players in question. They would be able to claim that they were being 'tried by the media'. Christ above, how could a case hold up when the *Irish Independent* had such pertinent material? It was a tactic designed to minimise the importance and power of my match report.

I felt exposed. The media will always get their hands on little titbits of information, but for this to appear was something else. I think that's what upset me most about the whole affair. You don't want something like that appearing in public. A match report should be a private affair between the referee, the top brass of the GAA and the players involved. The media should have nothing whatsoever to do with it. The case against the Dublin and Tyrone players later collapsed when the GAA's Central Appeals Committee overruled the CDC.

BOB HONAHAN: *'I was a member of the committee that suspended the Dublin and Tyrone players. We were very disappointed. It was an extremely time-consuming, tedious business, which suddenly unravelled, and we were left very disappointed and disillusioned. There were serious offences committed, and yet nobody served a suspension. No official reason was ever given as to why. I felt sorry for Paddy at the time, and I felt the same after Parnell Park. But the way he performed tells you a lot about the man. He has the courage of his convictions. I'm sure he learned a lot from Omagh, but certainly the Parnell Park episode was something that he could have done without. Once a referee goes through something of that nature once, he would like to think that's the end of it. May I add that I have always held Paddy in very high regard as a referee. He had a great rapport with players. He respected them, and they reciprocated. He's not a boastful, arrogant person. He doesn't worry about how he dresses or combs his hair.'*

Many people, myself included, were disappointed that the players got off. In the GAA, the rules are there, and they should be adhered to. If a player gets sent off for striking or kicking, he should face the music. I have never agreed with players taking their cases to the High Court or the Disputes Resolution Authority. Any young person who is willing to take up football or hurling should be made aware that he or she has to play according to the rules. When my playing career began, I knew the set of rules that I had to abide by, and I was always fully aware that if I stepped out of line, there were certain penalties there for me, and that I would have to accept them. There are some players in today's game who will not accept suspensions, and now it seems that everybody is challenging them because other individuals have escaped.

A referee's report doesn't seem to carry as much weight as it used to. It certainly carries little legal weight. There are solicitors and barristers who are au fait with the rules of the GAA. Fergal Logan, the former Tyrone footballer who was a central figure in the 1995 All-Ireland final, is a highly sought-after individual. He knows how to get players off, and county boards get him working hard behind the scenes.

There are times, too, when players escape more serious punishment because some referees water down their reports. Offenders are noted for less serious offences than those they committed. It happens more at club level, where, for example, a player might be suspended for a month on a charge of 'dangerous play' when they should have been charged with 'striking', which carries a heftier penalty. At club level, too, I've had the odd official asking me to dilute a certain incident in my report, but I've never bowed to that pressure. I would not be true to myself if I did. To my mind, if I diluted a report, that would be akin to taking a bribe.

Omagh eventually worked its way out of my system. Life became normal again, and I felt huge relief when the long-drawn-out saga finally came to an end. I wouldn't blame the

GAA or the people involved on the various committees for the players escaping the suspensions, but the rule book was certainly tightened up as a result, and suspensions dished out to the Meath and Dublin players in 2008 stuck. Of course, I expected that some would be contested, and this proved to be the case.

You might be wondering about my assessment from Omagh. The fact is that it never arrived. I was told that I was not assessed at Healy Park. It can work that way sometimes. It's a pity there was no official assessment of my work, if only for my own peace of mind, which can be fragile.

18

....

STEPPING OUT

You know you're getting old when the
candles cost more than the cake.

Bob Hope

Maybe I should never have left home on that bitterly cold
night in January 2008. I would have avoided all the fuss. I
thought I'd seen everything after the violent club brawl in 1983,
the 1995 All-Ireland final and the Battle of Omagh, but my final
season as an intercounty referee would have more than a few
surprises in store.

It began in Aglish, County Waterford, on Tuesday, 15 January.
During my previous 27 years on the intercounty circuit, I had
never once questioned my sanity before a match, but it was
bloody cold in that cramped dressing-room, and I asked myself,
aloud, 'What am I doing here?'

A new season has dawned, and the first round of the 2008
McGrath Cup, a pre-season competition for Munster teams, has
pitted Waterford IT against Limerick IT. It's hardly a fixture to set
the pulse racing. Only a handful of supporters brave the elements
on the exposed pitch. During the harsh winter months, Mother
Nature can be pretty unforgiving around these parts.

This cold night, it's hard to believe that yet another campaign
has rolled around, and it's a strange feeling, too, because I know

this one will be my last. My mind is made up that I won't be back this time next year. My umpires, Noel Cosgrave, Derek O'Mahony, Liam O'Dwyer and Paddy Noonan, know as much. This is the kind of night when I feel envious of them: at least a hooded white coat offers some protection against the elements.

This dressing-room is as bleak as any I can recall, and there's barely room to swing the proverbial cat. I am in the local GAA club's utility room, surrounded by an assortment of flags, whitewash, paint and netting. I've thought about quitting a few times, but this is the first time that I have ever truly questioned myself before a game. Then again, I am 49 years of age, fast approaching 50. Time I got sense.

There was the usual rush to get to the ground: home from work, a quick cup of tea, collect the umpires and dash to Aglish. Between work and other commitments, three of my regular umpires can't be here. Micheál O'Dwyer, Stevie O'Donnell and John O'Brien couldn't get away, but Derek, Noel and Paddy have kindly agreed to step in. It can be difficult to get umpires sometimes, because people have so many things going on, and I am grateful to the lads for being there.

I look outside; the floodlights are not the best and this makes me feel even worse. If it were a nice warm summer's evening, I would jump at the chance to referee a game, but darkest January is a different story entirely. Wouldn't I be better off at home beside the fire? No offence whatsoever to the Geraldines club, our hosts for the evening – their facilities are decent and the ground is well laid out – but I'm not feeling the love for a McGrath Cup game between two college teams.

It's time to grit the teeth, and once the ball is thrown in, I settle down. The game goes well; Limerick IT run out 1–10 to 0–7 winners, and there is little in the way of incident. That's just how I like it. My doubts have been banished; there's no turning back now.

The intercounty scene is a huge buzz for me. It gets me out running the roads on 1 January each year in preparation for the days of summer. It's hard to get motivated on those cold nights, but once the weather turns for the better, from April on, it's much easier.

I reached another career milestone later that month, on Sunday, 27 January 2008, when I refereed my very first McGrath Cup final. It's hard to believe that I was never awarded that game until then, especially as it's the pre-season showpiece in my own province of Munster. I would have expected an up-and-coming referee to be given that job, rather than a veteran like me, but perhaps the Munster council was aware that I had never refereed that particular fixture.

There was one big decision to make at the end of the final, when I penalised Limerick goalkeeper Seán Kiely for a foot block. Clare's David Tubridy scored the resultant penalty to clinch a 1–5 to 0–7 victory for his county. Stevie O'Donnell was back on duty with me, one of the umpires behind Kiely's goal.

STEVIE O'DONNELL: '*It was like an All-Ireland final for Paddy because he had never refereed a McGrath Cup final before. He made an important call in the dying seconds of that game, too. The Limerick goalkeeper Seán Kiely came out with his foot up, and Paddy awarded a penalty. Clare's David Tubridy drove the ball to the back of the net. I spoke to a Limerick supporter after the game. "Jesus, ye gave a penalty in the last minute of the game!" he exclaimed. "Well," I said, "that's the way the game goes. The referee judged that the goalie came out with his foot high. Dangerous play, penalty." He accepted that.*'

The list of referees for the opening rounds of the National Football League was released by the GAA's Central Referees Appointments Committee on 14 January. I scanned the list for my name but was left somewhat deflated. Standby referee and linesman for Waterford v. Wicklow in Division 4 on 9 February, referee for Clare v. Antrim in the same division a week later and referee for Wexford v. Down in Division 3 two weeks after that. 'Am I past it?' I wondered.

Maybe this was their way of shoving me aside, politely. I was philosophical about it. There are referees out there looking for games, the same as I was all those years ago. But when you're at the top, there's only one way down, and it seemed I was back to Division 4 again, where it all started for me in the early 1980s. In those years, a Division 4 match was manna from heaven, but now it felt as if the wheel had come full circle. Back where I started. That struck a chord with me.

When I began refereeing, the National League operated under the old 1 to 4 divisional system, a format that was revived in 2008. It brought back memories for me of countless trips to Askeaton and Dungarvan for fixtures involving those two counties. It seemed like a never-ending cycle for the first couple of years of my intercounty career: Limerick, Waterford, Limerick, Waterford. I suppose everyone has their own road to follow.

P.J. MCGRATH: *'We have a lot of young referees, and we like to blood them during the National League before making a decision on them ahead of the really serious stuff. The summer is where the likes of Paddy Russell, Pat McEnaney and John Bannon come into their own. They don't need ten matches to get into top-class form. They can just turn it on when it's needed most.'*

STEVIE O'DONNELL: *'Paddy was very annoyed when the first round of fixtures came out. He felt that he wasn't getting the games that he should be getting. But the younger referees coming up need these matches, and if they don't get them, they won't get the proper experience. For 2007's Tipperary county final, Paddy was back in there yet again when Moyle Rovers played Fethard. The county board plumped for an experienced ref, as they'd usually done before, but I would argue that it should have gone to a younger man coming through the ranks.*

'There is just the one big game that has always eluded Paddy – the All-Ireland Under-21 final. He had never taken charge of a Railway Cup final either, until 2005.'

The Wexford v. Down match, at Wexford Park on 2 March, turned out to be a lovely game. Wexford won by 2–8 to 0–9, and both teams just wanted to play football – a marked contrast to the Clare v. Antrim tie a couple of weeks earlier, a non-stop dogfight with loads of bookings. I was then called up to take charge of

Kilkenny v. Clare on 16 March. I felt sorry for Kilkenny; they tried their damnedest, but their standard of play was very poor, and Clare ran out comprehensive 4–19 to 1–4 winners.

Running the line for the Cork v. Monaghan Division 2 tie at Páirc Uí Rinn on Saturday, 5 April gave me a taste for the big time again. This was more like it. An evening floodlit fixture, a decent-sized crowd, a decent game, free-flowing with no major incidents. It couldn't have gone much better for Syl Doyle, the man in charge.

Just days later, like a bolt from the blue, I was notified of my next assignment. My son Shane broke the news to me after the fixtures were released on the Internet. Among them was a plum tie at Parnell Park in Division 2. Two bitter rivals, Dublin and Meath, set to go head to head in a crucial encounter. And there they are, those magic words: '*Réiteoir: Pádraig Ó Ruiséal (Tiobraid Árann)*'.

P.J. MCGRATH: '*In my book, Paddy is a referee who can really handle difficult situations. He's the one that features prominently on that shortlist, but there are others, too, like McEnaney and Bannon. You can send guys of that ilk anywhere and be confident that they'll do a good job.*'

Perhaps the fixture should not have come as a complete surprise to me. My assessment from the Down v. Wexford tie was particularly good. My assessor was Denis Guerin, a Dublin-based Kerry native. He is renowned as a pretty harsh assessor, a guy who brings a pair of binoculars to games when he is analysing a referee. Guerin was not particularly impressed when I refereed the Wexford v. Louth Leinster football quarter-final at Croke Park on 17 June 2007. In fact, I didn't get another game in that championship season, a direct result of a bad assessment. And yet Guerin gave me 85 marks out of 100 on this occasion. Anything in the 80s is considered good.

I was well aware that the rivalry between Dublin and Meath was massive. Even if the two counties met on the side of the road for a game of marbles, neither would relish the prospect of losing. Cork and Kerry are the very same. It was to be my first time refereeing Dublin since the classic 2006 All-Ireland football semi-final, which Mayo clinched with a late point from their gifted forward Ciarán McDonald.

Although I'd been involved in my fair share of controversy with Dublin down through the years, the prospect of handling this fixture against Meath didn't bring any bad memories rushing to the surface. However, I knew that I would have to be on my toes, as this was a game that could explode.

On the morning of Sunday, 20 April, Stevie took the wheel of my car to drive us to Dublin. Shane was there, along with three other trusted umpires, John O'Brien and Liam and Micheál O'Dwyer. Stevie knows Dublin pretty well, and if he drives, it takes a lot of pressure off my shoulders. I felt good but a little nervous. That was OK. Referees are like players: if I don't have nerves before a big game, there's something wrong. It feels like preparing for an exam in many ways. This was a big match for all the participants – and it was my biggest game of the year to date.

I sat back, relaxed and thought about the game. I thought of Omagh. Could something like that happen again? That was the last thing I needed. I certainly didn't want my picture on TV or my name in the newspapers again. Surely I'd had my share of all that.

19

. . . .

A FAMILIAR ROAD

Everything that happens once can never happen again.
But everything that happens twice will surely
happen a third time.

Paulo Coelho

It's all kicked off, but, strangely, I feel calm. Twenty-nine players from Dublin and Meath are embroiled in a mass brawl just five minutes after the start of this National Football League Division 2 encounter.

It sparked from almost nothing and quickly escalated until it was out of control. I sought advice from linesman Eugene Murtagh, as he had a good view of the initial outbreak, but more players suddenly piled in to add fuel to the fire. One word flashed through my mind: Omagh.

There had been no sense of impending doom. Sure, there was tension in the air, but nothing on the scale of Healy Park in 2006. I was up for it, just like the Dublin and Meath players, and prepared for whatever came my way.

I recall a referees' seminar after the Battle of Omagh when I said that I would handle things differently if a similar situation ever arose again. At Healy Park, I waded into a group of brawling players, attempting to prise them apart. I saw everything and yet saw nothing. It was a blur. It's been a habit of mine down through the years, stepping in between players. Break up the first two and it might stop: that was always my thinking. But in a mass brawl, it's the wrong thing to do, and Omagh taught me that valuable lesson. I was too close to what was going on.

This time, I stood back, let Dublin and Meath at it, and then moved in to act. I'd decided on another tactic after Omagh. In the dressing-room before every game since, I tell my umpires and linesmen that if a melee breaks out, they are to concentrate on one set of players only. For example, one umpire takes Team A, the other Team B. Linesmen are told to do the same.

STEVIE O'DONNELL: *'We had a meeting ten or fifteen minutes before the game. Paddy said, "We'll do our usual. Everybody keeps an eye on everything, and watch my back for any off-the-ball stuff. Linesmen, one of ye pick Dublin and the other Meath in the event of a row breaking out. Decide among yourselves." John O'Brien said that he would look after Dublin, and I said that I would go for Meath.'*

Stevie and John, my two umpires, had four names, those of the guys they thought were the worst culprits. I could have sent off eight from each side, but, logistically, that was a non-runner because you would have had no game worth speaking of then. After the melee petered out, I noted Dublin players numbered 4 and 15. Yellow cards were no use, because that would have given the players carte blanche to push the disciplinary boundaries to the limit.

STEVIE O'DONNELL: *'Dublin's number 4, Paddy Andrews, made a run from his own full-back line to contribute to the melee. Red card. The only man who stayed out of the whole thing was Dublin goalkeeper Stephen Cluxton. Paddy ran in to us: "Talk to me." He had Andrews picked out, too. We had Bernard Brogan, Dublin's number 15, and Meath numbers 2 and 17, Niall McKeigue and Shane McAnarney respectively. The four we pinpointed were the worst transgressors in our eyes. They were swinging wild. When there was no need to get stuck in, these guys really did.'*

MICHEÁL O'DWYER: *'Liam and I were at the other end and couldn't believe what was happening. It calmed down, and then it was off again.*

I was wondering if the game would finish. The only way that order would be restored was if heads rolled. If Paddy hadn't given red cards, that game might not have finished at all. He obviously learned from Omagh, and really put the foot down. That's the reason the game was completed.'

It could have been almost any four players, but, as a team, we had a general consensus about who had been the worst, and something had to be done. I marked the names of the four players in my book before returning to speak once again with Eugene Murtagh on the touchline. Dublin's captain on the day, Jason Sherlock, trooped over and asked me, 'Paddy, who are our fellows?' I named Brogan and Andrews, and Jason went to find the pair. In fairness, Jason couldn't have been more helpful to me that day.

STEVIE O'DONNELL: *'I recall that Jason Sherlock was cooperative all day. Before the game even began, he told Paddy, "If I can be of any help, just contact me."'*

McKeigue and McAnarney were supplied by Meath, and I dealt with the Dublin players first, taking their names before asking them to step aside. The way I sent the players off differed from the conventional manner. I took each player's name individually and then asked him to step aside while I noted the next man's name. Then they were all waiting together to find out what was to happen. They didn't know what to expect. I believe they were hoping for yellow cards, because they were absolutely gobsmacked when I pulled out the red card and flashed it at them. I had to point to the line and mouth the word 'off' before the message finally sunk in.

The reason I took their names individually before dealing with them collectively was simple, and I explained the logic behind it to my fellow passengers travelling home in the car that evening. If I had produced a red card for the first player, I would have had numerous players in my face arguing the call. I knew from past experience that this would have been a difficult situation. Issuing the red card to all four at the same time left no room for argument. I was thinking on my feet, and I felt that my actions were swift and decisive.

STEVIE O'DONNELL: *'I liked the way Paddy did that. If he had decided to show a red card after taking the first name, the others would have gone ballistic. The two Dublin players trudged off without muttering a word. In Omagh, it had been yellow cards and severe warnings, but Paddy had to lay down the law this time. If he'd given yellow cards, they would have laughed at him. "Ah, we had a good scrap, we let off a bit of steam, and the referee didn't have the bottle to send us off." But the referee stood up to the test and passed with flying colours.'*

With both teams reduced to 13 players, the pitch opened up. The difference was really noticeable. Minutes later, I issued Dublin midfielder Ciarán Whelan with a straight red card for a slap into Séamus Kenny's face. I had a clear view of it. He had to go off, no doubt about it. Before Whelan committed his offence, I had planned to book Dublin's Colin Moran for a challenge on Mark Ward, but I had no option but to let it go while I sent Whelan off. Moran escaped unpunished. 'I got a slap before that,' Whelan protested. He could have few complaints.

I endured a torrent of abuse from home supporters as I headed into the dressing-room at half-time. It was foul-mouthed stuff. I'm oblivious to supporters during a game, but coming in at half-time it's difficult not to hear them. 'A bollocks from Tipperary' was one of the kinder names that I was called. There has been a perception in the stronger football counties down through the years that just because I hail from Tipperary, predominantly a hurling county, I know nothing about football. It amuses me, because I played football from juvenile level right up until I was 47 years of age.

STEVIE O'DONNELL: *'In the dressing-room at half-time, Paddy came straight over to me: "What way are things going? Am I doing OK?"*

'"The worst is over, I think, Paddy. I can't see any more walking. But keep your eyes peeled in the second half."'

Seán Carroll from Westmeath, the linesman at the opposite side of the pitch, also assured me that I was doing a fine job and had handled the melee well.

The second half passed off relatively peacefully, although by the end of the game I had issued eleven yellow cards, seven to Meath and four to Dublin. They were for various offences – pulling an opponent, rough play, late tackles.

Dublin's Mossy Quinn scored a good point under real pressure from Meath defenders, and, after putting the ball over the bar, the forward jeered at his opponents to emphasise the point. It was real in-your-face stuff, but not enough to warrant a booking. I had a quick word with Quinn, telling him, 'I don't want to see any of that stuff.' He responded, 'Fair enough.'

One of the players I did book was Meath forward Graham Geraghty, who has caused me some problems down through the years. He was cautioned seven minutes after half-time for 'challenging the authority of an official'.

STEVIE O'DONNELL: '*Paddy must have been sick and tired of me calling him in during the game because I advised him to award five or six yellow cards. I called him in at one point and said: "Number 6 for Meath [Caoimhín King] – yellow card for him." I informed Paddy that King had been dragging his opponent, and he yellow-carded the Meath player.*

'*Graham Geraghty was actually pretty quiet during the game. I thought that his personality had changed somewhat. I felt that I was looking at a different Graham Geraghty, because he can be an arrogant type of player, but he was a bit more relaxed during the game. I did notice that some of the Dublin players were attempting to provoke a reaction from him, which they never got. He took unbelievable abuse from some Dublin supporters, too. They were calling him every name under the sun, and every time he gathered possession, he was booed and jeered. Maybe that's a mark of respect, in a perverse way, because he's the type of player who could tear any defence asunder. Graham shook hands with Stephen Cluxton after the game, and then he walked off the pitch. The Dublin fans were making obscene gestures right in his face and insulting him. It was really horrible stuff. I thought at one stage that he might lose the cool, but, fair play to him, he took it on the chin, kept smiling and walked off the pitch. He was quite relaxed* and happy when he reached the dressing-room, but, then again, it's probably water off a duck's back to Graham at this stage.'

I rang my wife Margaret after the game because I knew that she would be worried. She was 120 miles away, attending the National Hurling League final between Tipperary and Galway in Limerick.

MARGARET RUSSELL: *'I knew by his voice on the phone that he was fine. I was waiting for my sister Teresa in Limerick before we went into the Gaelic Grounds for the Tipp match. I have a transistor radio, and I was tuned in to hear updates from Parnell Park on RTÉ Radio 1. They spent more time in Limerick on the Division 2 hurling final, but I did hear that the game in Dublin would be 'remembered for all the wrong reasons'. Seven minutes of extra time in the first half. "Oh, God, what now?" I had no idea what was after happening up there. The presenters promised they would be returning to Parnell Park for further coverage in a while.*

'A fellow from Lattin spotted me. "Paddy's sending them off left, right and centre in Dublin."

'"Ah sure, he is. What's new?"

'I was trying to laugh it off. It was all bravado on my part. When she arrived, Teresa knew that something was wrong.

'"What's up?"

'"I am absolutely sick. I have no interest in going to the Tipperary game."

'"Why?"

'"Whatever is going on in Dublin, Paddy is after sending off five in the first half."

'I met so many people that I knew – and they all knew. I texted Shane: "How is Dad getting on?" He texted back: "Fine, five sent off in first half." I asked if Paddy was OK, and Shane assured me that he was. I felt better after that. Then I had a missed call from Paddy. I couldn't hear the phone at the Tipperary match. I didn't want to speak in there anyway, with people around me listening. When I left the Gaelic Grounds, we spoke on the phone, and I just knew that he was OK. Normally, he would ask, "Well, what did they say?" because

usually I would be watching his games on TV and in a position to let him know what the analysts were saying. The entire episode brought back a few old memories, though. "A week of it in the newspapers again," I thought.'

Before we showered and togged off, the linesmen, umpires and I came together as a group for a post-game assessment. My linesmen had their programmes open, and we formulated the contents of what would appear in my match report for submission to Croke Park. I jotted down the necessary information, and, satisfied, I popped the notebook into my gear bag. Then I heard a knock on the dressing-room door.

Dublin selector Dave Billings apologised, and he said that I had performed well, which meant a lot. He was really sorry for what had happened. Dublin manager Paul Caffrey arrived soon after. He said, 'I don't know what it is, Paddy. Omagh two years ago and this today. How much more of this can you take?'

'I just seem to be unfortunate.'

'You're good to stand up to it.'

It was a happy car on the way home to Tipperary. My four trusted umpires had performed admirably, Stevie and John O'Brien at the 'busy' end, Micheál and Liam O'Dwyer at the opposite end. I was satisfied that I had handled the game well, and said as much to the lads. And I knew that I could rely on these guys. Stevie turned to Micheál O'Dwyer, handed him a Dictaphone and told him to pass it to me. Stevie, who does a bit of work for local radio station Tipperary Mid West, had joined the media scrum after the game to record the reactions of the two managers.

Paul Caffrey's post-match comments, in which he praised my performance, meant a great deal to me. What managers say after a game can influence the way reporters view it. They interview managers after matches, and, as far as I can see, what they really want is for them to criticise the referee. That makes for good headlines. But Caffrey was having none of it. Here was a Dublin team with three players sent off, and yet their manager stated that I had had a good game. Media criticism through the years has affected my entire family, but this was not going to be one of those occasions.

MARGARET RUSSELL: *'I asked our son Mark if he was pleased that he went to the hurling league final or whether he would have preferred to have been at Parnell Park with his father. He replied, "Well, I'm glad I didn't see what happened, but I would have liked to have been there to tell Dad he did well." Shane will always tell his father that he did fine, but Mark wouldn't spare anybody. The footage of the melee was screened on* Sunday Sport *that night. I was somewhat apprehensive about the reaction from the studio analysts, but Mark said, "It's all right, Mam. Colm O'Rourke and Pat Spillane aren't on tonight."'*

SHANE RUSSELL: *'Dad was happy going home. He felt that he had done well. I know he's happy if he's not asking us what we thought or questioning his decisions.'*

MARK RUSSELL: *'He will ask his umpires questions at half-time in every match.'*

SHANE RUSSELL: *'"Was that right? Did he pick it off the ground? Was it hopping?" I think it's to help his own game too. If he gets caught out once, he's anxious that it won't happen again. It's like a hurler who gets hooked every time; he'll practise not getting hooked. A referee will try to get into a position where he won't make the same mistake again.'*

MARGARET RUSSELL: *'Shane being with Paddy at Parnell Park was brilliant for me. Paddy is very close to Stevie and the other umpires, but Shane is family. Without wanting to sound self-important, Shane was taking over my role. I wanted someone to be there with Paddy. Shane and Mark were in school the day after Parnell Park, and there were a few jibes. "Ah, your father was at it again." My back goes up when I hear that. Paddy didn't hit anyone. But children don't spare each other.'*

Paul Dorris, a former Ulster administrator of the National Referees Committee, rang at ten o'clock on the Sunday night. 'Well done today,' he said. 'I was watching the highlights, and you did a great job. I remember you spoke about Omagh at a referees meeting in Athlone and you said that you would do things differently if something like that happened to you again. You said that you would step back, take it all in and then move in to sort it out. I was looking out for that, and you were true to your word.' P.J. McGrath was in touch too, with more complimentary words. It felt like a redemption of sorts, after Omagh.

MARGARET RUSSELL: *'Still, neither Paddy nor I slept well that night. Paddy was tired, and we were worried about the Monday morning newspapers.'*

I knew from bitter experience that closure was not necessarily at hand just yet . . .

20

....

COCOONED

Experience: that most brutal of teachers.
But you learn, my God, do you learn.

C.S. Lewis

'Referee Russell praised for swift response' read the headline in Monday's edition of the *Irish Times*. It might, under different circumstances, have read 'Referee Russell slammed as brawl spirals out of control'. Fine lines: I know all about them.

Paul Caffrey, to his credit, had taken the sting out of the situation immediately after the game when he praised my handling of it. If Paul had criticised me, the newspapers would have had a field day. Caffrey was quoted as saying, 'Paddy Russell had a job to do and he did it. No complaints about Paddy, he did a very fine job on the game overall.' Interviewed on TV, Meath manager Colm Coyle took the Arsène Wenger stance, claiming that he'd seen nothing.

MARGARET RUSSELL: *'Colm Coyle couldn't understand how Paddy had picked out the four players. What I couldn't believe was that, for once, Paddy wasn't stuck in the middle of the melee! Jesus, he actually stood back and let them at it! He got a better view of that brawl than of any other.'*

It was the newspaper coverage that really got to me after Omagh. I couldn't stand seeing the headlines. Mickey Harte might have said that God Almighty could not have handled that match but I still didn't feel exonerated because the press were so negative. This time, the papers were much more reasonable, and that helped me not to get downhearted about it.

I had an important piece of business to attend to before I could put Parnell Park to bed. Late on Sunday night, around eleven o'clock, I completed my official match report. I knew that first thing on Monday morning the top officials at Croke Park would be looking for my version of events.

MARGARET RUSSELL: *'I faxed Paddy's report to Croke Park from Fitzpatrick's Printers in Tipperary town, my former place of work, on the Monday morning. That's the way it's done now. In the past, it could take three days to get to Dublin by post. Paddy had it written up on the Sunday night.*

The GAA referee's match report is hugely important in terms of discipline and, up until recent times, was viewed as almost sacrosanct. It was the final word, unchallengeable.

Under the heading 'Details of players ordered off the field', I had listed the five players sent off. I reported Dublin's Paddy Andrews for 'contributing to a melee', a relatively new offence brought in after Omagh, which is deemed worthy of a straight red card. Twenty-nine players were involved at Parnell Park, so technically every player on the field bar Stephen Cluxton could have walked; however, for reasons already stated, this could not have happened. The GAA could have charged all twenty-nine with the offence and handed down one-month suspensions across the board, but, instead, the perceived worst offenders were to be targeted.

I reported Dublin duo Bernard Brogan and Ciarán Whelan, along with Meath pair Niall McKeigue and Shane McAnarney, for 'striking with the hand'. The wording 'with the hand' is important here, as in the past players could escape the previous equivalent offence, 'striking with the fist', on a technicality, by proving that it was a slap, that they had struck with an open hand. Now, there is no room for ambiguity.

The front page of the modern-day referee's match report lists the fixture that the official has been appointed to, along with some basic requirements from Croke Park. The referee is expected to be on the pitch ten minutes before starting time and must supply his own umpires. Normally, he is required to complete the report, together with team lists, within three days of the match. However, any report involving a disciplinary issue must be faxed no later than midday the following day.

I made a note of the times that the teams took to the field before the game, Meath out first at 2.18 p.m. followed by Dublin at 2.20 p.m. The match started at 2.29 p.m. and ended at 4.05 p.m. The linesmen and umpires were then listed, along with the full-time score and the substitutes used by both teams.

It was then time to deal with the various offenders at Parnell Park, starting with the red-carded players before the eleven players booked were detailed. In three of the eight boxes supplied for bookings, I squeezed in two names. With eleven players yellow-carded, there simply wasn't enough room for everybody.

Then some more formalities: I submitted my travel and meal expenses and answered some standard questions as follows:

1. *If there was a delay in starting, what was the cause?* No delay in starting.
2. *Was a match programme provided? (Please check prior to the game.)* Yes.
3. *Were players' jerseys numbered in accordance with numbers on programme?* Yes.
4. *Were linesmen properly attired? (If not, give details.)* Yes.
5. *Was the pitch properly marked?* Yes.
6. *Was the grass cut short enough?* Yes.

The next section required me to: 'Give brief comments on stewarding, encroachment onto the pitch by officials, or any other matter of presentation which you feel should be highlighted.' I wrote: 'About ten minutes into the first half, a melee broke out between both sets of players. After consulting with my linesmen and umpires I sent off two players from both sides. There were no further instances of that nature in the game.'

Pierce Freaney, coordinator of the National Referees Association, phoned on the Monday morning and informed me that the GAA's Central Competitions Control Committee (CCCC) was meeting and that my report was at the top of the agenda. 'We might need you to clarify a couple of issues later,' he said.

As we chatted briefly, Pierce added, 'I never saw a referee get so much praise in the newspapers!' Eugene Murtagh called, too. He had been listening to local radio in Longford and the *Irish Independent* columnist Eugene McGee, a former Offaly manager, had also applauded me. According to Eugene, the general feeling in the midlands was that Dublin were more to blame for what had taken place than Meath.

Pierce rang back a while later and informed me that an email had been sent from Croke Park to Fitzpatrick's. I had to confirm by return that the only players that I had adjudicated on in the melee were the four that I had sent off. Then the CCCC would be free to take action against others they felt had a case to answer. An attachment with the email from GAA HQ, containing video footage of the brawl, could not be downloaded, but, in any event, I had seen it on TV. I informed Croke Park of this. Abandoning the match never once entered my mind; that's an extreme course of action, and I have never resorted to it during my career. The CCCC was swift in its actions, proposing suspensions for no fewer than 16 players. And this time, they wanted those suspensions to stick.

On the Tuesday evening after 'the Dust-up in Donnycarney', a referees' seminar was held in Athlone. Many of my colleagues made a point of shaking my hand and congratulating me on my performance. Chairman P.J. McGrath urged referees to 'apply the rules – like Paddy Russell did last Sunday'. As a man who has suffered from self-doubt in the past, this was music to my ears.

Further proof that I had performed well lay in store in the form of Noel Cooney's assessment sheet, which dropped through the letterbox just days after the game. Noel is a brother of Johnny, also known as Seán, who was a member of the great Offaly football teams I worshipped in the early 1970s. I ran the line more than once for Noel, a former referee himself who departed the scene a few years ago.

Since stepping down from the intercounty circuit, Noel has become one of the many referees who have taken up roles as assessors. Their job is to keep an extremely detailed account of the referee's performance before submitting a report to Croke Park. The referee in question is entitled to a copy of this report. It's often the case that a referee gets slated in the Monday morning newspapers but receives a favourable assessment on the following Thursday. I always pay great heed to assessments, not least because Croke Park officials place huge emphasis on them when finalising future appointments. I'm always slightly nervous before the assessment arrives, a bit like a teenager tearing open the envelope that contains exam results.

The Tipperary football board chairman Noel Morris publicly criticised assessors in December 2007, when he offered the opinion that referees are loath to apply common sense because there are assessors sitting in the stand watching their every move. I agree up to a point. The current assessment forms are so detailed that I often wonder if assessors employ secretaries to help fill them out. I really don't know sometimes how they keep track of everything.

P.J. MCGRATH: *'Assessors have been employed for a good many years, back before my time. In the past, they were picked at random, but now they're brought in and trained. They are all former referees and respected officials. The assessor will judge the referee on the rules of the game, nothing else. Referees might not like the rules of the game, but they have no choice but to implement them. Assessors have become quite professional. They take notes or speak into a Dictaphone during the game to record information. They have their own language, too, a form of shorthand to keep up to speed with the game. For example, 'D8 struck L4 12th minute unpunished' would mean that Dublin's number 8 struck Longford's number 4 in the twelfth minute of the game but that this indiscretion went unpunished by the referee.'*

A poor assessment is something a referee fears, because it can ruin an entire season. I know this from experience. Denis Guerin was my assessor when I took charge of Louth v. Wexford at Croke Park in the 2007 All-Ireland football championship. It was my sole championship outing of the year.

There were a few little things that I was not happy with during the game, but overall I felt that it was quite a solid performance. Guerin thought that I should have added on seven minutes of injury time; I played four. The Louth manager, Eamonn McEneaney, also insisted that I should have played more time. Louth had launched a late fightback that fell short, but I don't think they would have got back level even if I had added on the extra time. Guerin also wrote that I should have sent off two players for body-checking offences.

Nowadays, a referee does not know beforehand who will be assessing him during a game. There was a time when the assessor's name was listed along with those of the officials, but that is no longer the case. In the past, an assessor did not have to put his name on his assessment, but now he is identified, and a telephone number is also supplied in case the ref feels the need to contact him.

I took up the offer, and Guerin explained his take on some of the incidents in the game. There was no way that he was backing down. He felt that there were points when I should have taken stronger action. Guerin awarded me a mark somewhere in the 60s, and I didn't get another championship game that season.

For the Dublin v. Meath match at Parnell Park, Noel Cooney awarded me a mark of 81 out of 100. I felt a slight tinge of disappointment, but anything over 80 is in truth a pretty good assessment, so I should really have been happy. Noel wrote:

This team worked very well and they kept their cool during the melee. He took action after the melee and kept control of a very difficult game to referee. His experience helped him and overall I felt he handled the game very well.

Fair enough. That's good stuff. But under the heading 'Areas in need of improvement', he said:

I know it was almost impossible to keep an account of all that went on in this game but the two very late fouls mentioned should have been punished. Also noted a player for pushing with his hands, not a noting offence. Also noted two players twice.

I was awarded the following marks:

Teamwork	20/20
Technical	9/10
Aggressive	19/35
Dissent	5/5
Control	18/20
Positioning and fitness	10/10
Total mark	81/100

My linesmen received 4 out of 4 for their work on the day, while my four trusted umpires were awarded 12 out of 12. Noel noted: 'They all worked very well as a team between them. They correctly called the referee on eight occasions for off-the-ball incidents during the game.'

Having 16 marks docked under the heading covering the 'aggressive' aspects of the game annoyed me. It's all very technical stuff, but Noel pulled me up for not penalising Brendan McManamon and Jason Sherlock for 'rough play', Bryan Cullen for 'pulling down an opponent' and Colin Moran for 'preventing or attempting to prevent an opponent from lifting or kicking the ball off the ground by striking opponent's hand, arm, foot or leg with the boot'. Because of the above, I lost eight marks. Noel pointed out, too, that Meath's Peadar Byrne escaped three times for 'holding an opponent with the hand(s)', while Moran was marked on Noel's sheet for 'charging an opponent in the back or front'.

Noel also claimed that Dublin pair Paul Flynn and Sherlock were both noted twice. A player should not be noted twice. He should be booked for a second noting offence. My son Shane had his own book at Parnell Park. To aid the compilation of my match report, and to allow me to double-check some matters later, I asked Shane to record any player that I noted or booked. In fairness, Shane said to me after the game that he thought I had noted two players twice. I remember noting one of the players early in the game, but after I'd noted him a second time, a quick free-kick restarted play and I had to let the player go without a yellow card. These technicalities cost me six marks, while failing to pick up on pushing offences committed by Diarmuid Connolly and Caoimhín King knocked another two marks off my total.

The mark I was docked under the 'technical' heading was for a second-minute incident when Noel felt that Bryan Cullen had thrown the ball but I had allowed play to continue.

Under 'control', I lost two marks out of twenty for the following: 'Noted two players twice, also noted Meath number 6 (King) for a push in the back.' I know well that a push in the back is not a noting offence, but I felt that King's shove was more aggressive than your average push and warranted a noting. Noel added: 'He let two very late fouls go by Dublin no. 10 and no. 13 (Brendan McManamon and Jason Sherlock). Dublin no. 5 (Moran) should have been noted before sending off of Dublin no. 8 (Ciarán Whelan).' No complaints with the latter remark. I'll hold my hands up there. As I explained earlier, Moran escaped without censure because Whelan struck Séamus Kenny just seconds later. When that minor skirmish developed, the Moran incident went completely out of my head.

Noel believed that Moran should have been noted, but I was quite sure that the challenge on Mark Ward was dangerous and deserved a booking.

Although Noel explained his reasoning to me, the 19 out of 35 'aggressive' mark knocked the wind out of my sails. I was pleased with the manner in which I'd handled the game, and felt that sending off five players in the first quarter of an hour had taken the sting out of it and ensured that there would be no more serious messing around. There were no major incidents in the game afterwards – a couple of occasions when players came in late but no more offences that warranted sendings-off.

Noel's view of the melee was as follows:

> Twenty-nine players were involved in this melee. Dublin number 15 (Bernard Brogan) and Meath number 17 (Shane McAnarney) started it but the other players should have stayed away from it, as the referee would have sorted it out. Many more players could have received red cards but it was almost impossible to pick out the guiltiest players. I did feel that number 3 Meath (Darren Fay) and number 12 Dublin (Paul Flynn) were lucky to stay on the field, and Dublin number 22 (Diarmuid Connolly) was first in to restart the melee.

A few people have asked me if I would like to become an assessor now that I have stepped down from the intercounty scene, and the answer is that I don't know. I think that I would prefer to get into the coaching side of Gaelic football. I was in charge of the Lattin Under-12s who won a West Tipperary title this year, and that victory filled me with immense happiness. I believe that I have something to contribute on the other side of the whitewash, and surely more than 25 years of experience on the intercounty circuit, watching the very best players in action, should count for something. Years ago, I was player-manager of the Emly junior team, but that was more of a mercy mission than anything else. It was very difficult at the time to get guys involved, so I took charge of the training sessions.

I'd like to test my management skills at a much higher level, and it is a huge ambition of mine to be a selector with one of Tipperary's county teams. The Wexford hurling referee Dickie Murphy became a selector with his native county. Even at 50 years of age, I still have goals that I want to achieve within the GAA. This great Association is a drug I think I'll never have enough of.

21

....

STORM CLOUDS

Kerry county board has issued a statement in support of
Paul Galvin. Apparently, he was killing a wasp that had
landed on referee Paddy Russell's notebook. The wasp then
went after the linesman and finally turned on Tomás Ó Sé
before Galvin managed to get rid of it.

Text message circulated by supporters following
the Kerry v. Clare Munster championship semi-final
on Sunday, 15 June 2008, when Kerry captain Paul
Galvin slapped the notebook from Paddy's hands

Back where we started. You join me in the referee's room at
Fitzgerald Stadium in Killarney just minutes after I have
blown the final whistle on the 2008 Munster senior football
championship tie between All-Ireland champions Kerry and
Clare. It's quiet in here. I'm annoyed with myself for an error
during the game: I had to be reminded through my earpiece by
my fellow officials that Clare player John Hayes had already been
yellow-carded when I believed that it was his first booking.

But what's really dominating everybody's thoughts is what has
happened with Kerry captain Paul Galvin out on the field. The
Kingdom star slapped the notebook from my hand in the second
half, just as I was about to issue him with a second yellow card
for an incident with Hayes.

I had acted on the advice of my linesman Mike Meade, who indicated that both players should be yellow-carded for jostling off the ball. In the dressing-room, Mike tells me what happened between the two players, information that will appear in my match report. Mike says that he was not aware initially that it was Galvin who was involved in the jostling. He merely noted Kerry's number 10 and Clare's number 7 as the offending parties.

On his way out of the ground, Mike met the Kerry manager, Pat O'Shea, who said to him, 'Thanks very much, Mike. Good job.' Mike took those comments at face value. He didn't feel they were meant in any sarcastic way. Maybe O'Shea was trying to stay onside with Mike in case it might help Galvin's case.

In the car on the way home, not much was said. We couldn't find a reason why Galvin would react like that. It would have been a different story if he had been given a straight red, which would have ruled him out of the Munster final, but that wasn't the case.

MICHEÁL O'DWYER: *'Paddy was a bit down in himself. He just wanted the game to go off without incident.'*

I tuned into *The Sunday Game* on television later that night, waiting anxiously for highlights of Kerry v. Clare. They showed nothing, really. The jostling between Galvin and Hayes didn't feature, but the sole camera did, of course, capture Galvin's notebook slap and subsequent berating of Mike Meade. The pundits went easy on Kerry's captain. The general consensus was that Galvin should not have done what he did, but, rather than calling for heavy penalties, as they'd sometimes done in the past, they stressed that due process should be allowed to take its course.

This was in stark contrast to previous weeks, when the same pundits had come out and publicly urged the GAA to take severe action against other players for indiscipline. This had not gone down well at Croke Park; perhaps they discreetly asked *The Sunday Game* to tone down their analysis of amateur players.

Sleep was difficult to come by that night. I woke twice with the Galvin incident weighing heavily on my mind. I felt sick. There would be massive newspaper headlines again the next morning. I was sure of it.

And there it was again. That familiar feeling of dread in the pit of my stomach, a feeling I'd hoped I would never experience again. Paul Galvin and Paddy Russell were splashed all over the back pages of the daily newspapers. I wasn't surprised. I'd thought I'd seen it all, but knocking the notebook from a referee's hands was unprecedented at intercounty level. I remembered what John Moloney had once said to me: 'I've been refereeing for so long, but I will come up against something new every time I go out on the field.'

MICHAEL MEADE: 'The stupidity of Galvin's actions stuck with me. It was such a simple thing – an everyday booking for jostling – and because of his response, it exploded into a media frenzy. I can't believe the amount of newspaper coverage that was devoted to it. What struck me most was Galvin's reaction to Tomás Ó Sé. I didn't mind so much the abuse and the bollocking that I got, but his behaviour to Ó Sé was very surprising.

'One top referee texted me on Monday and asked if I would have been better off turning a blind eye to the Galvin incident. I replied, "Would I not have been better off sitting at home watching the match?" Like, where are we going with this?'

One particular newspaper photograph of me bending down to pick up my notebook was not very flattering. Galvin is stood above me, just a second after slapping the book from my hand. It's a humiliating snap.

The feeling I had when I saw the papers was one of complete déjà vu. It seemed that a fresh storm was always brewing when the last one had passed. Why the hell did this always happen to me? I couldn't find an answer. I thought that I might as well quit right now. I thanked God that it was my last year on the intercounty circuit, because I felt sick of it all. I wasn't sick of refereeing as such, but I'd certainly had my fill of the controversies that had punctuated my career. This was my final year, and already there had been a 29-man brawl at Parnell Park and now the Paul Galvin episode.

I found myself back in the eye of a storm again, and the entire family was affected. Margaret was upset, and although they wouldn't say it, I'm sure my sons Shane and Mark were too. Work was not an appealing prospect. I didn't want to face anybody, but I'm fortunate in a sense, because the majority of people working with me at Kiely's Coca-Cola Distributors Ltd in Tipperary town have no interest in Gaelic games. Then there are others who wouldn't read a match report but would notice the newspaper photos. Every Monday, I buy the *Irish Independent* and the *Irish Examiner* for their take on the weekend's GAA, but at work the tabloids are strewn across the canteen table. I decided to broach the subject before it was brought up by my colleagues, laugh it off and defuse the situation before they had a chance to comment. It's a tactic that has worked in the past.

I read the reports in the *Irish Examiner* and *Irish Independent* and was disappointed to see that my refereeing of the game was described as 'dreadfully fussy' by Cliona Foley in the *Irish Independent*.

The national referees coordinator Pierce Freaney rang to check that I had submitted my official match report to the relevant authorities. Margaret had faxed it earlier that morning, and the contents of it would go a long way towards deciding the penalty that would be imposed on Paul Galvin. I booked the Kerry captain in the first half for 'pulling down an opponent' and his second cautionable foul was the incident with Hayes, where he was 'jostling with an opponent'.

When a game includes a controversial incident, referees are encouraged to provide specific extra details. My addendum read as follows:

> During the second half of the match, my linesman Mike Meade reported Clare number 7 John Hayes and Kerry number 10

Paul Galvin for jostling off the ball. I called the two players together and I yellow-carded John Hayes and as I was about to yellow-card and red-card Paul Galvin (as I had yellow-carded him already in the first half), he knocked my book from my hand.

I picked up my notebook and showed him a yellow card and as I was taking the red card out, he ran to the linesman Mike Meade and began to remonstrate with him. At this point, Tomás Ó Sé (Kerry) led Paul Galvin away and he left the field of play. At the end of the match Mike Meade reported Paul Galvin for calling him a 'fucking bollocks'.

Pádraig O'Ruiséal, Réiteoir

By this point, the entire affair was weighing heavy on mind and soul. On Monday evening, Mark was playing for Lattin-Cullen in a juvenile match. I watched the game from my car. I didn't want to go out to the pitch because I was afraid of what people were saying. And I was seriously contemplating not travelling to Dublin on Tuesday evening for a fitness test organised for intercounty championship referees by the GAA.

Predictably, the worm began to turn as Kerry rolled out the big guns to influence public opinion. Eoin 'Bomber' Liston was in *The Star* newspaper arguing that officials were partly to blame for the Galvin incident, and the former Kerry manager Jack O'Connor stated that the player was being 'demonised'. I smiled to myself when I read Liston's comments. One of the match officials from the junior game in Killarney, the curtain-raiser, told me that when he was leaving Fitzgerald Stadium he saw Liston walking into the ground a quarter of an hour after the big game had started. I don't know if it was definitely him, but if it was, even though he would have seen the Galvin incident, it's my view that he shouldn't have commented publicly if he hadn't watched the entire match,

Those comments from Liston disappointed me. I always had the greatest of admiration for him as a player. He's in the rag trade now I believe, selling GAA merchandise, and when one of his contacts was in touch with me some time ago, I mentioned Liston's business to a few clubs around the local area in an attempt to generate some business for him. But I lost a lot of respect for him when he came out in the newspapers blaming officials for Galvin's actions. The linesman was wrong, the referee was wrong, everybody was wrong bar Paul Galvin, it seemed.

Liston is a big hitter in Kerry circles. He won All-Ireland titles as a player, and O'Connor won two in three years as a manager. So if Liston or O'Connor says something in the press, to many supporters it is the gospel truth. I don't think that mentality will ever change with the general public. I've seen a similar pattern emerge so many times: when a serious incident occurs, it's accompanied by wailing, gnashing of teeth and calls for heavy suspensions to be imposed; a couple of days later, and it's a case of 'ah, sure maybe it wasn't that bad'; and a few days after that, there are cries for the suspensions to be overturned. You see it in soccer: a big-name player does something seriously wrong, but he's still loved. It's called defending the indefensible, and, true to form, by Tuesday the spotlight had been turned on the officials who handled the game. It seemed that we were to blame for Galvin's actions. Mike Meade was particularly upset by an article in the *Irish Independent* that suggested that Galvin had been seeking protection from the linesman all through the game.

MICHAEL MEADE: '*The article stated that Paul Galvin had been looking for protection "all day" from the linesman, but at no stage during the match did Paul Galvin come next nor near me. The former Kerry manager Jack O'Connor was in the papers, too, saying that the linesman had a lot to answer for. I was in touch with the GAA on that Tuesday night. I made a phone call to make them aware of the fact that Paul Galvin never once spoke to me for 55 minutes of that match. The first time he spoke to me was when he was shouting and roaring at me after getting sent off. When it came to Galvin's disciplinary hearing, Kerry would need to back up their claims that he had been looking for protection from me "all day" with video evidence, I'm sure.*

'We only ever hear one side of the story. Under GAA rules, match officials are gagged. We're dummies; we don't have a voice. I was very pissed off on the Sunday night. I refereed a local Under-14 game on the Monday evening, and I got more enjoyment out of that game than in Killarney, which is wrong in a way. We all have families and close friends, so it's embarrassing when this kind of stuff is printed. I'll tell you the God's honest truth: I got a call from an uncle-in-law in Dublin about that article in the Independent. *I didn't want any of that sort of business. All we wanted was a good game, to enjoy the day out and to come home afterwards.*

'I also know in my heart and soul that this whole thing could count against me in my GAA work in the future, and it left me disillusioned. There's more to life than the GAA, and, at the end of the day, I have a young family, and I would be better off putting in time with them. It's grand to be involved in the GAA when things are rosy, but the Galvin business affected me and took away a lot of my enjoyment of it. Nobody wants to see their name in the paper in circumstances like that.'

Mike also heard from friends in Kerry that the well-known local broadcaster 'Weeshie' Fogarty, himself a former referee, had been critical of the match officials. Fogarty had made his feelings known on Des Cahill's RTÉ Radio 1 show on the Monday evening as well. He admitted that slapping the notebook out of my hands was wrong but played down the significance of the incident.

Personally, I never want to see players getting in trouble. They make huge sacrifices, and I don't like to feel responsible for causing them suffering. In many cases, it may as well be the ref who imposes the suspension, because the GAA will take his official match report into consideration when deciding on a course of action. However, through no fault of my own, I was involved in the Galvin incident. It was my notebook that he slapped. We all know that Paul Galvin is a player who plays on the edge and that he was geared up for this game as Kerry captain. What's more, he went on RTÉ news on Monday evening to apologise for his actions. But does any of that really matter when a player crosses the line by interfering with a referee?

When it came to the penalty that would be imposed on Galvin, video evidence would be important. Mike was hoping that footage would surface to prove that Galvin was deserving of a yellow card for his tangle with Hayes, but I believe that there was just one camera at the venue, which would have followed play when Galvin released the ball in the build-up to the Kerry score.

MICHAEL MEADE: *'That's the one thing I regretted in the immediate aftermath, that the jostling wasn't captured on video. A lot of people didn't realise what the second yellow card was for. You'd love all the facts to be out there, but the GAA in the counties have a lot of powerful people on their side, and at times you have to be careful about what you say. You worry that if you're too outspoken you won't get the games.'*

Naturally, the Galvin affair dominated conversation when Mike and I travelled to Dublin City University on Tuesday afternoon for a fitness test overseen by staff there, working on the GAA's behalf. News of Galvin's proposed suspension was imminent, and we kept our ears glued to the radio. Mike told me all about the phone calls from his Kerry-based friends, and it seemed to me that he was coming in for more criticism than me in the Kingdom.

MICHAEL MEADE: *'We had planned to travel together to Dublin since the previous Thursday night, but I wasn't sure if I would be able to make it due to work commitments. It would be a whole day gone, because we had to leave at two o'clock in the afternoon and wouldn't make it home until two o'clock the next morning. I decided to go in the end, though. Paddy had asked me to drive, and we had a good chat on the way up. We were apprehensive because we knew that the result of the Central Competitions Control Committee hearing would be out. We were listening to the radio for the outcome but . . . nothing. Then the text messages came through, and we were shocked at first to hear that Galvin had received a six-month ban. But after discussing the situation with our fellow referees in Dublin, we realised that he couldn't have got any less for what he did. Some felt that 12 months should have been the minimum for the offence.'*

We got to DCU around 5.30 p.m., had a cup of coffee and chatted with Professor Niall Moyna and the former Dublin manager Mickey Whelan, who guided St Vincent's to the All-Ireland club football title in 2008. They were the men overseeing the fitness tests for the referees ranked in the 3.2 bracket, the intercounty championship referees. The other guys began to arrive and the general feeling among them was that Galvin should have received a year-long suspension. I couldn't agree. 'It's all right for ye to say that because ye are not involved,' I told them. I argued that I did not like to see any player getting such a long ban because he could lose out on an entire season as a result.

GAA president Nickey Brennan was present, and he said, 'Well done on Sunday. You did what you had to do.' I told him that I didn't like being involved in incidents of that nature.

After the fitness test, we had a meal, followed by a meeting addressed by sports psychologist Canice Brennan. Nickey Brennan offered us some words of encouragement. It has struck me more than once during his three years as president that he has been very good to referees, standing up for us publicly on several occasions. There have been some good presidents in this regard, but, for me, Brennan ranks right up there as one of the most supportive.

MICHAEL MEADE: *'Discipline is a big thing with Nickey Brennan. And referees do need backing. There's a big problem with society in general: all authority is fair game; to challenge it is commonplace.'*

The support and camaraderie of my peers was most welcome, but when I returned to Tipperary, I withdrew deep into myself as the media storm continued to rage. Shane told me that when he was training with the Tipperary minor footballers, preparing for the Munster final against Kerry on 6 July, somebody passed a remark: 'Ah, Paddy Russell . . . controversy again.' Maybe this guy was having the craic, but I'm sure that Shane found that hard to listen to.

I narrowed my horizons after Killarney. Offers to referee

various challenge matches were declined. I was pencilled in to speak to referees in Midleton during the week, but I decided not to. I apologised to my contact in Cork and promised that I would attend the next monthly meeting.

Some will find this hard to believe, but I felt worse for Paul Galvin than for myself. I knew that what he'd done was wrong, but I didn't want to be the person responsible for him receiving a six-month ban. On the other hand, six months was not excessive. Rugby and soccer referees were interviewed on radio and spoke about how 12-month or even life bans would be considered in their codes. Close friends and colleagues kept on telling me that it wasn't my fault, but I felt guilty by association. I didn't want any hand, act or part in Paul Galvin receiving a six-month suspension, because he's a great player and had come across as such a nice guy when we'd filmed the Vodafone advertisement in Dublin.

I returned to refereeing a week after Killarney – a challenge game between Arravale Rovers and Pallasgreen from Limerick at Seán Treacy Park in Tipperary town. I felt ready to go back, and people couldn't have been nicer, in contrast to the guy I met in Cappawhite a few nights after who asked me if my hand was sore.

Those kind of jibes hurt, but they are part of the reason why I take refereeing so seriously. For me, it's not a case of going out there and doing exactly as I please. I question all of my decisions, and I would hate to do something wrong to a player or team. Some people could have walked away unaffected after the incident, I'm sure. Paul Galvin was sent off, OK, let's move on. But that's not me.

You may ask why I continued refereeing at intercounty level for so long when I have such an aversion to the controversy that appears to be more and more the norm in the GAA. It's because I never felt that something bad was going to happen in my next match. If I could have predicted the notebook-slapping incident, I would have retired after Parnell Park in April. I will never fall out of love with refereeing, but I was certainly sick and tired of the drama and headlines by the summer of 2008. I ask myself: was what happened at Parnell Park and in Killarney my fault? Why do these things not happen to other referees? Have players lost respect for me? I conclude that analysing is paralysing. These incidents are not related to or caused by my presence. I just seem to end up in the wrong places at the wrong times.

MICHAEL MEADE: *'Paddy's whole life has been the GAA. That's the big difference between me and him. He's been involved in the GAA since he was a child, in administration, too, along the way, and he can't walk away from it. And there are two types of referee. There's the ref who wants to go all the way to the top and it's a case of feck everything in his way – but Paddy is in the other category, among the guys that are in it for the goodness of the GAA. That's the way I see it. I've known Paddy a long time, although I'm a good bit younger than him.'*

MARGARET RUSSELL: *'When I looked at the Galvin incident on TV, he behaved just like a little boy. My first reaction, when the media got involved, was that Paddy had done nothing wrong so why was the story about him? He just happened to be there. The guys that came out and said that Paul Galvin was wronged did him no favours at all. He still has a few years left in his career, but he can't go through life like that. He's a teacher, and, in my view, that reaction to a booking set a bad example to children. I'm sure that he does his job very well, but I felt that that was as near as Paddy has ever come to receiving a belt. I've seen Paddy in the middle of melees, but Galvin was blinded by anger, and it looked to me as if he was capable of anything.'*

Friends have asked me why certain incidents during my career have affected me so much. They believe that a referee should be able to brush things off and get on with it. But how do I brush off what happened with Paul Galvin? If that didn't affect me, I wouldn't have feelings. If a work colleague of yours slapped a book out of your hands, wouldn't you feel bad about it?

Pat McEnaney rang me the day after the game in Killarney. He compared the initial jostling incident to what had happened in the National League final between Kerry and Derry, when Colm Cooper made a run, was blocked by an opponent but then booked. Cooper was later shown a second yellow card and sent off. Pat said, 'In cases such as these, I would only book the player who blocked the run.'

My philosophy is quite simple. I referee to the letter of the law; with independent assessors sitting in the stands, there's simply no other way. If I knew that there was nobody in the stand monitoring my performances, I'm sure that I would referee in a different manner. I would certainly let a lot more go. But it seems to me that referees apply the same rules differently, and this is where the thorny issue of consistency raises its head.

If I don't blow when a player picks the ball off the ground or if I neglect to hand out a yellow card for a jersey pull, I am docked marks by a guy watching me from the stands. But that doesn't matter to spectators and reporters, who want to see the game flow. They're not worried about the fouls. They don't want to see the referee constantly blowing and issuing yellow cards. If he does that, he's ruining the game. This is where I am confused.

I got hammered after that Kerry v. Clare game for blowing a lot in the early stages, but I'm damned if I do and damned if I don't. Although it was my final year on the intercounty circuit, I do wonder about the future. What rules are we going to apply going forward? The members of the National Referees Association change every three years, with the GAA president, so it might be difficult to find consistency. It could be an entirely different ball game under the next president.

MICHAEL MEADE: *'I'd love to go into every game and not blow the whistle at all and leave the cards at home. But there's a fella sitting in the stand watching a different game, reading the rule book and watching every lapse that you make on the field. It's a big distraction, and it means there's no such thing as common sense – only the rules.'*

Spectators and pundits alike bemoan the lack of common sense in refereeing, but I can't go on common sense alone if there's someone at the game assessing me. We are told time and time again at refereeing seminars in Athlone: apply the rules, blow the first foul. What's more, we all have different ideas about what common sense means, and that's why there is so much refereeing inconsistency. My view is that if we all referee according to the laws that are laid down, it will lead to greater consistency and players will know exactly where they stand. Problems arise if I let a particular infringement go on a given Sunday and a player is penalised for the same offence by a different referee at another venue. And that is exactly what is happening out there.

In the wake of the game at Fitzgerald Stadium, assessor Eddie Cunningham awarded me 83 marks out of 100, and I was pleased with that because a good score was confirmation that I had performed well. However, under the heading 'Areas of performance in need of improvement', he wrote:

> I felt that Paddy Russell, who is one of our best referees, in this game was not up to his usual high standard and, in trying to leave the game flow by playing advantage, left too many fouls go unpunished. Must be focused from start to finish.

So on the one hand, you have the media saying that I blew too much, and yet Eddie said that I let too many fouls go. Sometimes you just can't win.

For more than six weeks after the match, I felt like Bill Murray in *Groundhog Day*. It seemed that every day in the newspapers, there was some mention of the Galvin incident. The photograph that was used the most was the one in which I'm picking up my notebook and he's looking down on me.

I was out for an evening run on 23 July when a local man pulled up alongside me in his car and told me that the Disputes Resolution Authority had quashed Galvin's six-month suspension, while also stating that the case should be reheard.

The rehearing imposed a three-month suspension, accepted by Kerry, and the conclusion of the entire sorry saga came as a huge relief to me. It was dragged out so much that by the end of it public opinion had turned in Paul Galvin's favour.

There's a lesson to be learned here. It's high time to get rid of the various layers and have just one committee dealing with discipline. Ensure that a barrister or a solicitor sits on this committee, bring in the player, let him have his say and then let the committee members decide. Because of the legal representative on board, any decision would be final.

I had no major feelings one way or the other once the affair was finally put to bed. Once the referee's report goes to Croke Park and is accepted, that should be the end of the story as far as he is concerned. I didn't send off Paul Galvin for knocking the notebook out of my hand, I sent him off for a second yellow-card offence, which was reported by my linesman. I reported precisely what he was sent off for, what he did and what he said to the linesman, but I certainly did not enjoy the weeks that followed.

I received a phone call from the Kerry county board secretary Eamonn O'Sullivan, who apologised on behalf of the board. He said that they had wanted to ring me before this but couldn't while the case remained unresolved. Eamonn told me that he and his fellow board members were sorry and had always had great respect for me as a referee. I appreciated that. Paul Galvin himself never made contact, but I could see why, from his point of view. It could have affected the case if somebody heard that he had been in touch.

I felt sympathy for Paul, just as I do towards every player whom I send off. Nobody wants to do that, but referees are there to do a job. As it turned out, he in fact did become eligible for the All-Ireland final between Kerry and Tyrone on 21 September. But the original incident and what followed afterwards got to me in a big way, and my family were affected too. Some people I met asked, 'Have you a book there? I'll knock it out of your hands.' Childish talk that they thought was funny.

At referee meetings, the consensus was that Galvin should have got 12 months, but that was easy for them to say. They weren't involved in the situation. Every time Paul Galvin's name was mentioned on TV or radio or in the newspapers, mine was too. Nobody wants to be involved in something like that. I'm disappointed that that situation came about, especially in my final year as an intercounty referee. That plus the Parnell Park brawl left two dark clouds hanging over the year.

However, there is some consolation. I have done things wrong from time to time in my career and made wrong decisions on the field of play, but at Parnell Park and in Killarney, I was not to blame. Looking back, Omagh was different, to an extent, because maybe if I had sent off two players early on, it might not have boiled over later. However, I didn't look on it that way at the time.

The biggest thing that disappoints me, and Mike Meade feels the same, is that there were not enough cameras at the ground to show exactly what happened between Galvin and John Hayes. The media might have painted a different picture if that had been the case.

22

....

BOUNDARIES

Professionalism is knowing how to do it,
when to do it, and doing it.

Frank Tyger

My style of refereeing would come across as strict, but the
rules are there to be implemented, and my job is to ensure
that they are. I might not like some of the rules, but they must
be abided by. There are times when I will play advantage if
an attacking player is impeded, but Croke Park encourage us
to whistle for the first foul, and I like to keep a firm check on
proceedings throughout.

SÉAMUS ROCHE (REFEREE): *'Some people have said to me that,
sometimes, I look like I have a sneer on my face when I'm refereeing.
It's not a sneer; it's my way. I try to smile on the field, and I have no
intention of being arrogant. I don't smirk.'*

I don't want to come across as completely rigid, and there are
times when I speak to players on the field. If a player talks to
me, I will of course respond in a friendly, respectful manner. I
have refereed work colleagues, friends and relatives. Even then,
my demeanour will not change. If I have to book a player whom
I know, I will still ask for his name and then address him as if
he's a person I've never met before.

SHANE RUSSELL: *'When Dad refereed an Under-12 challenge game against Emly, he blew me for picking the ball off the ground. They're still talking about that one back in Lattin!'*

I often recall John Moloney telling me about a time when he sent off a player from Arravale Rovers. John was sure that he knew the identity of the player and didn't feel the need to take his name. However, it later transpired that he had in fact sent off the brother of the player in question! It was a good lesson for me. Always ask for the player's name, even if you think you know him.

SÉAMUS ROCHE: *'I spoke to a player once who told me that he always liked how I called him by his name on the field, and his teammates felt the same. The Dublin referee Aodán MacSuibhne is similar. Rather than "Number 4, come here", it's "Tom, come here". Sometimes that can defuse a player if he's wound up. Players have their numbers on the front of their jerseys now, too – a rule introduced in 2008 – so we don't have to spin them around any more to record their number. I thought that was an ignorant thing. I never liked grabbing a player by the shoulder and turning him around to see what number he was wearing.'*

I try to avoid banter with players, and if there is a flashpoint incident, it's not my style to crack a joke in an attempt to defuse the situation. In such circumstances, I must display an air of authority. When a game is going fine, players and spectators will accept a smile, but, to me, refereeing is a serious business and should be treated accordingly. I'm sure a player would take it badly if he was called by his number not long after seeing and hearing a teammate addressed by his name. In any case, I don't believe in that kind of familiarity. I know that some officials like to have a laugh with players and address them by their Christian names, but I believe that you have to know all 30 players on the field to get away with that.

I can't profess to be close friends with any of the GAA's top players, but I believe that as a referee that's the way it should be. In 1991, I travelled to Toronto in Canada with the GAA All Stars and spent time in the company of some of the Cork players of that era, like Shea Fahy, Dave Barry and the county's current senior manager, Conor Counihan. If I met those guys now, I would be delighted to have a chat with them. In 2008, I was linesman for an edition of the TV show *Celebrity Bainisteoir*, filmed in Mayfield, Cork. Dave Barry was on the sideline, acting as advisor to the well-known solicitor Gerald Kean. Dave had moved onto the field of play, and I asked him to move back. He joked, 'Are you still around?' Dave was one of Cork's key players when I refereed the All-Ireland final in 1990, in which the Rebels defeated Meath.

I have been told that I become a different person when I step onto the field, a strict, bossy type of individual. I never set out to be the centre of attention, but I do realise that I am out there to perform a specific role. I develop a kind of tunnel vision when I cross the white line. Once the gear is pulled on and I step out of the dressing-room, I switch into refereeing mode, and I'll take no nonsense. It has also been said to me that after a game I walk off the field with a certain air of assurance, irrespective of what has happened during the game. Believe me, this is far removed from how I sometimes feel inside.

I might come across as authoritative like that, but privately I don't have the greatest confidence in myself, and I can only rest easy when a good assessment arrives. I enjoy games best when I don't have to be fussy because the players are out to play football. The matches I hate are the niggly encounters that descend into dogfights. These matches require a tight rein, but there's nothing spectators dislike more than a referee's constant whistling.

I must admit; refereeing has become an obsession with me. There are people who can walk away from something after a few years and move on to something else. I don't work like that. I've been refereeing since 1976, and it has taken over my life. There are parallels, too, with the day job, which I've also been doing since the late 1970s. Refereeing is a second job to me, without pay.

I am friendly with many of my colleagues on the circuit, particularly guys around my own age. Our careers have been intertwined. Pat McEnaney, John Bannon, Maurice Deegan, Brian Crowe, Mick Monahan, Dickie Murphy, Willie Barrett and Aodán MacSuibhne are great fellows, but I must admit that I'm not really one for picking up the phone and ringing my fellow referees. In fact, one of the rare occasions when I stayed overnight at another referee's house was when my son Shane and I were on our way to Liverpool to watch a Premier League soccer match. However, I do know that some top referees ring each other twice or three times a week. In past years, the Munster referees would have met up for collective training sessions in Charleville or University of Limerick during the winter, but I haven't attended those for some time. I don't think the numbers are as big as they used to be. It takes up too much time to travel to these venues, particularly when I might just be home from a long day at work. I would prefer to run for an hour locally. If I were to travel to Limerick or Charleville, the whole evening would be gone. That's one of the reasons why I purchased a treadmill.

One of the main perks of this second job of mine is being afforded the opportunity to see some of the game's top stars in action at close quarters. For the most part, their attitude on the field of play has been exemplary. However, there have been some notable exceptions.

23

....

FLAK JACKET

Many a man's reputation would not know his character
if they met on the street.

Elbert Hubbard

Sunday, 7 May 2000. There are 13 minutes remaining in the
National Football League final when Meath captain Graham
Geraghty clashes with Derry's Kieran McKeever. Operating as a
linesman for match referee Mick Curley at Croke Park, I have a
clear view of the incident. Geraghty, leading with his elbow, hit
his opponent in the face. Curley was close to the incident but still
decided to consult with me. Geraghty had been booked earlier
in the game, but Mick and I agreed that this was a straight red-
card offence in its own right.

On his way off the field, Geraghty called me a 'fucking wanker'.
After the game, when Mick consulted with his fellow officials,
I told him what Geraghty had said, and this was included in
the Galway man's official match report. Geraghty was punished
both for the challenge on McKeever and for verbal abuse, and
he received an eight-week suspension, which meant that he was
ineligible for the replay against Derry on 20 May.

I was appointed as match referee for the replay, and I feared
that I would receive some terrible abuse from the Meath
supporters in Clones.

SÉAMUS ROCHE: *'There was a First Holy Communion the same day, I think, and Paddy was short of umpires. He rang me to know would some of my umpires go with him. John "Hotpoint" Hayes and I were at one goal, with one of my umpires and one of Paddy's at the other end. We headed off that day, stopping on the side of the road with flasks and sandwiches. It was some trip up to Clones. I'll never forget the booing Paddy got as he went out onto the field. It was from a group of Meath supporters around the tunnel area, because Graham Geraghty was missing for the replay. As that was my first time on the big stage, it felt a little bit intimidating. I'd rather referee a match any day than umpire. Somebody said that I'd signalled a wide ball that looked a debatable one, and the camera zoomed in on me seconds later. Key decisions such as that will be focused in on. But umpiring a match like that was a good experience.'*

Geraghty can be a tough customer to handle on the field of play. Pat McEnaney and I have spoken about him before, and Pat feels he's the type of player who needs to be coaxed through a game.

PAT MCENANEY: *'Graham was hard work for Paddy, but I always felt that with Graham you had to make him feel responsible. I remember Meath were playing a game in Leitrim, and Cormac Murphy was playing corner-back. Murphy was a tough cookie, and I think I had booked him at one stage. I had a word with Geraghty and told him, "The next time Murphy steps out of line, he'll be looking in." Graham went and had a word. I trusted him to do that, and Graham repaid my trust. Sure, if he had an opinion he would let you have it, but I have a lot of respect for Geraghty. He takes a lot of shit, but I have good time for the guy.'*

Armagh's Kieran McGeeney, the current Kildare manager, was another guy who tried to impose his will on me. 'You're riding us . . . you're giving us nothing . . . there are two teams here.' It used to go on and on. In Cork once, during a National League game, McGeeney questioned practically every one of my decisions. Some would argue that that's just good captaincy and leadership, and that if that type of chat works on a referee, a player is onto a winner.

Some teams will try anything to get on the right side of a referee. The former Kerry manager Mick O'Dwyer is a wily old fox. When he was manager of Kildare, he was aware that I was due to take charge of a forthcoming championship match against Dublin. I was on holiday in Tramore with the family when a call came through from Kildare, asking if I could travel to referee a challenge match against Cork in Newbridge. Micko would use any angle possible before a big game. I'm sure he was trying to soften me up by inviting me up to Newbridge, because being asked to referee a challenge game between two counties is quite an honour.

Management teams often launch an in-depth investigation into the man in black when the appointments are finalised for championship matches. They will look for what a referee is picky on and what he lets go, trying to work out what they can get away with during the game. I know for a fact that teams study videotapes of referees, and we are aware of that. They do their homework on the opposition, naturally, but it's become increasingly common to check up on the referee too.

In general, I can't remember having too much trouble with managers and selectors. Colm Coyle, when he was a selector in Meath with Seán Boylan, was giving it loads after a Westmeath–Meath game at Croke Park on one occasion, but I paid no heed. Louth's Eamonn McEneaney complained that I should have added on more time against Wexford in the 2007 championship, but nothing more serious than that springs to mind.

In July 2001, I did think that I was about to cop it big time after Westmeath edged out Louth in an All-Ireland qualifier in Navan. It was a real tit-for-tat encounter, and, as I made my way off the pitch, I spotted Louth manager Paddy Clarke walking towards me. 'I'm in for it now.' Clarke came across, arm outstretched, and we shared a warm handshake. 'Well done, Paddy.' Coming from Paddy Clarke, a man who was never afraid to voice his opinions, that meant an awful lot.

STEVIE O'DONNELL: *'That was a Saturday evening game, live on TV at 6.15 p.m. Paddy asked what time we should leave home for Navan, and I felt that if we got away by two o'clock, we would be fine. We hit the outskirts of Dunshaughlin at a quarter to five, but we had expected to reach Navan, some fifteen miles up the N3, at five o'clock. Sitting in a massive tailback outside Dunshaughlin, I knew that we were in trouble. Paddy was panicking, but I rang the Garda station in Tipperary town and spoke to Seán Moore, uncle of the former Galway hurler Cathal Moore, who does some work for TG4. Seán was not there, but the garda on duty agreed to help us out in our predicament. I asked him if he could ring Navan Garda station to send out a motorbike for us. By now, it was 5.30 p.m., and Paddy was really panicking!'*

I was sure that I would have to ring Croke Park and tell them that I was stuck in traffic and unable to make the game in time. In that case, the assistant referee would have had to step in.

STEVIE O'DONNELL: *'I told Paddy not to panic, and, shortly after, I received a call on the mobile from Navan Garda station.*

'"Where are ye?"

'"Outside Dunshaughlin."

'"Put the flashers on, and when you see the motorbike coming, flag it down."

'With just 35 minutes to throw-in, I'm sure Paddy was sweating buckets. He decided not to put on all of his refereeing gear in the car, but he pulled on the togs and socks. The motorbike arrived, and the garda on board told us to follow him. We ventured up some beautiful mountain roads, but the scenery was the last thing on our minds with an important match looming. We must have arrived at Páirc Tailteann at five past six, ten minutes before the scheduled throw-in time. But luck was on our side. The game was delayed by fifteen minutes. I remember saying to Paddy, "This could be one of your better games because you haven't had time to think about it." If he gets there an hour before, as is the norm, he's nervous. But that time, Paddy had just 20 minutes to get ready. It was one of the best games that I have seen Paddy refereeing, a truly great advertisement for football. Both teams played the game in the correct spirit, and Paddy gave an exhibition of refereeing.'

Dublin's former manager Paul 'Pillar' Caffrey had his critics, but he was always decent to me. He had two opportunities to criticise me: in 2006, after the Battle of Omagh and the All-Ireland semi-final, and again in 2008, following the dust-up against Meath. But Caffrey never rose to the media bait.

STEVIE O'DONNELL: *'The 2006 All-Ireland football semi-final between Dublin and Mayo was a superb game, one of the finest ever seen at Croke Park. When we came out on the pitch before the game, it was 3.15 and Mayo had gone to the Hill 16 end of the stadium to ruffle the Dubs. "There will be trouble here, Paddy."*

'"I wouldn't be surprised."

'The supporters on Hill 16 were going ballistic, but the tactic of warming up at that end, which is traditionally Dublin territory, seemed to work in Mayo's favour. Dublin were ruffled and their game plan was upset from the very start.'

MICHEÁL O'DWYER (MATCH UMPIRE): *'With five minutes to go in that game, the ballboy at the back of the goals was trying to tell me something. I couldn't hear a word that he was saying, such was the noise. I was due to undergo a medical at work later that week. Somehow I passed the hearing test. You have to be at pitch level for a Dublin game to fully experience the wall of noise.'*

I can never understand why players persist in arguing with the referee once a decision is made. I've never once seen a ref change his mind, and most players understand that. They get on with the game because there's no point in arguing. It's wasted energy that would be better used advancing the cause of the team.

There are guys that you know will accept the decision if you give a free against them, for example, but others will crib and complain. It's human nature. Advancing the ball forward 13 metres to penalise a team for showing dissent is a superb rule, because since it's been introduced you will hear the offender's teammates urging him to button it.

In 2002, Kildare and Offaly clashed in an enthralling Leinster championship replay at Nowlan Park in Kilkenny. I sent off Offaly's Seán Grennan for two bookable offences after just 23 minutes, and after Kildare won by a point, Offaly's Roy Malone dished out some unbelievable verbal abuse. I later received a brilliant assessment for my performance. I always found Malone to be a hot-headed character: when things were going well for him, he was fine, but if his team was losing and he wasn't getting on the ball, he turned aggressive and everything was wrong bar himself.

Kerry's Maurice Fitzgerald, the prince of footballers in my eyes, just got on with it. I've encountered so many players of that ilk during my career, guys that caused me no problems whatsoever. Different men have different make-ups, of course. Some are aggressive while others are more gentle in their attitude to the game.

One of the more bizarre episodes of indiscipline I've seen occurred during the 2007 National Football League tie between Clare and Longford. My umpires, Stevie O'Donnell and John O'Brien, were at the end of the ground where Longford's David Barden was attacking before he lost control of the ball. Barden fell to the ground and Clare cleared their lines. Play continued before my attention was drawn to the fact that John had his hand outstretched, signalling for my attention. We were not wired up because it was a league game, and some moments passed before I trotted in to John. My umpires informed me that Barden had had his hand inside the togs of a Clare opponent. I could take no action because Barden had been substituted, but I did include the incident in my official match report, and Barden received a two-month suspension. On appeal, the sentence was halved, and Barden escaped scot free following another appeal.

With players and managers, sometimes you get abuse and sometimes you get kindness, and it's not always easy to predict which is going to be coming your way. In 2008, Wicklow were playing Waterford in a league fixture and my fellow linesman told me that he had taken some awful stick from Kevin O'Brien, Wicklow's manager, on the bench on the far touchline during the first half. After the half-time whistle blew, the linesman said to him, 'Ye can have a go at Paddy Russell now in the second half.' O'Brien responded by saying that I would not be harassed. It struck me then that I had refereed the 1990 All-Ireland club football semi-final in Aughrim. O'Brien was playing with Baltinglass, who defeated Cork side Castlehaven. His team won by two points, and O'Brien must therefore have associated me with his club winning.

SÉAMUS ROCHE: *'I always like to get the ball after a big match, when I can. I have an awful lot of sliotars at home, with the score of the match written on them. After an All-Ireland final, one of the referee's duties is to present the match ball to the captain of the victorious team. At half-time in the 2005 All-Ireland hurling final, I put the ball in my bag, to be sure that I had one for myself. After the game, I went to the Cork dressing-room to present Seán Óg Ó hAilpín with the match ball. In my possession, I had the sliotar I'd finished the game with.*

'"Seán," I said, "I'm supposed to present this to you, as the winning captain."

'"No way, Séamie boy! You keep that, you deserve it."

'It was a lovely gesture on Seán Óg's part.'

If only all players could be like that. But then again, the criticism I have received from TV pundits down through the years cut far deeper than any jibe that's come my way on the field of play.

24

··

TALKING HEADS

It is easier to be critical than correct.

Benjamin Disraeli

Sunday, 5 July 1992. Kildare v. Westmeath in the Leinster senior football championship at O'Connor Park in Tullamore. TV commentator Marty Morrissey described it as 'a game that will have many talking points but will never be remembered as anything like a good match'.

Four gardaí escorted me off the pitch after the game – not a pretty sight. There had been a few flashpoint incidents during the match, but there was no disputing the result: a comfortable 4–11 to 2–5 victory for Mick O'Dwyer's Kildare. I sent off Westmeath's John Cooney for a second bookable offence, disallowed a Martin Lynch goal for Kildare and awarded a second-half penalty to Kildare, which was converted by Jarlath Gilroy.

Morrissey's co-commentator, Colm O'Rourke, the former Meath player, certainly wasn't impressed with my refereeing that afternoon. 'I couldn't see any reason for a free in a situation like that,' he said, after I had called play back before Lynch fisted to the net in the first half. And on the penalty incident, he raged: 'Tom Harris [Kildare] charges straight into Tom Darcy. It should have been a free-out straight away . . . the referee then gives a penalty. An extraordinary decision.'

Those were his opinions, and, as a TV analyst, he is required to express them. I will admit that it was a difficult game to referee, and it wasn't one of my better performances, but an exchange that took place after I had showered left me completely stunned. We togged off, and as my umpires and I were leaving the ground, we passed by O'Rourke, who happened to be standing nearby. He turned and addressed me, saying, 'Paddy, I'm after giving you a right going-over on TV today. I said some things about your refereeing performance, but I don't care. I won't be playing any more.' On reflection, I presume that O'Rourke was implying that there was no way that I could get 'revenge' because he was retiring from intercounty football, but that bitter outburst rendered me speechless. I thought about it later and wondered whether O'Rourke might be holding a grudge against me because of the 1990 All-Ireland senior football final, when he was captain of the Meath team beaten by Cork. Perhaps he was galled because he didn't have the entry 'All-Ireland winning captain' on his CV and decided to take it out on me. To this day, he has levelled criticism at me at almost every opportunity, both in his newspaper column and on TV.

MARGARET RUSSELL: *'It's a pity, in a way, because I held Colm O'Rourke in such high esteem. He suffered with injuries but I used to hope that he would be fit enough to line out in the big games. And I was concerned for him when I saw him running around with his knee heavily bandaged. He was such a workhorse for his team, and I had such admiration for him. But I was so angry when I heard about what he said to Paddy that day.'*

More than a year after that incident, Margaret and I were seated in the Nally Stand for the All-Ireland football final. I'd won tickets for the game through the Friends of Tipperary Football, and the old RTÉ TV gantry was situated in the Nally Stand. As O'Rourke made his way up, our eyes met, and we briefly acknowledged each other before he disappeared into the TV area. I've never met O'Rourke since, although he has often commented on my refereeing down through the years.

At the time, he described the 1995 All-Ireland as one of the worst finals in recent memory. Personally, I thought that some good football was played in that game, with some fantastic points kicked from long distance. On the Charlie Redmond sending-off, O'Rourke said on TV: 'I felt very sorry for Charlie. He has contributed a lot to Dublin over the last ten or twelve years, and in Dublin's greatest moment of triumph, it would have been nice if Charlie was on the pitch. I think Charlie felt that he wasn't sent off, because no player would stay on the pitch if he thought he had been. Obviously Charlie didn't understand what was going on.'

Charlie knew well what was going on. I suppose it would have been good for Charlie and the fans if he had remained on the pitch for Dublin's win, but I had sent the Dublin player to the line for an attempted head-butt, an offence that warrants dismissal.

Of course, O'Rourke's sidekick Pat Spillane had his say on the final, too, but he was more scathing in his criticism of me. He insisted that: 'Charlie is not a dirty player, and he was very unfortunate.' He also uttered those words, damning my performance and telling me to switch off the television, that rocked me to the core and helped to ensure that I was a national laughing stock.

MARGARET RUSSELL: *'Paddy's mother and father were so hurt in 1995. Paddy's mother doesn't listen to Pat Spillane any more, because what he said about Paddy hurt her so much. The cheek of him, telling Paddy to turn off the television. I remember the following December Spillane was handing out his "Christmas presents" in his newspaper column. He wrote that he wanted a big teddy bear sent to Paddy for comfort. "Good God Almighty," I thought to myself, "does Pat Spillane realise that people have feelings?"'*

Margaret was also annoyed by a comment from broadcaster Jimmy Magee, who suggested that Charlie Redmond's CV should have been taken into consideration before I sent him off.

MARGARET RUSSELL: *'If someone goes out tonight and kills someone else in town, and they have been very good up to that, do you take that into consideration then? A referee is not going to take a player's previous record into consideration if he commits a serious offence. He's not going to think, "Ah, no, sure he never did anything before. I think I'll let him off on this one."'*

TOM-JOE O'BRIEN: *'I don't think TV panellists give referees a fair deal any more. There isn't a player out there who doesn't make a mistake on the field of play, but if a referee makes one, he's picked on. It seems now that everybody is waiting to have a go at the referee. There's a lack of respect. Referees could probably accept that more easily if they were being paid.'*

In fairness, there was one time when O'Rourke spoke about me in complimentary fashion. It was in 2005, after I had refereed the classic Tyrone v. Armagh All-Ireland semi-final. Brian Crowe had been appointed for the final between Kerry and Tyrone, and, writing in his Sunday newspaper column, O'Rourke expressed his hope that Crowe would referee the big game in a similar manner. I took that as a real compliment because he was so often harsh in his judgements of me.

People tend to take what pundits say as gospel, but at the end of the day, an opinion is just an opinion. I remember what O'Rourke said about Brian Dooher in 2003, and those words certainly came back to haunt him. O'Rourke remarked that Dooher was one of the weak links in the Tyrone team and that he would 'eat his hat' if Tyrone won the All-Ireland with Dooher in the team. Dooher's response was typically modest. He stated that O'Rourke was entitled to his opinion but that he only cared about what Tyrone's manager, Mickey Harte, thought. Tyrone finished the 2003 season as All-Ireland champions, and any time Brian Dooher was not playing, I always felt that Tyrone were a much weaker team.

Many people will also remember the time when Spillane slated Kildare players Brian Murphy and Karl O'Dwyer.

SYL MERRINS (KILDARE COUNTY BOARD CHAIRMAN): *'What happened was, we were playing Dublin in the 2000 Leinster final, and the match was going out live on RTÉ. The two lads Spillane had a pop at were Brian Murphy from Cork and Karl O'Dwyer from Kerry. At half-time, we were losing by five points and getting well beaten. During his half-time analysis, Spillane more or less said that Karl and Brian wouldn't get on the junior teams in their native counties. Within ninety seconds of the restart, Brian had scored one goal and set up another. Dublin kicked just a point in the second half. I was county board PRO at the time, and Kildare snubbed RTÉ for 24 hours. It was embarrassing for Spillane. He had been so critical of the lads and it all blew up in his face within 90 seconds. But it's an amateur game at the end of the day, and things like that do affect players and their families. Karl and Brian were two of the most down-to-earth lads. But within 90 seconds, Spillane had his answer.'*

It does amuse me when Spillane comments about players playacting or making a meal out of a challenge from an opponent. In the 1980 All-Ireland final against Roscommon, he went down as if he'd been killed. He lay on the ground for nearly two minutes, but within seconds of getting up he was back to full health. I have seen the footage on TG4 a few times, and Micheál O'Hehir questions whether or not Spillane is injured as he lies on the ground, saying, 'The trouble with Pat is that Pat has been known to play it a little bit when he gets a knock, and it could be the case of the boy and the wolf again . . . Gerry Fitzmaurice is walking by and shaking his head, as much as to say, "Whatever I did there, it wasn't that bad."' Spillane gathered possession of the ball moments after his miraculous recovery and O'Hehir quipped, 'And there's Pat Spillane – was he really badly hurt or is he in line for an Oscar?'

Pundits are well paid to criticise players and referees, ordinary working-class fellas who have to get up for work the next morning. If I were being paid to referee a match, I would accept that I was fair game for whatever criticism came my way, but I'm not a professional. I remember, after I refereed Tyrone v. Armagh in 2005, a thriller at Croke Park in front of over 82,000 spectators, in work at eight o'clock the next morning, a colleague said to me, 'Imagine, you were in front of a full house at Croke Park yesterday, and here you are in here today.' That really stuck with me.

In fairness to the powers that be at Croke Park, they never seemed to take the opinion of the media on board, and continued to give me top games to referee even after I'd come in for a lot of stick. I've often felt that the level of criticism dished out to amateurs on national television and in the papers is wrong. I can move on from it now, though. My time has come and gone. Sadly for them, it's time for other people to suffer at the hands of the pundits.

25

··

LEST WE FORGET

And in the end, it's not the years in your life that count.
It's the life in your years.

Abraham Lincoln

It's one of the biggest regrets I have about my career. If I could
just turn back the clock, back to the evening when Sammy Ryan
passed away in Golden refereeing an Under-16 game between
Cashel and Aherlow. It still plays on my mind: would Sammy
still be alive had I refereed that game?

It should have been me in charge but I attended a funeral in
Emly that same evening. Jimmy English, an uncle of the great
Nicky English, had been a staunch club man for many years, and
his removal to the local church clashed with the Under-16 game.
I rang Sammy, informed him that I couldn't fulfil the fixture
and asked if he would fill in. 'Ah, I wouldn't be good enough!'
Sammy replied. That was his style – modest, self-deprecating
humour. Of course, he agreed to fill the gap.

On my way home from Jimmy's funeral, I stopped into Seán
Treacy Park in Tipperary town where a local game was in
progress. Teresa Ring, wife of West board secretary Jerry, came
over to speak with me. Just moments after receiving a shocking
phone call, Teresa was shaken. Sammy had had a heart attack
and passed away at half-time in Golden.

I was stunned. Sammy had been an umpire and linesman with me on many occasions. A thoroughly obliging fellow, he also drove the minibus we hired for trips to Fitzgerald Stadium in Killarney.

It was June 1994. I had refereed the drawn Leinster championship game between Dublin and Kildare on the previous Saturday, and Sammy had been one of my umpires at Croke Park. His burial was scheduled for the following Sunday, the same day as Cork v. Kerry in the Munster senior football championship at Páirc Uí Chaoimh. I was shattered emotionally and on the brink of pulling out of the Cork fixture until I consulted with Sammy's brother Paddy, who urged me to go.

My mind was at home during the match, but Sammy was with us in spirit on Leeside. I felt guilty, thinking that if I had refereed the game in Golden, he might not have died. At the morgue in Cashel, I had apologised to Sammy's daughter Catriona for asking him to do the game. Her mother had died a short time before, and now her father had passed away while obliging me. At the time, I felt truly awful.

That wasn't the only time that an acquaintance of mine had died in action. Timmy Hennessy, another former umpire and linesman, was thrilled by his appointment to take charge of the 1988 West senior football final between Golden-Kilfeacle and Galtee Rovers. The game was fixed for a Saturday night in Emly, and Timmy was buzzing. He arrived at my house to borrow a referee's jersey, which were scarce enough at the time, before travelling on to the Emly field. He was enjoying a fine game, up and down the field, before he collapsed and died instantly.

Ailbe Burke is another umpire whom I remember with great fondness. A match in Wicklow was Ailbe's last road trip before he lost a brave fight with cancer. Ailbe enjoyed the days out and stopping along the way for a sandwich, a biscuit and a cup of tea. Tipperary were playing Kerry at the Clonmel Sportsfield in May 1992, and I was ready to go to the game when the call came through that Ailbe's condition had deteriorated rapidly. I called to the house and stayed for a while. Ailbe passed away that night. He was a guy who would always speak his mind, and right from the start of my refereeing career, he had been with me. Weekends or weeknights – it didn't matter to Ailbe. He was always available. He was just 47 when he passed away.

There were others we lost along the way. Connie Lorigan and James O'Donoghue were so obliging. When Emly won the West SF championship in 1987, I marked 'Jayo'. You could ring him at the last minute and he would travel to a game. He died of cancer at just 35 years of age. Seán O'Brien, who allowed his four sons to skip milking to come umpiring with me in the early days, died young, too.

John Moloney was, without question, the single biggest influence on my refereeing career. I've never cried as much in my entire life as I did at his funeral in October 1996. He was such a decent fellow, and he reached unparalleled heights in his refereeing career.

MARGARET RUSSELL: *'Mick Maguire rang me to break the news. I just couldn't believe it, and when I was ringing Paddy to tell him, it just didn't seem real. It was almost like being in a dream. Paddy doesn't show much outward emotion, but it was obvious how bad he was feeling on the day that John was buried. He was suffering the huge pain of loss, even though he and John didn't live in each other's pockets.'*

Less than a week after John was buried, I was the referee for Galtee Rovers against Moyle Rovers in the county senior football semi-final. It was early in the game when John's son Cathal, the Galtee Rovers goalkeeper, hauled down one of the Moyle Rovers attackers. I had no choice but to award a penalty. It was a bookable offence, too, but I was torn on that one. Cathal placed his hand on my shoulder. He had no problem with the yellow card, but I hated waving it in his direction. It was one game I wished I wasn't refereeing.

John had always been there for me. He gave me the confidence to keep going, especially after the fallout from the 1995 final. He enjoyed a magnificent career but always insisted that a Cork

v. Kerry Munster championship game surpassed even an All-Ireland final for sheer sense of occasion. And what's more, he thought of it as a greater privilege to take charge of the almost annual Munster shoot-out between the ancient rivals. John took charge of eight Cork–Kerry Munster finals.

Whenever Cork and Kerry met before the introduction of the 'back door' in the championship, they were real do-or-die clashes, season-defining encounters in which the winners were virtually guaranteed a spot in the All-Ireland semi-finals while the losers retreated home with their tails firmly between their legs. There have been so many tales told down through the years from Cork v. Kerry matches. It is such an intense rivalry, just like Dublin–Meath and Tyrone–Armagh. It didn't matter to me if the venue was Páirc Uí Chaoimh in Cork or Killarney's Fitzgerald Stadium, the buzz was always the same.

My debut in the Munster championship was an Under-21 semi-final in 1983 – Cork v. Waterford in Dungarvan – and I was also appointed for the final of that year's competition, when Kerry beat Cork in Castleisland. Three years later, I refereed the Cork v. Kerry Munster minor final, and again in 1987, when a replay was needed to separate the two teams. Cork defeated Kerry on a 0–12 to 1–8 scoreline, but Mark Woods, writing in the *Examiner*, described my decision to send off Cork centre-back Stephen O'Brien as 'disgraceful'. I disagreed. O'Brien met his opponent full on in a dangerous frontal challenge.

I refereed four Munster senior football finals, and the first one of those, in 1989, pitted Cork and Kerry against one another. Pat Lane, Ray Moloney and John Moloney had dominated the Munster refereeing landscape prior to my arrival on the scene, but for a number of years it seemed that nobody else but I refereed Cork v. Kerry. Munster council officials were obviously satisfied that I could handle myself in that situation, and as a referee that was where I wanted to be: a massive game in a pressure-cooker environment.

In the 1991 semi-final, Kerry beat Cork, who were All-Ireland champions the previous year, in a classic game. I also took charge of the final, in which Kerry narrowly defeated Limerick in Killarney. That was Pat Spillane's final year as an intercounty player, and he captured his 11th Munster senior championship medal. I found him to be a moaner on the field, constantly looking for decisions from referees.

In many ways, the 1992 Munster final was an accident waiting to happen for the Kerry senior footballers, and Clare pulled off a sensational Munster final victory at the Gaelic Grounds. That was Jack O'Shea's final game as a Kerry player, and I consider it an honour to have refereed it, even though the great midfielder himself would have considered it an inglorious end. I had massive respect for O'Shea as a footballer. In 1998, incidentally, I was the man in the middle for Brian Corcoran's final game as a Cork senior footballer before he decided to concentrate on hurling only. In his autobiography, Corcoran wrote about how annoyed he was with himself when I penalised him for a 'double bounce' of the ball. It was an elementary mistake, but Brian admitted himself that he was not fully tuned in for the game.

In the 1994 Munster final, a row broke out between Cork manager Billy Morgan and Kerry selector Johnny Mulvihill. One of the players on the field told me to try to pull them apart, but I took one glance at the sideline and kept walking!

I sometimes regret that I never got to referee Kerry in an All-Ireland final. It would have been wonderful to have been able to take charge of the 2007 match, when Kerry and Cork met in the big game. However, it was not to be, and, on reflection, I'm more than happy with what I got.

26

....

KICK THE HABIT

The best way to stop smoking is to just stop –
no ifs, ands or butts.

Edith Zittler

My strange love affair with cigarettes ended with the dawn
of the new millennium. It began many years ago in the
typical way – a crafty teenage drag with a few friends. Step
forward Dermot Mulhall of the Golden Thatch in Emly, Pascal
Dawson and Seánie Lonergan! I used to pal around with those
guys at school, and the place to indulge in our early addiction
was the outside toilet of the local church. I had a keen interest
in football, but smoking was very much part of the social fabric
in the mid-1970s, especially when we went dancing in Dundrum
or Dromkeen. When Lattin-Emly won the 1975 county minor
football title, I was smoking regularly, and my refereeing career
began in 1976 under the influence of the weed. I could get away
with it to a certain extent in those days, but, in time, my chest
began to affect me, and I suffered from breathlessness during
games.

My habit developed a bizarre pattern. Let me explain: if I was
playing in a game at the weekend, I would give up the smokes
from Thursday until Saturday, but after the game, it was back
on the cigs again. This trend must have continued for seven or

eight years, but what followed when I joined the intercounty refereeing ranks really took the biscuit. Each December, all bets were off, from the 1st of the month right through to the 31st. But from 1 January, I was a non-smoker again until the moment that the November page was next ripped from the calendar. That first day off the cigarettes was hell, but as with any addiction, it was a case of taking one day at a time until the cravings subsided and finally died. Margaret would often comment that I was grouchy giving up the cigarettes, and I'm sure that any ex-smokers reading this can identify. How crazy was it, then, to go back on them each December?

At the height of my smoking, I could go through 30 Major a day. There was time off work over Christmas, friends called for card games, and we travelled all over the county for card nights. Slugging tea and smoking cigarettes in the halls was the order of the day. I smoked a lot at night-time. During the day, at work, I wouldn't smoke as much, but if we went to a dance, it was open season. I smoked for 25 years, and I have to admit that if I hadn't been so active in the GAA and therefore so conscious of my fitness, I would still be smoking.

Margaret used to smoke, too, but 19 years ago she gave them up for Lent along with a work colleague, Michael Fitzpatrick, and the two of them never looked back. When I was still puffing away, she didn't like the smell of smoke in the house. I can understand now how she felt, because the smell clings to everything.

Plenty of my umpires down through the years smoked as well, and the morning after a game, the ashtray in the car would be overflowing with butts and ash, and the smell of stale smoke would be hanging in the air. I still like the smell of fresh cigarette smoke, but that pungent, stale aroma really turns me off.

I recount my history with cigarettes because I believe that I would not have remained at the top for so long had I continued smoking. However, one or two guys on the circuit do enjoy the occasional cigarette. Pat McEnaney from Monaghan springs to mind, as well as Cavan's Joe McQuillan, a younger referee who smokes a greater amount.

PAT MCENANEY: '*I like to smoke a fag before a high-profile match. And while I'm bollock naked in the dressing-room after the game before I get into the shower, I have to have one. I must be left on my own to calm down with a ciggie. I still smoke the odd one, and if McQuillan was with me, I'd never hesitate. I love taking a fag off a Cavan man! Joe would be a heavy enough smoker, but he remains incredibly fit. The hoor is not carrying an ounce of weight!*'

I've always maintained a pretty high level of fitness, partly because I played football with Emly until I was 47 years of age. Of course, there is a moment in every player's career when he finally realises that it might be time to bow out. For me, that came against Aherlow in a junior football tie when Pat Burke met me with one hell of a hit into the chest! One of our guys on the sideline, John Leahy, was urged to run in with some water for me as I lay spreadeagled on the ground, badly in need of a drop. 'I'm not going in; I have my good shoes on!' John replied. It was late in the year, the grass was long and wet and John had no intention of getting his shoes ruined! Looking back, it's one of those funny memories, but I wasn't feeling too hot at the time, I can assure you. I thought that I was pretty fit from refereeing, but it's a different kind of fitness you develop. My legs would turn to jelly if I took a big hit from an opponent, but on the flipside I felt like I could run forever. Huge aerobic fitness levels are required for refereeing, to enable a ref to go hard for the entire game.

In 2008, for the first time, the GAA devised its very own fitness examination, having worked in other years with various FIFA versions. The National Referees Association worked in tandem with Professor Niall Moyna and former Dublin football manager Mickey Whelan at Dublin City University to devise a test specifically tailored for GAA referees. We've come a long way from an afternoon in Mallow many years ago when a fitness test was sprung on us out of the blue with a written assessment afterwards. Fifty questions, two points for each right answer. A 90 per cent score was required to pass.

P.J. MCGRATH: '*At the start of 2008, we examined referees on their personal fitness and then gave them a programme to follow for their own benefit. The referees received another assessment rating a couple of months later, and any guy who harboured hopes of progressing during the year should have at least maintained or preferably raised his standards. The new test is relevant to the game they are now refereeing, and our refs got something they never had before – a totally free medical examination. It's costing the GAA a lot of money, but it's very well spent. There's also a written exam that referees must pass, which was introduced less than ten years ago. The pass rate is 94 out of 100. All of the referees officiating in the All-Ireland championships are in the high 90s.*'

I always aim to reach peak fitness in May, just in time for the championship season, but, just like the leading intercounty players, we need to be at a pretty decent standard when the National Leagues begin in February.

This year, we underwent unprecedented health checks, overseen by Dublin City University's School of Health and Human Performance. The data collected during these screenings is then used to develop fitness norms for GAA referees. All grade 3.2 referees, the leading intercounty guys, are expected to have a maximal aerobic power of at least 50. I measured 42.8 on the test, but I had plenty of time to get up to speed. The recommended body fat measurement is 15 to 20 per cent, and I did well on this score, with 18 per cent recorded. Our body composition was examined under the headings of height (1.72 metres in my case), weight (79.6 kg), body mass index (26.9) and body fat (18.1 per cent). Flexibility, power and speed levels were also recorded as part of a pretty rigorous NCT for referees! In 2007, GAA President Nickey Brennan stated his desire to bring referees to higher levels of fitness, and a series of sprints and treadmill exercises certainly pushed us to our limits.

Margaret joked that she stopped paying life insurance when

she read the report sheet, and I have to admit that I was pleased with my results. In 2008, I felt fitter than ever, and at Parnell Park in April my breathing was spot on. Sometimes you might end up chasing the game, but I was right up with the play. My high levels of fitness came as a pleasant surprise, because I think I put in a lot more work in previous years.

Refereeing at intercounty level now places huge physical and psychological demands on the match ref. The intensity of the game at this level is ever increasing because of the emphasis that is now placed on players becoming fitter and faster. This in turn requires referees to work harder on their fitness to enable them to keep up with the play without getting tired out. Research has shown that referees can optimise their performance levels by undertaking a training programme that reflects the demands of the game. The best training is described as high-intensity intermittent (stop–start) training interspersed with multiple changes in direction. As well as staving off fatigue, this type of training should also help the referee to maintain psychological focus and engage in effective decision-making.

The Munster referees completed an outdoor or 'field-based' fitness assessment at Limerick Institute of Technology on 29 March 2008. This also differed from previous years, as the usual punishing 3,200-metre run was dispensed with in favour of a sprint-based examination. The battery of tests for the assessment, which took place on the Institute's running track, was as follows: height and weight, blood pressure, skin folds, 5-metre/20-metre sprint tests and the 'yo-yo' intermittent recovery test, similar to a 'bleep test'. Since the Dublin tests, my weight had dropped by over 4 kg from 79.6 kg to 75 kg, along with my body-fat percentage, from just over 18 per cent to 16 per cent, below the referee average of 23 per cent.

The tough yo-yo test assesses an individual's ability to perform bouts of high-intensity aerobic work. We began at the starting line of a grid and covered a straight-line distance of 40 metres in the form of two 20-metre shuttle runs in a specific period of time. Once this was completed, a recovery time of 10 seconds was allowed before the next set of 20-metre shuttle runs. The time in which the individual has to complete the 40-metre distance decreases as the test progresses, but the rest period remains at 10 seconds throughout. This is designed to give a realistic idea of a ref's match fitness.

I measured up quite well on the field tests. For the 5-metre sprint, 1.06 seconds is considered 'very good', but I managed it in 1.03 seconds. My time of 3.30 seconds for 20 metres is considered 'average', while I would have come in between 'poor' and 'fair' for the yo-yo test. Still, I'm not exactly a spring chicken any more.

KARL COGAN (DUBLIN CITY UNIVERSITY): *'Paddy's yo-yo test result in March was 800 metres, but in June he had improved to 960 metres. That's pretty good and in line with the intercounty referee average. FIFA international soccer referees would score anywhere between 1,300 and 1,800 metres, which means the GAA refs are still a bit off, but they are now averaging beyond 1,000. Players will obviously surpass referee averages. For example, a top club team we measured during 2008 averaged 1,600 metres.'*

The field tests this year were gruelling but nonetheless far preferable to the old 3,200-metre run. Still, I was pleasantly surprised when I dug out some old results from previous years. In 1998, I completed 3,200m in 14 minutes and 50 seconds, but I ran the distance 9 seconds quicker in 2002. It seems that you can teach some old dogs new tricks!

Back then, a 45-metre forward sprint, a 45-metre backward sprint and a bleep test completed the examination. It was difficult, and I remember our second test of the year in Ballymahon in 2006, on a desperately warm day. Two referees pulled up injured and were unable to finish. You got a second chance if that happened, but if you failed again, you could kiss goodbye to the championship.

The country's top players spend long hours working on their bodies and minds, but they're not alone. Our first seminar of the year, which took place in January, was a very interesting evening. A leading sports psychologist, Canice Kennedy, warned that we are being pushed to our mental limits by the almost professional demands associated with modern-day Gaelic games.

CANICE KENNEDY: *'There's no doubting that the standard expected of referees has increased, and it's mainly due to the media spotlight. Some referees struggle when they make the huge leap from local club matches to the goldfish bowl of the country's top stadiums to take charge of glamour championship matches. Many of the referees are covering club games in front of small numbers, and then they are thrust into the national limelight, perhaps in front of 60,000 or 70,000 people at Croke Park. That puts mental pressure on them that they are not normally used to, and they need strategies to prepare for that challenging environment. Of course, the rules of the games are the same, but the pressures are much greater. If a referee makes a mistake, it will be highlighted and they will be criticised on* The Sunday Game, *and they need to have techniques in place to ensure that this criticism does not affect them. The same goes for players, in many ways. I find the referees to be an extremely professional group of people. The sad thing is that a referee could give an excellent performance and make 49 good calls, but the 50th might be an error that turns the game. There is huge pressure associated with that.'*

After the tests, we faced an anxious wait to discover who would be officiating during the 2008 championships. Separate hurling and football panels were drawn up based on performances during the National Leagues. Just like players up and down the country, we were fighting for our championship lives. In January and April, all referees on the national panel attended the Athlone seminars, but just a chosen few were invited to attend on 13 May. If you got the call, you were on the championship panel. Thankfully, I was there.

FATHER SÉAMUS GARDINER (NATIONAL REFEREES ASSOCIATION): *'The top grade of referee in the country is classed as 3.2, and for the early seminars in the year they were joined by those ranked in the 3.1 bracket. Some felt that the seminars were too big, so from May it was just the championship referees who were invited to attend.'*

The number of 3.2 referees was itself reduced in 2008. I thought that made sense. Before, as was the case with me in 2007, a referee might only get the call once during the championship. I remember a few years ago that Longford's John Bannon refereed a first-round championship match but didn't get another game until Cork met Kerry in the All-Ireland semi-final. John didn't think that he was going to get another game, and when the big one arrived, he didn't feel as ready as he would have liked to have been. A ref needs something to keep him going, the prospect of another game a few weeks down the road. Three is my ideal number of championship games in a season, but if you have a massive pool of referees, not everybody can be accommodated.

Refereeing is serious business these days, and we cover so much ground. I watch my soccer counterparts on TV, and I believe they have an easier job. A soccer pitch is shorter, and it's easier for them to spot a foul. They are also full-time professionals. They really are under intense scrutiny, and I can certainly relate to that.

I found it increasingly difficult to get fit as the years went by, but I've always managed to get up to speed in time for the championship. Religiously, I began training on 1 January, working away on the treadmill until the bright evenings arrived. Fifteen minutes walking, fifteen minutes running, back to walking and then running again. A six-mile run takes me from my house into Tipperary town and back out again, and I would complete that three nights a week, which is pretty good. Sure, it was tough going, but if I didn't do the training, I could forget about refereeing. For years, I trained every single evening for an hour at a time, but this year I went at it only every second night.

I have always been quite fortunate with my fitness, but a knee injury did threaten my participation in the 2007 championship, which was short-lived in any case. I refereed a National Football League tie between Kerry and Cork in Tralee on 10 February, a high-intensity game under lights on a Saturday evening. I was fine during the game and experienced no discomfort whatsoever, but when I arrived home, I was barely able to walk. The next day, I was scheduled to referee the hosts Ardfinnan against Cahir at noon, but it was too late by then to find a replacement, and, after receiving a rub from the Ardfinnan physiotherapist, I went ahead. I should never have refereed that game. I went for several sessions with Aherlow-based physio John Ryan after that.

Apart from a painful run-in with Deep Heat rub, applied too liberally around the groin area before a match with Emly many years ago, I've generally been quite lucky in terms of injuries during my playing career. However, I have been operating with a collapsed disc in my back since 1985. I had just refereed a game between Golden-Kilfeacle and Arravale Rovers when my back seemed to collapse, leaving my body slumped to the right. The problem recurred many times before I finally visited a specialist in the Mater Hospital, who performed a CAT scan. I was told that if it happened again, the disc would have to be removed, but it never came to that. I visited a chiropractor in Kilworth for some corrective work, and running and walking also strengthened my back considerably. Thankfully, I have had no major problems since the early 1990s.

It's not just players who make the sacrifices and dream about the big days out at Croke Park. It bugs me when people complain that a wrong decision from a referee costs players who have been training three or four nights a week for six months. We're not just sitting at home by the fire waiting for a phone call or a letter to tell us that we're refereeing a big championship game. Referees put in huge efforts too, and it is never our intention to ruin a player's season with our decisions.

27

MEN IN WHITE COATS

Nobody made a greater mistake than he who did
nothing because he could only do a little.

Edmund Burke

Umpires. The four men in the white coats. Two situated at
each end of the field, one behind each goalpost. It might
appear that they don't do an awful lot, but a referee needs four
guys whom he can trust, because a wrong call can lead to a
whole lot of trouble.

The main duties of an umpire are to signal for a 45-metre free
in football or a 65-metre free in hurling to the attacking team if
the ball is diverted wide by the defending team; he also indicates
a score by raising a green flag for a goal and a white flag for a
point; and he is required to indicate a decision to disallow a score
by crossing the flags, while a wide ball is signalled by crossing
both arms above the head.

It sounds simple enough, but a referee can live or die by the
decisions of his umpires. And there have been many occasions
when the men in white have got it wrong.

In May 2004, Westmeath defeated Offaly by just a single point,
0–11 to 0–10, in a Leinster SFC tie at Croke Park. Controversy
reigned afterwards when video evidence clearly showed that a
shot taken by Westmeath's Brian Morley in the 21st minute was

wide of the post. A point had been awarded, and Offaly, naturally enough, were hugely aggrieved by the decision.

STEVIE O'DONNELL (MATCH UMPIRE): '*Pádraic Kelly was in goal for Offaly, and he roared at me that the ball was a mile wide. But it was Richard O'Connor's call. The ball came in at a low trajectory. I could have taken a step back to help Richard, but it fizzed across the square. I couldn't make the call because I would have had to be situated at the opposite post for a clear view. Richard was put off because the Offaly full-back rushed in on top of him and waved his hands wide, trying to influence his decision. I felt that the ball had gone over Richard's head at that side and could not have gone over the bar. Paddy mentioned the incident later and asked if the ball had gone wide or over the bar. I told him that I felt it was wide, and it was proven on TV later that it was indeed, by two or three feet. I waved the white flag to indicate a point, but I was hesitant. Richie pointed to me to put it up. I crossed my hands beneath my knees to indicate to Richie that I felt the ball was wide, but he was adamant. I had to take his word for it. The crowd went ballistic.*'

I never knew how big a deal this was until I picked up the newspapers the next morning. I knew that Stevie was troubled by that decision, but because it was Richard's call, he didn't want to bring it up in the car on the way home. It was one of those things, human error, and we have all been guilty of that in our lives. Richard didn't do many more games with me, but it wasn't as a direct result of that call at Croke Park. He had enough on his plate, as he was making a name for himself as a referee on the local club circuit and in ladies' football.

STEVIE O'DONNELL: '*I think a lot about umpiring, and some of them out there are not fit to do the job, both mentally and physically. I'm not saying for one minute that I'm a great umpire, but I do work on it, and if I make a mistake today, I hope I won't make the same mistake tomorrow. I've often seen umpires awarding a point when the ball is blatantly wide. Why? Because they are badly positioned, standing right beside the upright. You move back two yards if the ball is coming in from the opposite angle, but some umpires are not fit enough to do that. The white coats don't even fit some of them. These guys should not be umpiring at intercounty level, because the stakes are too high. The players are putting in a phenomenal effort. Umpires are not vetted or tested in any way.'*

MICHEÁL O'DWYER: *'There are seminars for umpires, but I haven't been to one for the last couple of years because other things have clashed. But from what I heard, I was better off not going anyway, because the umpires weren't allowed to ask questions. It seems to me that it was a case of tell us what to do and finish up early.*

STEVIE O'DONNELL: *'The onus is on a referee to supply the umpires, and therefore he ultimately carries the can for any wrong decisions. But the championship is serious business, and a referee needs his trusted four, not guys who are not up to it any more. I've often seen referees staying loyal for years to a fella who might be over the hill, a guy who's related to him in some way or is a family friend. It's difficult for a referee to give somebody the flick, but he must be strong enough to stand up and take action when necessary.'*

During the 1998 Munster minor final between Limerick and Kerry in Thurles, Limerick scored a perfectly legitimate goal, but my umpires ruled that the ball did not go into the net. Two of the umpires were situated at the Town End of Semple Stadium and claimed that the ball hit the crossbar and rebounded back into play.

Limerick's county board secretary quizzed me about the incident, and he was insistent that the ball had hit the stanchion. Video evidence proved conclusive. TV footage showed that the ball had cannoned off the back stanchion and come out again. Goal. Limerick had been denied a perfectly good goal, and, to rub salt into their wounds, Kerry ran out 2–11 to 0–8 winners.

I am very happy with my present umpires. However, there are some out there not doing their job properly. You'll sometimes see one umpire waving a ball over the bar while the other waves it wide. And when an umpire makes a mistake, it's Paddy Russell, Pat McEnaney or John Bannon who must face the music.

The issues have been discussed at various seminars in Athlone. You sometimes have an umpire or linesman, for example, who is over-eager and calling the referee in for even the most innocuous of incidents. They are not supposed to do that. Umpires have limited powers in the vast majority of cases. When there is a break in play, an umpire can alert a referee to an off-the-ball incident, but he cannot signal for a foul during open play, even if, for example, he sees a player touching the ball on the ground and the referee is blind-sided. A rule change at Congress would be required to give more power to umpires.

During the McGrath Cup final in 2008, I awarded a free to Limerick to a player who had handled the ball on the ground before he was fouled. The Clare players argued, but I couldn't blow for the first foul because I didn't see it. Although Stevie and John O'Brien did see what happened, my view was obstructed by a group of players.

The good umpires are the ones who will tell a referee straight if he is performing below par. Stevie is particularly good in this regard. Also, before matches, he plots the route to a particular venue, and more often than not he does the majority of the driving on match day.

I find that driving to Dublin can be a nightmare. Not making the game on time is a constant worry with traffic congestion. Travelling by train removes a lot of hassle. We went by train to the All-Ireland semi-final between Armagh and Tyrone in 2005, and it was so relaxing. There was no pressure. Jump on the train at Limerick Junction, get off at Heuston Station and then grab the LUAS or a taxi to Croke Park. A relaxed frame of mind will help a referee on the field of play.

Having umpires whom I can rely on is a huge advantage, and Stevie is good at noting whether or not a guy operating locally at club level will cut the mustard in the white coat. In the heat of championship action, I need guys who are on the ball and tuned in to what's happening on the field of play. My umpires generally are not drinkers; I can count on one hand the guys who have worked with me who took a drink. And if they did, they would never venture out the night before a match.

The men working with me take pride in what they do, and working at important league and championship games is a big thing for them. Micheál O'Dwyer is more nervous than me going out on the field! Everything has to be perfect with Micheál, who is an invaluable help to me. He records the times the respective teams arrive out on the field, which must be included in my official match report, and he will keep an eye on players booked and noted. Micheál also notes the times the teams reappear after half-time (counties are fined if they are late) and what time the game finishes. He is meticulous.

I would argue that umpires are every bit as important as linesmen now.

STEVIE O'DONNELL: '*As umpires, we don't have enough powers. If a ball goes wide, we wave our hands. If there's a 45, we give a 45, or a 65 in hurling. If there's an off-the-ball incident, we are allowed to draw the referee's attention to it. We keep a check on time for the referee and we also keep a check on the score. What I often see in the game is a defender standing behind an attacker and digging the toe of his boot inside his opponent's boot, to agitate him. If the attacker retaliutes, the defender will go down in a heap in an attempt to get the attacker booked or sent off. Another popular one is holding an opponent's jersey. The attacker goes to run but he can't because he's being held back. Paddy might not see it because he doesn't have the same view that we have, but still we can't call a free. If a player is fouled and the ref can't see it, the onus should be on the official with the best possible view. It's high time the authorities at Croke Park gave umpires more authority on outfield decisions. That's how you help referees, and that's how referees will improve. What are we there for otherwise? Just to wave the flag – and that's no good to us.*'

Perhaps it is time for an overhaul in umpiring. The Mayo football manager John O'Mahony advocated this as far back as 2004, but in the GAA the wheels turn slowly. A referee needs the best type of support from all officials, and umpiring needs to be made a higher priority across the country. I'm just lucky to have such good guys fighting my corner.

28

....

TIME FOR CHANGE

Change the changeable, accept the unchangeable, and
remove yourself from the unacceptable.

Denis Waitley

I am GAA president for a day. I cast my eye over the Gaelic
football landscape and formulate my blueprint for change.
There are three key points:

* Introduce a second referee, who will be seated in the stand
  and wired up to the man on the field;
* Bring back the 'sin-bin' rule, whereby players are ordered off
  for ten-minute periods for bookable offences;
* Take timekeeping out of the referee's hands.

I am not in favour of having two referees on the field of play,
but it is time for the GAA to bite the bullet and place a second
referee in the stand for all major intercounty games. I realised
that this is the way forward in 2008 when I watched Tipperary
play Cork in the Munster senior hurling semi-final from a fine
vantage point in the uncovered stand at Páirc Uí Chaoimh. The
view from the stand is so much better than it is at ground level,
and I could see so much more.

Having a second referee is something that I have thought about for a while now, and it could be done quite easily. Looking down from a height, the man in the stand has a better view of the game, and if he were to communicate with the on-field official via microphone and earpiece, it would lead to much more consistent refereeing. If something happened behind the referee's back on the field of play, it could be caught by the man in the stand because he would be able to see so much more.

During the 2006 All-Ireland semi-final between Dublin and Mayo, I booked Dublin midfielder Ciarán Whelan for a challenge on Mayo's Ronan McGarrity. When I saw the incident on TV later, I cringed. I had seen it from a different angle, and it hadn't appeared to be as bad as it actually was. Whelan was fortunate to escape with a yellow card. I should have sent him off. A second referee in the stand could have taken a quick glance at a TV screen and given me the nod to issue a red card. One final point on this: one umpire at each end of the field might well do if we had somebody in the stand, because he would have a much clearer view than an umpire standing at ground level beside an upright.

I was a big fan of the sin-bin rule, which was introduced for a short spell during the National Football League of 2005. It was a deterrent to a lot of players. They thought twice about making a rash challenge that could have seen them booked and ordered off the field for ten minutes. I refereed the league opener between Dublin and Mayo at Parnell Park, the first ever floodlit competitive game to take place at the venue, and it was just an unbelievable game of football.

It was such a free-flowing encounter, and players who looked about to pull or drag an opponent stopped themselves because they knew the consequences of resorting to such tactics. I had Westmeath v. Donegal soon after, and that was another fine game. However, the media couldn't get enough of the sin-bin rule, and the negative press contributed to its demise. Quite a few managers were dead set against it and weren't slow about making their feelings known in print. The GAA was forced into a rethink, but to my mind that was one rule that was done away with far too quickly.

Taking timekeeping out of the referee's hands would certainly make life easier for the overworked man in black. You have heard the old saying many times, I'm sure: 'Ah, the ref played for a draw.' An independent timekeeper in the stand or a countdown clock with a siren to signal time up would lighten the referee's load and prevent such speculation. In more recent times, the fourth official on the touchline has indicated the amount of time to be added on, and this has been a big step forward. In previous years, nobody knew how much time the referee was adding on for stoppages, and more often than not the conspiracy theorists had a field day. With 32 or 33 minutes played in the second half, the linesman on the fourth official's side of the pitch will run in to find out from the referee how much time is to be added on. This is then indicated by the fourth official on an electronic board and relayed to the crowd over the public-address system at the stadium. Of course, a referee is not going to blow the final whistle bang on time if a player is winding up for a shot at goal, but we are advised that if two minutes extra have been allocated, that should not mean two minutes and thirty seconds. We have to stick as rigidly as possible to the two minutes that have been announced. During any game, a referee must keep an account of players noted, booked and sent off, while at the same time trying to ensure that the game flows as well as possible. Handing timekeeping to an independent body would grant the referee an extra bit of breathing space.

'So if the poor old referee is under so much pressure, why not have two of them on the pitch?' I hear you ask. I don't think it's necessary, especially with the increased emphasis on handpassing and keeping hold of possession. If the game shifted towards more direct, 'old-style' football, combined with modern-day fitness levels, I would definitely make a case for two referees on the field. But the way the game is right now, a fit referee should be able to manage just fine. And spectators would argue, with some justification, that seven officials on the field of play (referee, four umpires and two linesmen) are more than enough.

A question I am regularly asked is whether or not referees should be paid. I've heard the argument that if we were paid, we would have to accept that we were fair game for any level of criticism; but even though we're amateurs, we get slated anyway, so I don't see that as an important consideration. My view is that as long as referees get their expenses and are looked after properly, payment will not become an issue.

We get a set of refereeing gear before every season, along with a pair of football boots. Before Nickey Brennan's arrival as GAA president, some referees were disgruntled because they were knocked back when they requested a second strip. I sympathised with them because most referees are doing more than one game a week, and they need plenty of gear. Nickey's message was loud and clear: 'I don't want any of this petty stuff. If you need gear or boots, we'll get them for you. End of story.' It shouldn't be a problem. There is more than enough money swirling about in the GAA. Today, there is better communication between referees and Croke Park than ever before. Every season, two refs from each province meet the GAA to discuss any matters that need addressing.

However, some fundamental problems remain. Physiotherapy should be freely available to referees, and, as for players, compensation for loss of earnings needs to be looked at. I have often taken half or full days off work to travel to Athlone for refereeing seminars. I have never looked to make money from the GAA – I'm happy as long as the basic requirements are covered – but I'm sure some younger referees coming through the ranks feel differently.

I've often wondered how Michael Collins in Cork feels when he travels to Athlone. He's living 50 miles outside Cork city. There are often times when I don't arrive home until one o'clock in the morning, but I can only imagine how it is for Michael having to travel all the way down to Clonakilty. It's heavy going. On a seminar day, I'll finish work at four o'clock, head home for a shower and leave at five. It's a good two hours to Athlone from my home, and the road isn't great either. Into Dundrum, Ballycahill, the Ragg, over to Templemore, into Roscrea, Birr, Ferbane and on from there.

Tuesday can be a busy day in work, too, but I have never had a problem getting a couple of hours off, and my employers are more than understanding. I started work with Kiely's in Tipperary town back in 1977, bottling 7-Up and Coca-Cola soft drinks. Kiely's closed in 1989 and I was transferred to the Limerick depot for four years. Operations then moved to Cork, and I spent seven years with Connacht Minerals before Kiely's opened up again in Tipperary town and I was asked back. The wheel had turned full circle. Michael Twomey, Billy Kiely and Charlie Fitzgerald have been very good to me through the years. Billy was my first boss; he's retired now, and his son Michael has taken over the business. Michael's son Robert played at centre-half-back on the Tipperary minor football team in 2008, with my son Shane just behind him in the full-back position.

There's an obvious GAA link there, but I know that other referees on the circuit are not as fortunate. Some of them work night shifts and are unable to get time off to attend the various seminars. Refereeing is like a second job for all of us. It's virtually a full-time occupation now because of the increasing fitness demands placed on the top officials. Although I would not advocate going down the road of seeking payment, it can't be ruled out. Fifty cents per mile travelled is the current allowance for covering an intercounty game, and I consider that to be quite a low rate. Rising fuel costs are an obvious concern, and the four umpires travelling to a game with a referee might not be the smallest guys in the world, so there are wear and tear issues. I sometimes wonder about the insurance implications for the GAA if a referee were ever involved in a serious accident. On the road, we are entitled to a €40 per head meal allowance, umpires included. The total bill might touch the maximum €200, but receipts must be included with all claims, and I don't abuse the system. If Shane and Mark are with us, their meals are paid for separately.

A major bugbear of mine is the controversial International Rules concept. The series between Ireland and Australia sees one referee from each country on the pitch at the same time, and yet chaos still reigns. I'm no lover of this hybrid sport because the elements that we want removed from Gaelic football – the pulling, dragging, fighting and throwing opponents to the ground – are very much part of International Rules. It's my view that Australia play the series because they want to protect their relationship with the GAA in order to continue poaching our best young players.

The Irish lads would argue that it's their only opportunity to represent their country, but so much hypocrisy surrounds the entire concept. We throw our arms up in despair when we see the brawls at Omagh or Parnell Park, but there are 60–80,000 people travelling to Croke Park to witness similar scenes when Ireland and Australia collide.

We all remember the front-page headlines that followed the Australian violence on these shores in 2006, but after a year, when the dust had settled, the clamour for the series to be revived began. I will concede that there is some fine fielding and little things that we can learn from and implement in Gaelic football, but the majority of the people going to Croke Park to watch Ireland play Australia want to see a fight.

I refereed the interprovincial final between Ulster and Leinster at Parnell Park in 2005. It was a terrific game and extra time was needed to separate the two sides, but the 10,000 people present on that evening would have been lost in Croke Park. When the GAA HQ was opened up in 2007 for both the hurling and football interprovincial finals, just over 10,000 turned up. These are the best players in the country, but for the interprovincials the attendances are truly pathetic. And yet Ireland v. Australia at Croke Park will attract 80,000 fans. Go figure it out.

Discipline remains a huge problem for the GAA. There are too many avenues of appeal open to players when they receive a suspension. Surely the day will come when just one committee deals with disciplining players. At present, there are too many layers. But the root of the problem is a general reluctance within clubs and counties to accept the punishment that comes their way for offences committed. Perhaps all counties should sign a charter before the start of the intercounty season promising that they will abide by the rules and regulations of the GAA and steer clear of the legal route.

There has been talk of using independent disciplinary panels, made up of people with no vested interest in the GAA, to rule on cases. There is merit in this suggestion, because these neutral people would have no specific allegiances within the GAA and could not be accused of bias.

As things stand, there are too few people within the Association willing to stand up and take responsibility. I have great admiration for the Waterford hurler John Mullane, who accepted a lengthy suspension after he was sent off in the 2004 Munster hurling final, a suspension that ended his season. Mullane's motto was 'If you do the crime, you do the time', but there are not enough players out there with a similar mentality.

I'm proud of my record that no yellow or red card that I have issued during a game has ever been rescinded, although Westmeath midfielder Rory O'Connell challenged a red card all the way to the High Court in 2004.

I did not see the incident, which happened during the Leinster championship game against Offaly, but my linesman, Fintan Barrett from Kildare, called through on my earpiece and told me that he had seen O'Connell stamp on Offaly's Pascal Kelleghan. I approached O'Connell and issued the red card. 'For what?' he protested. 'You're off,' I replied. If a player asks why he has been sent off, a referee is required to explain his decision, but because I hadn't actually seen the offence, I could not.

Rory O'Connell received an initial three-month suspension, and I felt sorry about that. He had been a great servant to Westmeath for many years, and now he faced the prospect of missing out on the Leinster final. But there was nothing I could do, and it was an open-and-shut case as far as I was concerned.

As it transpired, O'Connell didn't miss a game because he succeeded in his bid for a High Court injunction. Mullane could have travelled down a similar road, but he was man enough to put up his hand and admit: 'Yes, I did it.' I have not played at intercounty level myself, but I have quite a bit of experience from club level. Sure, we all lose the cool from time to time – it's only natural – but if we step beyond the boundaries, we should suffer the consequences. Instead, a rash of High Court injunctions has led to the establishment of the independent Disputes Resolution Authority. I remember that the former Tipperary footballer Derry Foley was the first man to explore the legal avenue, many years ago.

DERRY FOLEY: *'It was a South championship game between my club, Moyle Rovers, and Clonmel Commercials at Grangemockler in 1994. There were five minutes left when I was sent off. The referee indicted me for striking, which carried a mandatory month, but I contested this on the basis that I felt the offence was rough play, which carried a two-week ban. I was due to play in the biggest game of my career 17 days later, the Munster senior football final with Tipperary, and I took the case to the High Court. The big controversy prior to the Munster final was about whether I would or wouldn't start, but I received the injunction on the Thursday before the final. The manager, Séamus McCarthy, and his selectors had direction from the county board not to play me, a direction they considered before deciding that the most appropriate course of action was to see how the game progressed. Twenty minutes in, the game was going away from us and I was brought on.*

'After the case ended, the GAA and I had discussions, and it wasn't in our best interests to pursue the matter to its conclusion, both from my own economic perspective and also because the GAA knew that I was setting a precedent.

'I'm in no way embittered by the whole thing. It was a real learning curve. But would I go there again? No. I don't think any sporting occasion warranted the pressure I put myself under prior to the game, or the allegations and misquotes that went with my decision to appeal. I felt vindicated by virtue of the injunction being upheld, but it would have cost me £100,000 to pursue the case to its rightful conclusion. I did not have the wherewithal to challenge the GAA as a hierarchy, and, besides, the Association has been exceptionally good to me. I played Compromise Rules against the Australians and represented Munster in the Railway Cup. I'm even more passionate about the GAA now, and I know more about the intricacies of politics having become involved in that field. In 1994, I felt that I had a duty, as an individual, to challenge the GAA's rules, and a fairer procedure has subsequently been put in place. I'd like to think that I started the ball rolling from the players' perspective. It might not sound like something to boast about, but the right of a player to challenge a decision he deems to be unfair is now in place. Players can use video evidence now and there is an appeals process, but before it was a kangaroo court. The referee made his report and that was it. I won't deny that there was an incident in that game against Grangemockler, but the magnitude of it was a matter of personal interpretation. P.J. Corby was the referee, a really nice man, and I still get on really well with him. There was never any animosity.

Following the case, I received many phone calls from clubs asking about the procedure, but my first response was 'Don't go there.' It cost me £12,000. A solicitor was employed from day one, a junior barrister for High Court papers and when the injunction was being requested. I wasn't naive, but I didn't expect the cost to be on that scale. Several people felt that I had a case and did support me. Those backing me had been at the match and seen the incident, and they assured me that I had a case. But I was the person out in front of the media, challenging what was deemed sacrosanct. I actually considered giving up football because of the pressure. What really put it to bed was playing with Munster in 1996. I met the GAA hierarchy of the time and there were no recriminations. The chairman of the Munster council was Seán Kelly, and he showed a willingness to be objective. If they were prepared to be *objective with me, I was more than willing to engage with them. I don't believe in harbouring grudges, because anger can weigh you down.'*

O'Connell and Foley did not have video evidence to back up their cases, but their points were obviously well argued. Such successes account for the willingness of county boards to go to any lengths to get players off the hook, particularly if their player will otherwise be ruled out of a big game.

On a related issue, is it time to introduce a 'video ref', which is used to good effect in rugby, in Gaelic games? I believe the answer is no. It would slow down football and hurling too much. People don't want to see stop–start games, and, besides, installing big-screen technology into every major intercounty ground would be very costly. And surely the video ref would have to filter down to all levels of the GAA, down as far as the clubs? However, I would like to see a microchip inserted in sliotars to determine whether or not a point has been scored in hurling.

I fell foul of the big screen at Croke Park when Wexford's Matty Forde was involved in an incident with Offaly's Shane Sullivan during the Leinster championship game between the two counties in 2006. Footage of the clash between the two players, which appeared to show Forde stamping on Sullivan's head, was mistakenly repeated on the big screen, which should only show repeats of scores.

I did not see the footage, but it was obvious from the reaction of supporters around me that something serious had been shown. I was the linesman on the Hogan Stand side of the pitch, and some Offaly supporters were shouting at me and pointing towards the screen. The situation could have become very nasty indeed, as the Offaly people were incensed by what they had seen. I was in a difficult position because they were sure that I had seen the Forde incident, and they wondered why I wasn't acting on it. Even if I had seen it, I could not have mentioned it to the referee because video replays are not part of the rules. We were told later that the person in the control room who decided to replay the incident did so because he thought the referee had caught it and he wanted to show how good a spot it was. That was a big mistake, because the referee hadn't seen what happened.

Hindsight is a great thing, particularly with the assistance of video evidence, but it is a totally different ball game at ground level when officials are up close and personal with the players. It is easy to get blocked by a player and miss out on a foul, while the cameras, zooming in from above, capture everything. Communication with linesmen and umpires is a help. We are wired up for most championship games to both linesmen and one umpire at each goal. I was never too impressed with the actual quality of the technology, though. At times, it was very difficult to understand exactly what was being relayed through the earpiece, and I would have preferred a higher standard of equipment with a clearer sound. Croke Park is so vast, and, with the huge noise levels from spectators, I always found the signal there desperately crackly. To speak with a fellow official, the referee must also push a button on the microphone, and it can be quite an unwieldy system to use. However, any advances such as this are to be welcomed, and as the technology is relatively new, I'm sure that it will be perfected in time.

Turning to the use of video evidence specifically, I'm not in favour of referees being asked to review certain incidents that they have already adjudicated upon during the course of a game. It is a double-edged sword. Croke Park's disciplinary people are trying to preserve the power of the referee's judgement, but, as a result, referees are coming under huge pressure.

A high-profile case occurred in August 2007 when Cork defender Noel O'Leary was cleared to play in the All-Ireland senior football final after referee Brian Crowe stuck with his original decision to issue him with a yellow card during a game against Meath. O'Leary had been caught on camera striking Meath's Graham Geraghty in the face, and under new guidelines the CCCC are entitled to review controversial incidents and contact referees to determine if they are satisfied with how they were dealt with.

The problem was that Brian didn't see the incident. He was alerted to it by a linesman during the game and opted for the yellow card. But if Brian had looked at the video and upgraded the offence to a red card, O'Leary would have received a four-week suspension and missed the All-Ireland final as a result. It wasn't fair to ask Brian to make such a call. At the time when he handed out the yellow card, nobody knew for sure that Cork would be in the final, but a few days later, Brian was effectively deciding whether or not a player would be allowed to line out in the biggest game of his career.

Since then, Brian has taken charge of just one league match, during the spring, Sligo and Leitrim in Division 3. You can draw your own conclusions as to why this is the case, but many believe that it is as a direct result of his refusal to upgrade the O'Leary offence to a red card. I can see where the committee is coming from when they ask referees to have another look, because they want to preserve the power of the referee's word, but in cases such as the O'Leary one, surely it's better to let sleeping dogs lie. I would not like to find myself in a situation where my revision of my own ruling deprived a player of a chance to line out in an All-Ireland final, particularly when he had not been sent off in the semi-final that preceded it.

29

....

THE LONG GOODBYE

Other things may change us, but we start
and end with family.

Anthony Brandt

The night I have feared most is finally upon me. The night
before my final championship game as an intercounty football
referee. I can't really complain, I suppose. Twenty-seven years on
the circuit has been a good innings, but this is a difficult habit
to break.

At least I'll have the club scene to fall back on. I can't stop
completely. I've been doing this since the age of 17. I've thrown
everything into it, absolutely everything.

Match-day gear is always prepared the night before, ready in
time for a National League or championship morning. I'm not
overly superstitious, but if a previous game has gone well, I'll
pack the same jersey or togs – washed first, of course! I'd say
there are 100 pencils in the bag, along with erasers and a topper
in a Coca-Cola pencil case.

Time for a quick confession: when it comes to whistles, I am
something of an anorak. If I walk into a sports shop, I have to look
at the whistles. My personal favourite is the Fox 40, described on
one Internet site as 'the whistle of choice for professional sports and
Olympic competitions'. I'll try not to bore you, but this particular

whistle has a patented three-chamber design and comes without a 'pea', which can sometimes stick and impede sound. The harder you blow on the Fox 40, the louder the sound. Fox 40 struck gold with the pea-less whistle, because moisture and too much air-flow can cause traditional whistles to perform poorly.

When I worked in Limerick, I often dropped into the well-known Gleeson Sport Scene shop. I must have driven the staff in there mad, constantly enquiring about the Fox 40 whistle. When the whistle finally arrived, I took it for a test drive at a local game in Tipperary town. John Moloney was particularly impressed. 'Where did you get that whistle?' he enquired. 'There's a fine blast out of it!' I believe that Gleeson's became the official agent for the Fox 40 once they started getting them in.

STEPHEN GLEESON: *'It must be 20 to 25 years ago now, but we were bringing them in direct from Canada at the time and supplying them to Croke Park and refereeing associations up and down the country. We sell plenty of them still, but we only sell them from the floor now, on a retail basis. The Fox 40 whistles are unique. There is the classic whistle and the mini, which is used for mountain rescue and by women for protection. To the best of my knowledge, the Fox 40 is widely used in the Premier League and by rugby referees. It was the first whistle to use a lanyard, the length of twine clipped onto it so that it can be worn around the neck. There was a finger holder, but they were not as popular because some referees reckoned they chipped their teeth. Some would also wear them on the wrist rather than around the neck, where they bob around and sometimes it can be difficult to get to them quickly to blow.'*

I always carry three or four whistles in my kitbag, along with a pouch containing yellow and red cards. Two watches also, one running and the other a stopwatch so I know exactly how much injury time to play. A pair of garters (to hold up my socks), sweatband, comb, socks, togs, jersey and coin. Check to all of the above, and we're ready to go.

I'm not a hugely religious person, but my faith is important to me, and I carry holy water in my kitbag, too, water from

Knock or Lourdes. I call for my parents at eight o'clock on a Sunday morning, to bring them to Mass at half past eight. My mother lights a candle before taking her seat, and if I have to leave home on a Saturday evening for a Sunday fixture, I bid her a fond farewell along with a gentle reminder: 'Don't forget to light a candle for me, Mam.' If I'm there on a Sunday morning, the familiar clack of the coins dropping into the box assures me that I'm in her thoughts.

In our own house, there's a three-day novena before a big game. Margaret instigated this particular practice, and we pray for the match to go well. I'll always say a couple of Hail Marys the night before, or the morning of the game itself. I have often prayed silently in the dressing-room's toilet cubicle just minutes before making my way onto the pitch.

STEVIE O'DONNELL: *'When we reach the dressing-room, we throw the gear bags to one side, sit down, relax and have a cup of tea. Then we discuss the match and how we're going to approach it. Before heading out onto the pitch, Paddy will say, "Is there anybody who wants to ask me any questions? It's a big game; this is what I have trained all year for. Watch my back; I don't have eyes in the back of my head." Paddy also asks the umpires and linesmen to concentrate on one team only in the event of a melee breaking out, like what happened at Omagh or Parnell Park. We decide among ourselves. It was a new tactic Paddy employed after Omagh in 2006 and worked particularly well when history repeated itself at Parnell Park in 2008.*

'Ten minutes before throw-in, Paddy glances at the watch and then it's into the light with his linesmen and four umpires. We will talk briefly before the game. I look around the ground and check what direction the wind is blowing in by throwing a few blades of grass in the air.'

At intercounty level, football has dominated my career, but on the local scene, my commitments have been split pretty evenly between hurling and football. The highlight for me as a hurling referee was taking charge of the drawn 2002 county senior club final between Mullinahone and Thurles Sarsfields. In addition, I have refereed county hurling finals at intermediate and Under-21 levels.

My experience as an intercounty hurling referee has been limited to challenge games, including Wexford v. Limerick in 2007 and Tipperary v. Limerick in 2008. Another proud moment was refereeing Tipperary and Limerick in a tournament game back in 1998, a match played on my home pitch in Emly.

Hurling's a much easier game to referee, I believe. There are not as many fouls and much less pulling and dragging. Would I consider myself a good hurling referee? That's not for me to answer. I would never say about myself that I'm good at this or that. I just love refereeing, and I'm not one bit envious of the adulation and the attention that the players attract. For me, it's a privilege to go out in front of those guys, an honour to take charge of a game involving thirty of the best players from the two competing teams. And, as always, I will referee the game to the best of my ability, irrespective of who's playing.

Of course, my club remains dear to my heart. I am still a member of the Emly committee, the representative to the West board for the last number of years. Emly is where it all started for me, and the likes of Father Robert Mullally, Jim English, Paddy Clancy, Mick Frawley, Jack Hennessy, Seán McManus and Eamonn O'Meara were always a huge support.

Eamonn and I used to train juveniles, and in our late 20s we were bringing them to games while other people were heading off to dances. The club meant everything to us. At one time, I would have envisaged my children playing for Emly, but Lattin is their home. The boys adore Lattin, and I can't imagine how I would have felt if I had been uprooted from Emly and taken to play with another club.

What an incredible journey it has been from Emly to Croke Park on All-Ireland final day. I could never have imagined that a Bord Na nÓg refereeing course would help to create a lifetime of memories. Refereeing took over my life, just like work takes over with other people. I sometimes feel that if I had no job in the morning, it wouldn't bother me as long as I had refereeing.

I have refereed not only in Ireland, but in America, Australia, Canada, England and Scotland. I was appointed to referee an exhibition match between Cork and Mayo held at Brentford City's soccer ground in 1990. I was amused when the chief of police visited me before the game and handed me a pass code to signal the abandonment of a game if crowd violence got out of hand. The English police were truly amazed as Cork and Mayo supporters happily wandered into Griffin Park, chatting freely with each other.

The Skydome in Toronto, Canada, is the home of the Toronto Blue Jays baseball team and the Argonauts from the Canadian Football League. When construction was completed on this stadium in 1989, it was hyped up locally as one of the wonders of the world. An artificial pitch was laid down for the visit of the 1991 GAA hurling and football All Stars. It was quite a surreal experience refereeing there, as the game was of a stop–start nature for the benefit of the local TV networks. When there was a break in play, we were told to keep the ball behind the goal until we received the signal to resume.

We take the GAA so much for granted in Ireland, but it is truly something to see how people attempt to keep the Association alive in far-flung destinations. When I refereed in Chicago, I was told that teams travel huge distances to compete in the North American championships. For example, San Francisco's players and officials paid their own travel and accommodation expenses for the weekend. I think we can learn a lesson here. Can you imagine how a club or county team invited to Dublin to participate in a tournament would react if asked to cover their own expenses in the capital?

In 1999, I travelled to Perth in Australia and was honoured to learn that I was the first Irish referee invited to take charge of their games. An Australian delegation had travelled to Ireland for the 1998 International Rules series and the GAA president at the time, Joe McDonagh, had promised to send a hurling and football referee from Ireland on the return trip in 1999, to take charge of their local games.

Of course, there have been times when refereeing has left me wholly demoralised. After the 1995 All-Ireland final, I was in the pits of despair and afraid to face people. Then there was Omagh, Killarney and Paul Galvin. But refereeing has taught me coping mechanisms, how to survive and how to restore the level of my self-esteem.

SHANE RUSSELL: *'Sometimes we wonder why he's out every night running on the road if he's just going to be abused. But he enjoys it, and it keeps him fit. It's like a drug to him. And he has two All-Ireland senior football medals. He may have got them refereeing, but they're still All-Ireland medals.'*

SEÁN MCMANUS: *'Paddy acted as he saw it. He had his own convictions about things. He would take advice and listen, but when he went out to referee, he was in charge. He wanted to referee as well as he could and was fiercely conscientious. He would have worried a lot about his refereeing, too. He's an intense kind of person, he wouldn't be too laid-back, but he's very sincere and very honest. He must have a fierce record for dispatching players to the line, but, by and large, he's been right.'*

'Red Russell', an Antrim native living in Tipperary town calls me, because of the number of players I have red-carded. But I'd like to be remembered for those All-Ireland semi-finals in 2005 and 2006, two classic games. The first ever floodlit game between Dublin and Mayo at Parnell Park was another superb encounter. Donegal and Westmeath soon after was a great match, too, even though I was as sick as a dog. I'd got up twice during the previous night to take cold remedies. I would have done anything to be right for the match.

MICK MAGUIRE: *'Paddy was always fit, and, like John Moloney, he had that authority, even though he wasn't as big a man as John. I always thought that Paddy was equally good at hurling and football, terribly sharp. Both teams will see a foul their own way, but I always thought that Paddy read situations excellently. He's very decisive, and be it junior football or a county senior football final, it's the same Paddy*

Russell with the same whistle and the same way of going about his business.'

MARGARET RUSSELL: 'We have had some great times. I do feel that Paddy has lost out sometimes on family life, and that's why I'm delighted that he's involved down in Lattin with the juveniles. Night after night, it was me taking the boys to training because Paddy was away. Now, any night he is free, he can go down to the field with his "children", as he calls the Under-12 team, and train them with Tom Neville and Roddy Crehan. We all go, and I really feel that we are a family doing what we love.'

SHANE RUSSELL: 'There's a great group involved in the club now. There was always underage activity but never the numbers. Now they have the numbers and the skill. The club would have contested West finals in the past, but getting to county finals and semi-finals, which has happened over the last three years, is unheard of. I think he enjoys the coaching as much as the refereeing. And I've noticed that even if it's an Under-12 match down there, the youngsters can have a laugh at the same time. Training isn't as pressurised in that age group.'

MARGARET RUSSELL: 'One can get caught up in the bad times, but when I think of the hundreds of games that Paddy has been part of, there have been fantastic times, great memories and, most of all, great friends made along the way.'

SHANE RUSSELL: 'The intercounty stuff can be heat of the moment, but at club level it can be worse. Some places are notorious for abuse, but others just get on with it. Would I become a referee? Maybe later, after I have finished playing. It could be something to do to stay involved in the GAA.'

MARK RUSSELL: 'I have no interest in becoming a referee. It doesn't appeal to me. I would prefer to continue playing. And who knows what the future holds?'

Refereeing has consumed me, taken over my life for the last thirty-two years. Five or six games a week and sometimes two in the one day. It will be hard to walk away from that.

Watching the 2009 Munster and All-Ireland championships will be hard, knowing that I won't be involved. I'll feel the loss, and I'm sure the longing will be there again next year to pound the roads when the evenings stretch. But I'm not getting any younger. It's time to get off the intercounty carousel, time to explore new avenues.

I'd love to do this forever. I had my bad days but the good days outweighed them all. If I had my time back, I would go through it all over again. If I didn't love refereeing, I would never have come back after 1995, Omagh or Killarney. And I'm not going to blow that final whistle just yet.

EPILOGUE

The trouble with retirement is that you never get a day off.

Abe Lemons

Saturday, 9 August 2008. All-Ireland senior football championship quarter-final. Armagh v. Wexford. My final championship game at Croke Park. The match provides some redemption after a difficult year, and it's a famous day for Wexford as they record a 1–14 to 0–12 victory.

The newspapers had picked up on my appointment for this clash when it was announced earlier in the week. Eight weeks had passed since the Paul Galvin incident when I ran out at Croke Park for the first time since June 2007. The papers wondered why I hadn't been given a game in eight weeks. I wondered too, since my marks from the assessors had been good all season.

Whether they were waiting until the Galvin affair was over or whether I was getting my own suspension for my part in it, I don't know. Nobody from the National Referees Association said anything to me, but the chairman, P.J. McGrath, was quoted as saying that I had done nothing wrong.

I was happy to get another game, but I felt under pressure going up there. I hadn't had a big game since 15 June, and you need matches to remain in top condition. A referee needs to be on top of his game, especially with the huge levels of media scrutiny, which means that errors are ravenously pounced upon.

It was only natural that I should feel nervous. I had expected that Clare v. Kerry would pass off without too many problems, but the most talked-about incident of the entire summer had erupted. Wexford are not renowned for physicality; Armagh are tough, but these teams have never met before in the championship, and, apart from recent league meetings, there is no major historical rivalry to speak of.

On the way to Dublin, my mobile phone was hopping with phone calls and text messages. Brian Crowe texted good luck wishes before he jetted out on a family holiday. My Tipperary colleagues Brian Tyrell and Donie Cahill were in touch, and Pat McEnaney, Aidan Mangan and Mike Meade called, too.

Vincent Neary and Rory Hickey were my linesmen, and they wished me the best of luck going out before the game and congratulated me afterwards. Joe McQuillan was the man in the middle for the Galway v. Kerry quarter-final, the second game on the Croke Park double bill, and he ran out before the first match to offer me words of encouragement. We're a tight-knit bunch, us referees. We all like to get the big games, and we do discuss fellow refs and assessments between ourselves, but when other guys received high-profile appointments, I was always genuinely pleased for them.

Before we got out of the car outside the stadium, I told my umpires to savour the day. 'This will be our last day in Croke Park. Enjoy it.' I knew there were two semi-finals and a final to come, but I wouldn't be in the shake-up for those games. I was sure of that.

Professor Niall Moyna from Dublin City University was waiting for me when I arrived. I was to be wearing a special vest under my kit for the game, the 'belly-warmer', as I called it. I later discovered that the exercise was a bit more hi-tech than that. I was actually part of a groundbreaking experiment being conducted by DCU staff in conjunction with the American Department of

Defense. Professor Moyna is the head of the School of Health and Human Performance at DCU, and he told the *Irish Times* in a subsequent interview that I was the first referee to be fitted with this version of the vest. My two linesmen also wore the vests, and our movements during the game were monitored via GPS (Global Positioning System).

NIALL MOYNA: *'Cameras were fixed on the individuals to track their movements via satellite. The GPS system tracked Paddy's heart rate and respiration, as well as the standing, sprinting and jogging that he did during the game. The information records the movement patterns of the referee, how he ran, for how long and the intensity of each run. The vest gives us the information and the physiological data, which we can then use to design referee training programmes. In five years' time, every single sports jersey will have a form of this vest embedded in it. What we're doing at the moment is part of an ongoing experiment with the American Department of Defense. They use the vest to track military personnel in the field, so if an individual is shot or put down, his or her state of health can be tracked by detecting the vital signs. They can then decide how quickly medical assistance is required, because medics could also be placed in danger if they go to help.*

'I should mention, too, that Paddy was always willing to look outside the box, and anything that could be done to improve the quality of fitness in refereeing, he never shied away from. I only found out late on Friday night that we would be getting into Croke Park, and even though Paddy only discovered on the morning of the game about the vest, he had no problem doing it. This vest is by far the most advanced prototype in the world and will be used much more extensively on referees during next year's National League. At the end of the day, if they're going to train, it's important that the time spent training is quality time. The next step will be for players to use the vest. We want to be in a position to measure and assess the appropriate things, and in five years' time, we should be able to pick up ECGs. [An ECG (electrocardiogram) is used to measure the rate and regularity of heartbeats as well as the size and position of the chambers, the presence of any damage to the heart and the effects of drugs and devices used to regulate the heart (such as a pacemaker).]

'It is very much in its infancy at the moment, but we also did this on Paddy a few years ago in a National League game. It has moved on considerably since then, and it's possible to wear a shirt now and not even know that you're being monitored. We can see the ups and downs in the heart rate, and I have to say that Paddy is very fit and has always kept himself in great shape.'

Thankfully, the game went well for me, but I felt sorry for Armagh. They've been a superb team over the last decade, but they just seemed to run out of steam. This was Oisín McConville's last year, and I'm sure he was disappointed not to get a run on the Armagh team. I brought Oisín's book *The Gambler* to Dublin with me on the day of the game. Mark was with me, and he ran down to the former Armagh goalkeeper Benny Tierney before the match. Benny was pitch-side, and Mark asked if he could get Oisín to sign the book.

I didn't want to go near the Armagh personnel or be seen talking to any of them before the game. If I was seen chatting with one of them and they went on to win, the conspiracy theorists would have had plenty of ammunition. Oisín signed the book with the following message: 'To Paddy, best wishes, Oisín. Luckily we are both retiring in the same year! Meet you for golf some time.'

I felt sad for Oisín but delighted too for Matty Forde. The Wexford man and former All Star has experienced many low points in his career, but his late goal set his team on the way to a famous victory against Armagh. Wexford's joy strikes me on an emotional level when I think back to my early days of refereeing when the county struggled to stay afloat in Division 4 of the National League. I recall games between the Model County and other minnows in Gorey, but now I can notice a lovely symmetry. I'm sure this is my final game at Croke Park, and here are Wexford competing for the right to contest an All-Ireland semi-final. Like me, they've come a long way.

It was a nice game to referee, but when I checked the Monday newspapers for the free count, I couldn't believe it. Just ten to

Armagh and sixteen to Wexford. That's low. Did I leave that much go? The doubts crept in again, but my umpire Stevie said that it was one of my better games, and the *Irish Independent*'s Monday 'Ref Watch' praised my display:

> In what was his first championship engagement since the Paul Galvin incident, there was always going to be an intense focus on Paddy Russell's performance. Despite calling back play on a few occasions when he could have let it run, Russell was solid and, more importantly, consistent.

Eight players were booked, including Armagh's warhorse of a full-back Francie Bellew. Some of the stuff I have read about Francie down through the years is not in line with reality. In all my time refereeing, I've found the Crossmaglen man, a clubmate of Oisín's, to be an absolute gentleman. Whenever I booked him, it was always the same. I asked Francie for his name, he gave it and accepted his yellow card without protest. Sure, Francie played the game close to the borderline between what he could and could not get away with, but if he did something wrong, he accepted the consequences. The majority of players would plead their case, even if they didn't have a leg to stand on, but Francie never did.

After the game, Armagh midfielder Paul McGrane came over and shook hands, saying, 'Well done.' That meant a lot to me. I've always found the Armagh team to be fine sportspeople, and they live for their football. It's a shame that they never won that second All-Ireland title. That squad of players certainly deserved it.

I always said that I wanted my intercounty career to finish on a high, and that match was a good way to bow out. It's a pity the year as a whole didn't go according to plan, but in sport you can never tell what's around the corner.

Another surprise lay in store just a few days after Margaret and I returned from a short break in Donegal. The phone rang and on the end of the line was Bernie Connaughton from Boston GAA. I had met Bernie in Chicago in 2007, and he wanted me to referee the Boston championship semi-finals on 17 August and the final on 24 August. Galway's Alan Kelly, who took charge of this year's All-Ireland minor hurling semi-final between Tipperary and Kilkenny, was drafted in to look after the hurling matches.

I want to put on record my thanks to Bernie and his fellow officials for inviting me to Boston. I am grateful to Bernie for putting me up in his house for the duration of the ten-day visit. The GAA facilities in Boston are absolutely superb, and many people will recall that the club hosted the 2005 M. Donnelly interprovincial hurling final, along with the football decider a year later. The matches I refereed in August were hugely competitive. I took charge of nine in total, and I thoroughly enjoyed my time there.

Of course, there was time also to reflect on an intercounty career that has provided me with pleasure and pain in almost equal measure. Twenty-eight years and a multitude of memories. Finally, I have decided that it's time to step off the merry-go-round, but it's funny, I swear I can still hear the music.

Appendix A

··

THE UMPIRE'S TALE

I never questioned the integrity of an umpire.
Their eyesight, yes.

Leo Durocher

Allow me to introduce myself properly. My name is Stevie O'Donnell, an Arravale Rovers club man who has been on the road with Paddy for the last ten years, working alongside him as an umpire.

I often said to Paddy that when I was young, it was my dream to play at Croke Park. For me, umpiring is the next best thing. Growing up, I only ever saw Croke Park on TV on All-Ireland final day, but during my first full year working with Paddy – 1999 – I umpired six times at the famous stadium. I have always assumed the same position there: Hill 16 End, white flag, at the Cusack Stand side of the field.

I never imagined that I would follow in the footsteps of my wife Siobhán's late father Matt, who umpired at four All-Ireland finals with the great John Moloney. It is a lovely link, but, unlike Matt, I have never umpired on All-Ireland final day. I have been there for four semi-finals (1999, 2000, 2005 and 2006), as well as senior provincial deciders in each of the four provinces, but the big one eluded me.

I was attending a local referees' meeting at the Royal Hotel in Tipperary town when Paddy called me aside and asked if I fancied umpiring with him. That was back in 1998, and I've been with him ever since. A good eye is crucial for umpiring, and I'm sure that my years as a darts player stood me in good stead.

I won London championships in 1984 and 1985, and was picked for the London and Home Counties team that was beaten in the English championship in 1985–86. Darts over there at the time was of a very high quality, and I put an awful lot of practice in.

I haven't thrown a dart competitively since 1987, when I won the area final of the *News of the World* competition and later collected a bronze medal in the All-Ireland finals. There were two qualifiers from the Tipperary/Limerick/Clare/Waterford region. The other was a cult figure whom many GAA fans will know quite well: 'Effin' Eddie Moroney, the voice behind the famous amateur video commentary, was a left-handed darts player, just like me.

In 2000, former Tipperary player Brian Lacey was in action for Kildare against Dublin in the Leinster senior football final at Croke Park. I was umpiring with Richard O'Connor at the Hill 16 end. Brian was tugging at Jason Sherlock's jersey as the pair raced across to contest possession. We had a word with Brian, but it didn't stop him testing the quality of the fabric on Sherlock's back.

Richard warned Brian, 'Listen, you're on the verge of being booked for jersey pulling.' Brian replied, 'Richie, give me a chance.' Sherlock was surprised and asked Lacey, 'How do you know those guys?' Brian, Richie and I all hail from the same native club – Arravale Rovers! So, for the 2000 Leinster senior football final, you had two Arravale Rovers men at the Hill 16 end of the ground, with an Arravale Rovers man playing for the Lilywhites!

We survived a bomb prior to the 2000 Ulster SF semi-final replay between Antrim and Derry at Casement Park. We stayed in the Carrickdale Hotel, six miles north of Dundalk, the night before the game, and I almost cried as I left Tipperary on that

Saturday afternoon, because the following day, Tipperary were due to play Cork in the Munster senior hurling final in Thurles. We stopped in Thurles on the journey north and spent some time in Lár na Páirce, the GAA museum and shop in the town. I was close to pulling out of the trip, because the craic in and around Liberty Square was superb.

However, we enjoyed our evening in the Carrickdale. We had a meal, and the atmosphere was good in the hotel. It must have been 1.30 a.m. when Richard and I heard an almighty bang. 'Oh, good Jesus! Is it a bomb?' A car had been blown up in the car park outside, and it wasn't long before sirens could be heard and flashing lights seen as police cars and fire engines converged on the area.

The next morning, helicopters hovered around the area. I had originally planned a helicopter ride to Belfast that morning, scheduled to leave Seán Treacy Park in Tipperary town, but Liam O'Dwyer's fear of flying had scuppered that idea. I had discussed it with Paddy earlier in the week, and it made both practical and financial sense. By the time the GAA had paid for petrol, hotels, dinners, evening meals and breakfasts, it would have worked out cheaper to hire a helicopter. Irish Helicopters in Shannon had quoted €800 for a return trip to Belfast from Tipperary.

I met the Sinn Féin leader Gerry Adams before the Antrim v. Derry game. I had my umpire's jacket on and Gerry winked and said, 'Be good today, my son is playing.' Gearóid Adams was indeed number 5 on the Antrim team. We were delayed by five minutes coming out of our dressing-room before the game, as Gerry Adams and Martin McGuinness were conducting a live TV interview just outside the door. Gerry was in the Antrim corner while McGuinness, deputy leader of Sinn Féin, was very much in the Derry camp.

I have rarely been subjected to abuse from players at intercounty level, because they know that they have to watch themselves. At club level, I have received the height of it. I was once grabbed by the throat at an inter-firms match before match referee Paddy Lonergan sent the offender from the field of play.

On the intercounty scene, it is not unusual to see umpires working with various referees. I recall umpiring a Kerry v. Dublin National Football League game with Pat McEnaney in Killarney. Pat would be in touch if he was short an umpire. Paddy Russell was linesman that same day. I also umpired for Armagh referee Jimmy McKee at an All-Ireland Under-21 semi-final between Cork and Laois.

What makes a good umpire, then? I will always point out Paddy's mistakes and flaws to him, and I think he appreciates that. I don't believe that a referee will ever become a good one if he has four umpires who will just agree and nod their heads all of the time. I've often pulled Paddy up on poor decisions, and hopefully he won't make the same mistake when he takes charge of his next game.

The two best referees that I have ever seen both hailed from West Tipperary. Paddy is one, but I don't rate him as the best ever. That accolade must go to the late John Moloney, who stands head and shoulders above the rest. Paddy learned from the master, but he will never be his equal, in my view.

I like Paddy's style of refereeing. He's not intimidated by any player, and his fitness levels are consistently good. He approaches every game in a professional manner, and I have often predicted that Paddy would be handed certain games because they promised to be tough encounters.

But I would argue that Paddy should not now be doing so many games at local level. New referees trying to break through should get these matches. I told Paddy a couple of years ago that he should not have done a county minor football final in Cashel between Thurles Sarsfields and Killenaule. Why? Because he has done enough, and, what's more, he can see where I'm coming from.

How can referees improve standards if the same guys keep getting the big games? I'm thinking of younger guys like Ger

Riordan from Solohead and David Grogan from Aherlow. They can't move onto the provincial scene and beyond if they don't get the plum fixtures at divisional and county level.

But it is a combination of Paddy's professionalism and dedication to his craft that has kept him at the top for so many years. Even if it's an Under-12 match at Seán Treacy Park in Tipperary town, he will go out there the very same as he would for an All-Ireland final. And those young kids look up to Paddy Russell. I've seen him interact with them, explaining to them where they're going wrong and encouraging them for doing the right things.

I will never forget a match in New Inn one evening when Paddy demanded that the team manager bring three young guys off the bus to apologise to him. An incident took place during the game, and Paddy was called a wanker. He embarrassed those young kids by demanding an apology, but he also helped them. Christy Peters, the groundsman in New Inn, said it was the best thing that he had ever seen a referee do. The three boys all said sorry to Paddy, who replied, 'It's not sorry I want at all. I don't want you to do that again. It's no good to the referee, and it's no good to you. You are lovely young kids. Keep playing the game, and don't let your mouths destroy you.'

TOM-JOE O'BRIEN: '*I played football alongside Paddy with Emly for many years. Paddy played half-back and I was half-forward. Paddy was a handy enough footballer. He always wore the number 5 jersey. The only point I can remember him kicking was as a senior player, and he chose his moment brilliantly, in the 1987 West senior football final. We knew that it would be our day when Paddy got forward to kick a point! The next score he got was some 20 years later – as a junior footballer against Aherlow!*

'*As an umpire, I had some great days out with Paddy. I recall a Munster Under-21 final between old rivals Cork and Kerry in Castleisland. Ambrose O'Donovan and Tom Spillane would have been major players for Kerry. Cars were bumper to bumper, and as we left the ground, Paddy spotted the former Kerry manager Mick O'Dwyer. "Ye had a good win, Micko," he said.*

'"*Ah, it was. It's great to beat that crowd.*"'

MICHEÁL O'DWYER: '*I love going to Croke Park with Paddy. It's such a Mecca now, since the redevelopment. It's a fabulous set-up, but there are other venues where referees and umpires struggle to get ready for a game. At Breffni Park in Cavan, the referee's room is very small, and at St Tiernach's Park in Clones it's not much bigger.*

'*I was 14 when I began umpiring. My club, Éire Óg Annacarty, were playing Seán Treacy's in an Under-16 hurling match; my uncle Liam was involved with the team, and he asked me if I would stand at the goalpost. It snowballed from there. Liam himself was one of the longest-serving referees in West Tipperary.*

'*My first intercounty game with Paddy was a Munster minor championship game in Killorglin, Kerry, against Waterford, I think it was. A semi-final on a wet June evening. Liam had to milk the cows, and I ended up getting the call. My first full year on the intercounty scene was 1998–99. The first game was Waterford against Wexford in Lemybrien.*

'*There are some games and moments that stick out in my mind. Oisín McConville's penalty for Armagh in the 1999 Ulster final; Dublin and Roscommon in a National Football League tie when the former Leitrim player Declan Darcy, plying his trade with Dublin at the time, took some ferocious abuse from Dublin's supporters.*

'*And then there was the time in 2003 when a re-fixture was ordered between Sligo and Kildare. That was the one day I dearly wanted to pack in umpiring.*'

PADDY RUSSELL: '*That was an awful day. Kildare were already relegated. There was real needle between the two teams. I could tell by their attitude even before the game; they wouldn't so much as acknowledge each other. I awarded an early free, and Kildare's Glenn Ryan went berserk. Ryan was sent off later for two yellow cards. "We shouldn't be here today." They did not want to play football at all, and it was one of the worst games I ever did. Sligo won by a couple of points, but if Kildare had concentrated on their football, they might have edged it. The two dugouts were arguing with each other from the very start, and before the match started, players who knew guys on the opposing team were told not to talk to them.*'

MICHEÁL O'DWYER: *'I'm lucky that as an umpire I haven't been involved in any controversies over the years. I came close at one stage during an Ulster championship game when Fermanagh's Paul Brewster swung a ball towards the Armagh goal. I watched the ball as it looked to be heading over the bar, but I lost it for a moment in the blazing sun. The ball swerved just outside the post, and I waved it wide. There were no complaints from Fermanagh players, but it was a close call.*

'Tyrone blitzed Cavan in the Ulster championship a few years back, but in the first half of that game I gave a wide against Peter Canavan. It was Tyrone's only wide of the half as they ran riot. The ball drifted over the top of the upright; it wasn't in, and I waved my arms to signal a wide. Canavan was beside himself with anger. He argued with Paddy, but to no avail, and I wasn't budging. That's the best thing about Paddy. He will always side with his officials.'

TOM-JOE O'BRIEN: *'We've had some close calls with Paddy! On the way home from an Under-16 challenge against Austin Stacks of Tralee, road resurfacing works were in progress in Newcastlewest. A white lime substance was down on the road, before the coat of tar was applied. Paddy was tailgating Seán Mackey in front, with Jimmy Cunningham following behind. It had rained, and as Seán hit the white lime, we could see nothing through the front windscreen. We did hear the screech of brakes behind us, though, as Jimmy Cunningham shot out through a line of empty tar barrels. But for Jimmy's evasive action, seven cars would have clattered into each other.*

'Closer to home, Paddy drove around a bad bend to be faced with a digger with its loader down on the wrong side of the road. The paint was literally taken off the car. To cap it all off, as we approached the Old Hall in Emly, a car came straight out in front of us, and Paddy had to stop to avoid it. Three times in the space of twelve hours; somebody was certainly smiling down on us that day!'

Appendix B

··

MARGARET'S STORY

If ever two were one, then surely we.
If ever man were loved by wife, then thee.

Anne Bradstreet

I knew what I was getting into from the very start. We had been going out just a very short time when Paddy informed me that the GAA would always be number one in his life. People say that circumstances change when you get married, but I never tried to change Paddy. In truth, I was the one who changed.

My two brothers were heavily involved in the GAA, and I went to all of their matches from when they were at Under-12 level and up through the ranks from there. My late father wasn't part of any team, but he was a great supporter of our local club, Cappawhite. My two brothers Noel and Mike wore the blue and white with distinction for many years.

I had a certain amount of interest but nowhere near the almost fanatical level I have today. The local fields were more of a place to spot talent, and not just in a football sense! I had never heard of Paddy Russell and didn't know who he was, even though he was a player when Emly made a huge breakthrough in my native Cappawhite in 1983, with victory in the West intermediate football championship. He also refereed the West junior championship final in 1981, when Cappawhite were victorious over Knockavilla Kickhams.

I played ladies' football myself with Cappawhite, winning two county junior titles along the way, and I still follow the club today in various grades. The highlight of my life was in 1987 when Cappawhite won the Tipperary senior hurling championship. I can honestly say that there has been nothing, apart from the births of my two children, to compare with that day.

I had no great love of football until I met Paddy, but now I would choose it over hurling if the two games were clashing. Paddy helped to instil a love of football in me, and I thank him for that. He took me to Croke Park in 1984 to see Tipperary playing Dublin in the All-Ireland minor football final. It was my first ever visit to the famous stadium, and in the senior final Kerry defeated Dublin. We had brilliant seats, and in my mind's eye I can still see Pat Spillane scoring some fantastic points.

They don't understand me in Cappawhite any more. They wonder where this love of football has come from, because back home football is a second-class game compared to the hurling. However, our sons Shane and Mark would rate football as their number-one sport.

Paddy and I both worked in Tipperary town, where we first met. I happened to be friendly with Mick Kennedy, who worked with Paddy, and I found out that Paddy was unattached.

One day, I asked Mick if Paddy was going to a dance in Dundrum, our ballroom of romance, one particular night, and I was told that he was. Furthermore, I knew by now that Paddy had expressed an interest in me. We met and got on very well. After going out on a few casual dates, we became an item in October 1983.

We were engaged in August 1985 and married a year later. People were sure that us getting married on a Sunday was a set-up – so that Paddy couldn't escape to referee a local game! But I always wanted to get married on a Sunday. We've never looked back, and we celebrated 22 years of marriage in August 2008.

Neither of us drinks alcohol. We're not pub people; we're match people – even though the two so often go hand in hand.

We need two cars on the road with the GAA, as there are so many evenings when Paddy is refereeing a game and I am elsewhere, at a different game or at training with Shane and Mark.

During the summer, we live at matches. Paddy would admit that the GAA has taken over his life, but I wouldn't be able to live without it now, either. I hate it when the summer ends, and especially when the darkness of winter descends.

I couldn't tell you how many birthdays we have had when Paddy has been absent. Paddy's parents would be there, my parents and extended family present – but no Paddy. This annoyed me at times, but I had to get over it, because there is always another match that he needs to go to.

For the first five years of our relationship, I went to all of Paddy's matches with him, but that changed when Shane arrived in 1991. We had just the one car, and every Sunday Paddy took us to my mother's in the morning and collected us in the evening. I do believe being a referee is a huge commitment, but there was never once a time when I said to him, 'This has to stop.' Mam knew that I wanted to be with Paddy, and one day she said, 'If you wrap Shane up, there is no reason for you to stay at home.' That was music to my ears, and Shane became our travelling companion.

I don't know too many other referees' wives to compare experiences with, although I would have met Willie Barrett's wife, Joan, and Pat Lane's wife, Anne, often at matches. I never met John Moloney's wife, Betty, at games. As far as I am aware, she was at home rearing a fine family and saw that as her role. That is my role too, but often it is done at matches, where we are all together.

I recall an evening earlier this year when Paddy took a phone call out of the blue and agreed to fill in for a referee who was unavailable for a match in Emly. I had planned to attend a course in Tipperary town, and, on top of that, family friend Nora Cunningham was due to take out stitches from Mark's ankle, which he had damaged playing in a match. One of us needed to be here at nine o'clock, when Nora was due to arrive, but the ball was very much in my court because Paddy drops everything when refereeing duty calls. I could have picked a row over that, but it wasn't worth it. I rang Nora and asked if she could wait until half past nine. By then, at least one of us would be home.

One Saturday, Maggie Crosse, a work colleague of mine, got married. She doesn't understand the GAA, but she knows our form, and, to be perfectly honest, she thinks we're a bit crazy. She was married in Holycross, and, half-joking but half-serious, I said to her, 'You'd better not be late for your wedding. I have to get back home to see Paddy's match on television. I'll be back for the reception when the game is over.'

Of course, she was late, and the moment the wedding concluded in the church, I was gone. After breaking the speed limit to get home in time for the throw-in, I closed the blinds, took the phone off the hook and watched the game. Afterwards, it was back into the glad rags again and away to the reception. The priest who'd married the couple had me sussed. He grinned, 'Who won?' Paddy made the reception at eleven o'clock that night. Really and truly, nothing interferes with his refereeing career, and I have travelled alone to more than one wedding. Paddy joins me later in the evening, when he arrives back from the match.

But from the beginning, I've never made an issue of it. Maybe in some cases when people are going out together, they make efforts that they don't make later, but I walked into this thing with my eyes wide open. The next generation in this house think the very same way about the GAA. There are no two ways about it. The GAA comes first. The Association has been good to us and will be good to them also, I'm sure.

In 2007, Paddy and Mark missed out on a holiday abroad because of an Under-12 county football semi-final. Shane and I went ourselves. I had the holiday in Portugal paid for, but I said to Paddy, 'If you and Mark want to stay, Shane and I will go.' I contacted my dear friend Ella Cunningham, who is always ready to travel anywhere at the drop of a hat, and she came to Portugal with us. Shane was reluctant to pick one friend or relative to travel, in case anybody was offended.

PADDY RUSSELL: '*I was manager of the Under-12 team, and Ballina wouldn't switch the game. I even rang their club chairman, but there was no way they would budge. I also put in a call to the county board secretary, Tim Floyd, but there was no room for manoeuvre. We lost the game, but, although I missed the family holiday, I had the consolation of refereeing at the North American championships in Chicago later in the year.*'

Some people really thought that I had lost the plot and were asking if I would be looking for my money back after Paddy and Mark missed the holiday. There was never a question of that. Paddy and Mark were doing what they wanted to do, and I was sending text messages right through the game. All that bothered me in Portugal was what the score was. Shane was 16 at the time and it was probably the last chance I will get to take him off on my own on a holiday.

In May 2008, I planned a surprise weekend away in Prague from 3 to 6 May. Paddy celebrated his birthday on 8 May while I reached the half-century exactly a fortnight later. Prague brochures littered the house, but Paddy was totally oblivious. The flight tickets and other travel documentation could be lying on the dressing table, but it would never once enter Paddy's head that he might be going somewhere. The only sheet he reads is the local GAA fixture list. 'Any post?' Paddy will ask when he arrives home in the evening. Unless there's a GAA crest on the envelope, it's not considered important as far as Paddy is concerned!

I always wished for him to bow out after a top-class game, just like Armagh v. Tyrone in 2005 or Dublin v. Mayo in 2006. He is ambitious, too, in his day job, but with refereeing he is always striving for that little bit extra.

If I have to push him out the door, he will keep doing the club games now that he has stepped down from the intercounty circuit! I worry about the day when his legs give up. He only let go of intercounty because he finds it more difficult to get fit each year. He could not bear to have a charge of lack of fitness levelled against him.

The most difficult aspect of being a referee's wife is attending games and hearing the verbals dished out. There are certain individuals at club level whom I would have no respect for because of their behaviour on the sideline. You won't hear the barbs at intercounty level as much because of the larger numbers attending the games, but the local guys can be vicious. At a minute's notice, Paddy will go and referee a match for them, and yet these people still think that it's perfectly OK to call him what they like.

I've felt sick inside at work on a Monday morning when he's been involved in something over the weekend, particularly when it has made an appearance on *The Sunday Game*. The shutters come down, and I always try to shrug it off with a smile. 'Paddy was in the wars again yesterday?' they'll say. 'Ah sure, what's new?' I respond. I feel that I have to knock it on the head before it goes any further. Maybe I shouldn't. Some people would give you . . . sympathy's not the right word, maybe understanding; but others are not so genuine. I am well able to differentiate now.

I think he feels a twinge of regret now and then about the GAA having such a hold on him. I have said it to him: 'Paddy, this has taken over completely, and I just hope, down the road, that you won't have regrets about what you missed out on, family-wise.' That's as strong as I would ever get, but he won't have regrets. The two boys are mad into the GAA – and into him. We have a strong bond even if Paddy has been missing out of the house a lot. When he's here, he spends quality time with the boys. Mark won't sleep until Paddy comes home and gives him a rundown of the game. Mark then reads the match programme and files it away in his drawer along with the countless others. He has developed a great knowledge of various players from many different counties.

SHANE RUSSELL: '*After the Battle of Omagh in 2006, I would have noticed around the house that everybody was a bit down. People were talking about it. A big fight like that in the GAA is rare enough at that level, and Dad was refereeing. That brought it home. He's usually so easy-going and has a laugh, but he was down in the dumps, and we were trying to help him forget it. Around that time, he was that bit quieter. People were trying to cheer him up, telling him that he did well, but they were still talking about it, and he couldn't get it out of his head. If they'd just said nothing, it might have passed off quicker. But slowly things returned to normal.*'

I have noticed that a referee doesn't have many friends on the losing side after a match. Paddy always has great time for the players who shake his hand after any game, but especially if they have been beaten by a narrow margin.

To me, it should not matter if it's one point or ten between the sides, because I can honestly say that Paddy always went out with an open mind to every match. I can't understand the idea that the referee is out to 'do' a player or a team, or that he favours one team above another. Why would he?

I have often asked spectators, and not just at Paddy's games, 'What in God's name do you think that the referee has to gain from one team winning over the other?' I remember an agitated Fethard supporter at one particular game. 'Isn't the referee a proper bollocks?' he raged. Shane and Mark were with me. I paused for a moment before replying: 'And do you know what else? He's their father.' It didn't register with him at first, but then the message began to sink home, and he edged away down the sideline. My two brothers feel the same. They hate to hear of a ref being abused – and they are former players themselves. I am proud to say that I have seen them leap to a referee's defence on many occasions.

Some people believe that I think that Paddy can do no wrong, but on several occasions we have travelled home from matches and the debate has been lively in the car. I'm not there just to admire Paddy. I'm also a critic, and we discuss match situations and calls that he has made. When he's refereeing a televised game, he asks me to watch it, and we'll talk about it when he gets home. I have seen him make incorrect calls, and I've seen several other referees do it, too. It's the way they see it at the time. They only have a split second to make a judgement call, so they won't get it right all of the time.

I was sick when I heard on the radio that trouble had erupted at Parnell Park in April 2008, but it didn't affect me so much afterwards, because I knew that Paddy had been out there doing the best job he possibly could. As well as rearing the two boys, I've had to keep Paddy going, too, because it has been an emotional roller-coaster ride, with the various incidents. He's had supportive phone calls when things have gone badly wrong, but the funny thing is that not an awful lot ring to say 'well done'. I hope this is not too cynical on my part, but I think that some people ring just to be in on the act. You'll have the genuine well-wishers, but there are others who like to get the inside line.

I worked at Fitzpatrick's Printers in Tipperary town, a great GAA house. My boss for 25 years, Michael Fitzpatrick, has more affection for hurling but would watch both games. We had great debates, and the Monday morning banter was most enjoyable after a weekend of top action on the fields. A regular Monday caller was the late Hugh Kennedy, former chairman of the Tipperary football board. Hugh loved nothing better than the chat about the various games.

Tipperary football was at such a low, but Hugh never saw lows, he always looked for the positives, minuscule as they might have been. Tipp might have been beaten by seven points, but Hugh could pinpoint eight moments during the game that, had they worked out, would have seen Tipp win by a point. That is why I love Tipperary football. The people who follow our county football teams do not have huge expectations, but they have loyalty, a trait I admire.

Make no mistake, there have been some really terrible times

during Paddy's career, especially when he has found himself at the mercy of the TV analysts. The likes of Micheál O'Muircheartaigh and Marty Morrissey will make an on-the-spot call, but the guys on *The Sunday Game* have the chance to watch certain incidents numerous times before forming an opinion. That's a nice luxury for them and far removed from the referee's reality. He has a split second to make a call. The TV guys will play and replay the key moments. I would really like to know what they think the home life of a referee is like, because, in my opinion, players do not receive the same levels of criticism if they make mistakes. If a referee makes a bad call, of course it can affect the outcome of a match, which in turn affects the referee himself. But it is human error. There are no ulterior motives. And how many mistakes does a player make during the course of a game that go unmentioned or unnoticed? At the end of the day, Paddy Russell comes home to a wife and two children, and he is entitled to some modicum of respect.

The Charlie Redmond affair in 1995 was truly horrific. It was the first time we had ever encountered anything like that. During that All-Ireland final, there was only one person on the field as far as I was concerned. I watched his every move throughout the entire game, and I prayed through the whole match. Some people ask after big games, 'Had you a good seat?' It's actually the worst seat in the world.

I think Omagh was worse for Paddy in some ways. He was desperately low afterwards. Paddy is deep. He doesn't talk an awful lot, but he always tries to keep the bravado up. The last thing that Paddy wants to do is wrong a player or team out on that field. He is so aware of the efforts they are putting in and how hard they are training. The pressure was even greater in recent years, because it's all about winning nowadays. Merely competing means nothing any more, and that applies as far down as juvenile level. In the times we live in, if you didn't have an interest in the GAA, there is no way that you could be married to a referee.

I am fortunate to be so deeply involved. I remember a day when Paddy was refereeing a game in Cashel and he left me in the nearby village of Golden to take in another match. 'I'll tell you about the game in Cashel, and you watch the game in Golden. We'll compare notes later.' I can't complain; I have fostered this environment. I go to every training session with Shane and Mark, and I'll sit and wait for them until they're finished. I have served as secretary of the juvenile club in Lattin-Cullen, and I will always support the boys at their club and school matches.

The GAA may have taken over in the Russell household, but, in so many ways, it is the cement that has bonded us together. On the other hand, some of Paddy's family members would have no great interest in the GAA, but that doesn't stop them worrying about him.

With Paddy, what you see is what you get. There are no hidden agendas. I love his honesty, his integrity and the way he operates as a referee. When spectators are having a go at him, I often feel like shouting, 'Do ye know? Do ye have any idea? None of ye know this man. He wouldn't do a wrong to anybody.' He is a quiet man who you wouldn't hear boo from, but he has a bit of a strut on the field; he gives off an air of confidence. In my opinion, he is a good referee, but, most of all, he is the best husband I could ever wish for, a wonderful father, too, and a brilliant provider. It hasn't been such a bad deal at all.

Appendix C

....

PADDY RUSSELL: A TRIBUTE

By Seán Ó Costagáin, Cathaoirleach an Choiste Chontae

We here in Tipperary are rightly proud of the many fine ambassadors of the GAA that our great county has produced over the years.

The Association was founded in 1884 in Hayes Hotel, Thurles, and Tipperary men were at the helm on that historic day. Over the years, players from our county have graced the scene with distinction. On the administrative scene, we have produced many of the best, and in the difficult world of refereeing, Tipp has not been found wanting either. I remember that when the late John Moloney stepped down from refereeing after almost 40 years of honourable service, in a local radio programme I stated my belief that his contribution to the GAA in the county and country was worthy of the same recognition gained by men who have won many All-Ireland honours in the blue-and-gold singlet.

It is my belief that Paddy Russell, an ordinary Tipp man with extraordinary skills in the refereeing area, with in excess of a quarter of a century of service in that difficult field and still going strong, is indeed worthy and deserving of similar recognition.

Paddy was a football player of above-average ability and has won many divisional and county awards with his beloved Emly as testament to that. However, it was as a referee that Paddy gained the national recognition that he so richly deserves.

Paddy's career as referee began in 1976 when he availed himself of a Bord na nÓg training course under that doyen of moltóirs John Moloney. He moved from there to referee many games in the West division. He was invariably called upon to referee needle games, and he was never afraid to call it as he saw it.

He made his name in the 1980s in the West with his expert handling of many difficult games. His concise reporting of incidents enhanced his reputation. Gradually, his talent was recognised in the county and within the province, and he was called upon to officiate at four provincial senior football finals involving Cork and Kerry, which he did with style and authority.

The decade saw him recognised at national level as a young talent on the move, and he ran the line on that famous September Sunday in 1982 when Séamus Darby's last-minute goal denied the Kingdom what would have been an unprecedented five-in-a-row.

The highlights of what has been a tremendously distinguished career were his appointments to two All-Ireland senior football finals, the 1990 Meath v. Cork match and the Dublin v. Tyrone game in 1995.

In both of those finals, Paddy was confronted with situations where firm decisions had to be made, and the man from Emly always had the courage of his convictions and did what he thought was correct. I admire him tremendously for that wonderful characteristic. At county board level, we are deeply indebted to Paddy Russell for his tremendous service for over 30 years. His punctuality, his authority, his decisiveness and his honesty have enabled him to officiate effectively at the most difficult of encounters in both hurling and football.

He commanded the height of respect from players at all levels, and seldom have I witnessed his decision-making being questioned. Paddy is a man of tremendous courage, and even after the most difficult of assignments, he would walk off the pitch amongst players, mentors and officials, yet rarely have I seen him become the target of unwanted attention.

Now, in the twilight of a glittering career as a moltóir, Paddy has done himself, his family, his club, his county and his division proud, and he stands beside Seán Hayes, Bill O'Donnell, George Ryan and John Moloney as men from the West who have refereed All-Ireland finals.

We at the board thank him for his service and hope he will serve for many more years as the 'man in the middle' within the county, even though he has called time on his national career.

As I pen these few words in recognition of the wonderful service of Paddy Russell to the Association so dear to us all, it is great to see him in action at Croke Park for the 2008 All-Ireland SFC quarter-final between Armagh and Wexford.

As this phase of Paddy's career comes to a close, I have no doubt that his wife, Margaret, and he will have many enjoyable GAA occasions in the future, watching the next generation of talented Russells carve out their own particular niche in our wonderful Association.

Molaim thú, a Phádraig, agus go n-éirí go geal leat sna blianta atá romhainn.

Seán Ó Costagáin,
Cathaoirleach an Choiste Chontae